# *A*llegories of

## COSTERUS NEW SERIES 146

*Series Editors:*
*C.C. Barfoot, Theo D'haen*
*and Erik Kooper*

# *Allegories of Telling*

## Self-Referential Narrative in Contemporary British Fiction

Lynn Wells

 Rodopi    Amsterdam-New York, NY 2003

ISBN 90-420-1114-9

© Editions Rodopi B.V.
   Amsterdam - New York, NY 2003

Printed in The Netherlands

# Acknowledgements

Since the original work for this book was done as my doctoral dissertation at the University of Western Ontario, I would like to take this opportunity to thank the teachers there who had a formative influence on me: my supervisor, Alison Lee, as well as Thomas Carmichael and Tilottama Rajan. Also, I would like to thank Linda Hutcheon and Frederick Holmes for their friendship and good advice over the years. I am very grateful to my parents Ben and Lillian Wells, my husband, Michael Trussler, and my children, Annie and Jesse, for all of their support during the long process of preparing this manuscript for publication. I would like to thank The University of Regina for giving me a comfortable academic "home" in which to continue my research, as well as my indefatigable copy-editor, Donna Achtzehner. Finally, I am grateful to Rodopi Press for giving me this opportunity to bring my work to a wider audience.

Parts of this work have previously appeared in print and are published here with the permission of the editors and publishers of the respective works. Part of Chapter Four appeared as "*Corso, Ricorso*: Historical Repetition and Cultural Reflection in A.S. Byatt's *Possession*" in *Modern Fiction Studies*, Volume 48, Number 3. Part of Chapter Five is derived from my essay "Virtual Textuality," in *Reading Matters· Narrative in the New Media Ecology*, Eds. Joseph Tabbi and Michael Wutz, Cornell UP, 1997.

# Contents

# Introduction

> One of the important powers of fiction is its power to theorize the act of
> storytelling *in and through the act of storytelling.*

Ross Chambers, Story and Situation

> Any narrative is primarily the allegory of its own reading.

Paul de Man, Allegories of Reading

Since the loquacious narrator of John Fowles's *The French Lieutenant's Woman* stepped out of the shadows to engage his audience in a discussion about the modern novel, British fiction has had as one of its conspicuous preoccupations the state of literary narrative in an age of textual self-consciousness. If, after the emphasis on signification in modernism and its successors—post-war experimentalism and the *nouveau roman*—novels must call attention to their own fictionality or risk being dismissed as either naive or anachronistic, how can they avoid becoming superficial artifices, unrelated to the real world in which their readers exist?[1] Critics frequently deal with this problem by studying the texts as examples of "metafiction," which Patricia Waugh defines as

> fictional writing which self-consciously and systematically draws attention to its status as an artefact in order to pose questions about the relationship between fiction and reality. In providing a critique of their own methods of constructions they not only examine the fundamental structures of narrative fiction, [these texts] also explore a *theory* of fiction through the *practice* of writing fiction. (2)

This critical approach—particularly as elaborated in terms of "historiographic metafiction" by Linda Hutcheon in *A Poetics of Postmodernism* and applied by Alison Lee in *Realism and Power* specifically to postmodern British writing—concentrates on elements of the works (narrative voice and style, subject

---

[1] A.S. Byatt attests to mounting some "[d]efiance of the aesthetic imperative that all good fiction now is overtly fictive and about fictiveness" (*Passions* 18), a position that her own writing would seem to contradict.

.tter, etc.) that openly address the permeable boundary between historical and
.ctional discourses. For instance, both Hutcheon and Lee analyze how the
clearly thematic "yarn-spinning" of the history teacher who narrates Graham
Swift's *Waterland* points out the discursive, essentially "literary" nature of all
historical representation.

Some recent British novels, however, contain self-referential textual structures that are not immediately apparent and that must undergo an act of
hermeneutical translation in order for their significance to be perceived. These
implicit structures theorize contemporary narrative's relation to various historical and cultural realities in ways different from those suggested by the texts'
overt metafictional form and content. It is these "allegories of telling" that are
the focus of the following pages. This study examines novels by five British
authors—Fowles's *The French Lieutenant's Woman*, Angela Carter's *The
Infernal Desire Machines of Doctor Hoffman*, Swift's *Waterland*, A.S. Byatt's
*Possession: A Romance* and Salman Rushdie's *The Satanic Verses* and
*Midnight's Children*—all of which allegorize contemporary literary narrative's
profound connection to the world outside its textual borders, notwithstanding
its self-acknowledged status as metafictional construct.

The underlying autoreferentiality of each of these novels is brought to light
by means of one of two related methods. The first extrapolates an embedded
textual model or passage that reflects the relationship which the surrounding
narrative is formulating for itself with regard to its audience, other literary
works, or the external world. As Lucien Dällenbach clarifies in *The Mirror in
the Text*, such *mises en abyme* tend to occur in texts "that, conscious of their lit-
erariness, 'narrativize' it," texts in which "reflexivity appears as a theme [...]
guaranteeing some sort of systematic view" (48, 50). In Chapters One and Five
concerning Fowles's and Rushdie's texts respectively, I examine how embedded scenes of seduction and various spatial metaphors shed light upon those
novels' self-conscious demonstration of their ideal interactions with their readerships, their intertexts and their historical referents.

My second method identifies pertinent metanarratives that reveal self-
reflexive implications that may seem to be at odds with the texts' apparent
meanings. This critical approach is a form of what Fredric Jameson calls "metacommentary" which, "not unlike the Freudian hermeneutic [...] is based on the
distinction between symptom and repressed idea, between manifest and latent
content, between the disguise and the message disguised" ("Metacommentary"
15). In *The Political Unconscious*, Jameson develops this concept to encompass

the part that metanarratives, in his case Marxism, can play in divulging repressed textual material: "Interpretation is here construed as an essentially allegorical act, which consists in rewriting a given text in terms of a particular interpretive master code" (10). By "rewriting" Carter, Swift, and Byatt's novels with the aid of certain "master codes" adapted from psychoanalysis and the historiographic theories of Walter Benjamin and Giambattista Vico, I disclose aspects of the texts that would otherwise remain concealed. These metanarratives are not used to illuminate the texts at the level of plot or character; that is, the application of psychoanalytic theory to *The Infernal Desire Machines of Doctor Hoffman* in Chapter Two or Benjamin's historiography to *Waterland* in Chapter Three does not produce a Freudian or a Benjaminian "reading" *per se* of either novel, but rather makes visible the texts' self-referential deliberations about the reading and writing of fiction. The fact that these metanarratives, suggested by the texts themselves, are often strikingly modernist in derivation underscores their role in mediating the self-conscious textuality that persists from that period as both an inescapable component and a lingering problem.

With neither method do I seek to deny or ignore the texts' "manifest content," whether that content be specifically metafictional or less formal in nature (feminist, post-colonial, etc.), though the surface content (for example, an historical event) is often directly informed by the latent (how the depiction of history in an artificial form can nonetheless produce "real" effects in readers' perceptions of that event). Instead, in my readings of each of the authors' works, I look beyond what the narratives *say* to how they *talk about themselves subliminally*, recognizing in the process that several different levels of interpretation, including the allegorically self-referential, can be brought to the same text.

A question that must be confronted regarding these novels' tendency to comment on their own condition in this way is why such compelling speculation frequently takes place, as Jameson would say, in the textual "unconscious," where it is not readily discernible. As we shall see, readerly participation is the subject of much of these texts' ruminations, both overt and covert. But while open metafictional gestures speak superficially about the reader's involvement in the narrative process, hidden self-reflections of the sort considered here actually necessitate a deeper level of readerly hermeneutic engagement at the same time that they define its parameters.

From my interpretations of these novels there arises a picture of some of the predominant issues that contemporary British fiction raises in and about itself in the process of telling stories. While the need for readers to be actively

engaged and self-conscious about their role is one of these texts' recurrent fas-
cinations, others extend beyond the general postmodern context to that of
British contemporary writing in particular. The British novel's ambivalent intertextual connections with its literary heritage, primarily with the antithetical representational impulses of its realist and modernist antecedents, reappear in various forms throughout the works. Although the challenge of historical representation is a topic prevalent in recent fiction worldwide, it takes on added significance in British writing, which has a distinctive affinity with the past, both in
the literary and social senses. These thematic points linking the texts are
explored in detail in this introduction.

The novels under scrutiny here have been chosen for their interest in these
interrelated ideas, but especially for their common characteristic of conducting
their self-theorizing in allegorical terms. Consequently, the subsequent chapters
comprise neither an author-based study nor a comprehensive survey of current
British fiction, but rather selective readings of representative works carried out
using a shared methodology. In each chapter, a theoretical approach adapted to
the individual text(s) at hand is developed which brings the self-referential content to the surface while relating it to one or more of the following concerns of
contemporary British fiction.

## 1. The Reader's Role

As various theorists of reading have argued,[2] the reader had been internally represented, either directly or indirectly, in literary narrative long before the recent
revival of metafiction. After the explicit appeals to, and figurations of the reader in early novels such as Miguel de Cervantes' *Don Quixote* and Laurence
Sterne's *Tristram Shandy*, the textual audience became, with nineteenth-century realism, a generally more tacit presence, a shift that suited the reader's new
role as "the subject-position of [a text's] coherence, the point of its view, the
knowledge of the common reality" (Heath 110). This implicit reader, a realist
formulation, eroded under the influence of modernism's emphasis on subjective
perception and its increasingly self-referential textuality, until late modernist
works such as Virginia Woolf's *Between the Acts* began once again unmistak-
ably to symbolize their audiences within their textual worlds.

---

[2]For extensive bibliographies of theories of reading and their applications, see Susan
Suleiman and Inge Crosman, Eds., *The Reader in the Text: Essays on Audience and Interpretation*
(Princeton: Princeton UP, 1980), and Jane P. Tompkins, Ed., *Reader-Response Criticism: From
Formalism to Post-Structuralism* (Baltimore: Johns Hopkins UP, 1980).

With many recent novels, it would seem that we have returned to the apparent clarity of early metafiction. The reader's position is frequently articulated as part of the self-conscious text's overall foregrounding of its fictional status, achieved, Hutcheon says, partially through its "emphasis on its enunciative situation—text, producer, receiver, historical and social context" (*Poetics* 115); the reader is either openly addressed (as in Fowles's famous Chapter 13 in *The French Lieutenant's Woman*) or provided with an easily discernible intratextual surrogate (such as Padma in *Midnight's Children*). Yet as Hutcheon makes clear in *Narcissistic Narrative*, the invocation of a "reader" still does not refer unproblematically outside the fictional world: "The reader is, then, a function implicit in the text, an element of the narrative situation. No specific real person is meant; the reader has only a diegetic identity and an active diegetic role to play" (139). Despite being fictionally generated, though, such textualized figures still do not necessarily correspond with the preferred readers and modes of reading that the texts implicitly theorize for themselves, and may in fact be clues to the hermeneutic effort required to uncover that repressed information. To differentiate between the readers-as-constructed in these novels and the fictive readers who can be inferred allegorically, we need first to review the terminology used to describe internalized depictions of textual audiences.

According to W. Daniel Wilson's lucid summary of the theoretical field, the basic distinction that applies to fictional representations of readers is between the "characterized" and the "implied" or "ideal," neither of which can be equated automatically with people in "real life." The characterized reader has perceptible features, sometimes not very admirable, which are inscribed within a text in either direct or indirect terms, and it usually acts as a "narratee," which Susan Suleiman defines as "the necessary counterpart of a given narrator, that is, the person or figure who receives a narrative" (Suleiman and Crosman, 13). Conversely, the implied reader, especially as conceived by Wayne Booth, may or may not be clearly delineated, and may or may not be identical with the characterized reader, but is always deducible through interpretation as an abstract figure that embodies "the behavior, attitudes and background [...] necessary for a proper understanding of the text" (Wilson 848). Since the real reader must recognize this idealized position in order to make sense of the text, the implied reader, as Wilson indicates, is both a purely aesthetic entity and an intermediary to actual historical acts of reading:

> It must be interpreted as a property of the text, without allowing extra-textual aspects to dominate. At the same time, the implied reader is an essential link in the line of communication between the author and every

(real) reader, one that determines to a large extent the success and quality of the communication. (859)

Of course, as Wilson is also careful to point out (858), the implied reader is
itself a product of interpretation, and its traits will vary with individual readings
and contexts, as will the definition of a "proper understanding."

With contemporary fiction, the temptation exists to be unwary of characterized positions, particularly those denoted through direct address, and to
accept them as signs of a newly democratic textuality that includes the reader
in the act of creation, on the same footing with the equally textualized "author."
In fact, the seemingly most liberated "readers," as Hutcheon suggests, are
sometimes subject to "overtly manipulative narrators and narratives" (*Poetics*
206), as is the case in *The French Lieutenant's Woman*. Hutcheon's summary
contention that such displays of narratorial control mark the unavoidable exercise of power accompanying every gesture of freedom, however, does not
explain how one looks past the characterized reader to reveal the implied role(s)
it disguises.

That degree of penetration involves an interpretative process which
reworks certain facets of texts with a view to discovering their inferences
regarding reading. In some instances, the hermeneutic attention is focused on
the intratextual portrayals of the act of storytelling by means of which a text
establishes its "narrative situation," the contextual components needed for it to
be understood, which include, as Ross Chambers outlines, "minimally, a storyteller and hearer together with the agreements constitutive of relevance" (22).
Chambers asserts that such self-referential representations should not be taken
at face value:

> [O]ne should not allow one's own mode of reading to be determined by
> the text's situational self-reflexivity [...]. On the contrary, by reading
> this self-situating as part of the text, one should free oneself to recontex-
> tualize it (that is, interpret it) along with the rest of the text. (27)

The real reader should never therefore simply passively identify with an internally characterized figure, but should actively interrogate a text as to the forms
of implied reader and reading it is advocating. From the analyses in Chapters
One, Two and Four, the portraits of the implied readers that emerge suggest the
importance of combining self-awareness about the act of reading with a willingness to probe vigorously beneath surface appearances.

In my chapter on *The French Lieutenant's Woman*, I examine embedded
models both of narration and of seduction, which is a specialized sort of

storytelling, to demonstrate how the novel sets up its first-level (or general) narratee as what Wilson calls a "negative foil" (856) for a contextually appropriate implied reader's position. This interpretation yields a profile of an ideal reader who is able to see through the narrator's manipulation to appreciate the manner in which he is craftily readjusting contemporary British reading tastes.

In my commentary on *The Infernal Desire Machines of Doctor Hoffman*, on the other hand, the object of interpretation is specifically the characterized reader. Although Carter's novel is not as manifestly metafictional as Fowles's, it presents its hero, Desiderio, as an allegorized figure of reading, based, as I elaborate, on a modernist intertextual precursor from Marcel Proust's *Remembrance of Things Past*. Using the metanarrative of psychoanalytic theory to connect repressed textual material, I argue that Desiderio only seems to be the reader's intended representative, when in fact he, too, is a "foil" designed to show how readerly desire can be coerced by narrative, and to block the kind of narcissistic identification that characterized positions can elicit.

Narcissism also comes under attack in *Possession*, a novel in which reading is the main activity of all of the central characters, as they attempt to enhance their historical understanding through the perusal of documents. Not all of these characterized readers are successful in their pursuit, however; those who impose their personal and contemporary priorities on the past are denied access to its secrets. By rewarding those internal readers who recognize their hermeneutic prejudices and acknowledge the past on its own terms, Byatt promotes an ideally dialogic form of interpretation that can lead to the restoration of postmodern culture.

What my interpretations in these chapters reveal, then, is that this kind of self-conscious reading, which also figures prominently in the intertextual and historiographic concerns studied in the chapters on *Waterland* and Rushdie's two novels, is one of the prevalent ideas that contemporary British fiction theorizes subtextually. In the terms proposed by Jacques Lacan (1973), the self-conscious reader plays the role here of "*le sujet supposé savoir*" [the subject supposed to know], a fantasy position associated with psychoanalysis, in which the analyst, by virtue of his or her presumed ability to interpret and understand what will be said, endows the analysand with the authority to speak. That is, these novels project for themselves fictive readers who, by assuring a precondition of active and self-aware interpretation, in turn invest the texts with the authority to tell stories with meanings that often extend beyond, and may even contradict, those suggested by the texts' metafictional exteriors.

Unless otherwise specified, the "readers" mentioned in the following pages therefore do not refer to "real life" consumers, but rather to the imaginary occupants of fictive positions, produced by the novels themselves, that can be reconstructed through "allegorical" interpretation along the lines described above. Except to the extent that is readily textually justifiable, these abstract readers have not been historicized or gendered. Rather, they serve as positions with whom actual readers can identify in their attempts to understand the texts on the level of latent autoreferentiality.

## 2. Intertextuality and the Literary Tradition

One of the key demands placed on readers by contemporary writing is to detect the presence of intertexts, especially those evoked by an author for the sake of parodying certain literary conventions. The parodic recasting of conventions, however, is only one means in which postmodern British fiction deals with intertexts. In the novels studied here, earlier literary works appear in ways and for reasons which become evident only with attention to subtle self-referential signals. The intertextual affiliations disclosed by such interpretations are predicated not on parodic subversion, but on compromise and internal dialogue: the contemporary texts invoke canonical works associated with specific periods in order to grapple with issues which continue to intrigue writers in the present, most tellingly the symbolic polarity of realist representationalism and modernist anti-representationalism. This unapologetic rehashing of past texts and ideas exemplifies a peculiarly British attachment to the literary tradition, as Byatt suggests: "[I]t seems that much formal innovation in recent English fiction has concerned itself, morally and aesthetically, with its forebears, and in a way for which I know no exact parallel in other literatures" (*Passions* 149). While Byatt singles out the nineteenth-century realist novel as still having great sway over British authors, the high modernist tradition, as we shall see, also has a considerable on-going presence. In this section, I sketch out why the formative periods of realism and modernism are of such particular interest to contemporary British fiction, and how their intertextual relationships are figured allegorically in the novels under discussion.

First, though, it is necessary to contextualize my use of the bedevilled word "intertextuality" in connection with postmodern writing. Since Julia Kristeva (1969) introduced it as an alternative to author-centered notions of influence, intertextuality has principally come to designate the immanence of discourses other than the literary in any given text. This anti-literary bias derives from Kristeva herself, who rejects the term's use "in the banal sense of 'study of sources'" (*Revolution* 60), and focuses instead on discursive codes from other aspects of culture: the law, social practices, and so on. Michel Foucault's definition of intertextuality in *The Archaeology of Knowledge* continues in this vein. He characterizes a "book" as "a node within a network" (23) which varies according to the book in question, but which always potentially includes, as Jay Clayton and Eric Rothstein point out, both "discursive and non-discursive formations—such as institutions, professions, and disciplines" that are instrumental "in shaping what can be known and, more radically, what can count as 'true'" (27); the network is thus a web of the power relations at large in any society. Yet these more expansive concepts do not take into account the unprecedented and widespread tendency of contemporary fiction to refer overtly to literary intertexts, in forms ranging from allusion and direct citation to such obvious embeddings as the poker game, played by characters from several Latin American texts, at the end of Carlos Fuentes's *Terra Nostra*.

According to Hutcheon, this postmodern predilection for bookish inter-referentiality marks an acknowledgement that, after the self-conscious "autonomy" of the modernist work of art, it is impossible for literature to return to a seemingly unmediated relationship to empirical reality: "the 'world' in which these texts situate themselves," she says, "is the 'world' of discourse, the 'world' of texts and intertexts" (*Poetics* 125). In Hutcheon's view, then, the primary function of postmodern literary intertextuality, including parody, is to alert the reader to the inherent discursivity of all representations, and by extension, of the world itself as we know it. And while Hutcheon follows Roland Barthes and others in relocating the site of intertextual activity in the reader rather than in the author,[3] her explanation, like Kristeva's, tends to downplay or generalize the particular affinities between works of fiction.

John Frow's formulation in *Marxism and Literary History*, on the other hand, recognizes the special status of literary intertexts. He contends that "[i]ntertextuality is always in the first place a relation to the canon (to the 'specifically literary' function and authority of an element) and only *through* this a relation to the general discursive field" (128). From this viewpoint, the literary intertext has a double role: first, it indicates some internal negotiation

---

[3]For an overview of reader-based theories of intertextuality, see Clayton and Rothstein, pp. 21–26. Also of note is Michael Riffaterre's definition of intertextuality as "an operation of the reader's mind" (142–43) in "Intertextual Representation: On Mimesis as Interpretive Discourse," *Critical Inquiry* 11 (1984): 141–62.

between the "host" text and one from the past on the level of literary history; and second, it acts "as a metonymic figure of general discursive norms" (128)—that is, of the cultural structures and historical world-views covered under Kristeva's broader term. Like Kristeva, Frow draws on Mikhail Bakhtin's theories; he thinks of literature as a "play of voices" (159), with various positions being articulated not only by characters and narrators but also by intertexts. It is this more inclusive, dialogic understanding of intertextuality that I am applying to contemporary British fiction.

The realist and modernist intertexts that appear in the novels studied here function in the doubled, literary sense described by Frow. On the one hand, they are "metonymic figures" for the various ideologies connected with the periods from which they originate: the bourgeois capitalist ethos of nineteenth-century Europe, for example, or the cultural elitism of Bloomsbury modernism. More importantly for my purposes, though, they stand for opposing sets of ideas that boil down, in Jameson's phrase, to "the old modernism/realism dispute" ("Ideology" 232), in which the periods become aligned, in a somewhat over-simplified manner, with two extreme positions regarding representation. For Jameson, period formulations always "imply or project narratives or 'stories'" (*Political* 28) which supersede actual historical practices. How realism and modernism came to be designated by the representational "stories" that are so influential on contemporary British writing will be apparent after an examination of the prevailing thought about their conventions and places in literary history.

Realism's basic premise is confidence in art's ability to reflect or imitate the external world. As Andrzej Gasiorek points out in *Post-War British Fiction*, the implementation of this belief can be charted as a transhistorical "general mimetic orientation" (14) dating from Aristotle's *Poetics*, or localized as a period in nineteenth-century European aesthetics, widely associated with liberal humanist principles and art's responsibility to depict the social realities of certain groups, notably the lower classes. In the literary context, nineteenth-century realism involves several conventions and assumptions, which Lee helpfully summarizes in her first chapter. Literary realism is supposed to be stylistically objective, impersonally and impartially narrated (the stories should seem to "tell themselves," without diegetic interruptions), and committed to a documentary presentation of the "facts." Behind these customs lie a number of presuppositions about the nature of literary representation:

> The first of these is that "empirical reality" is objectively observable
> through pure perception. The second is that there can exist a direct

> transcription from "reality" to novel. Implicit in this is the idea that lan-
> guage is transparent, that "reality" creates language and not the reverse
> [...]. Finally, there is the notion that there is a common, shared sense of
> both "reality" and "truth." (12)

Owing to this unimpeded intercourse between world and text, the novelist, who is conventionally a person of uncommon sensibility, should be able to convey a picture of reality which is not only mimetically faithful and "true," but also morally edifying.

Among the problems with this conception is the fact that literary realism in the terms outlined above, as Lee makes clear, "does not exist" (8) except as a critical fabrication. All so-called classic realist texts, including the standard English example of George Eliot's *Adam Bede*, lapse from one or more of the listed tenets, perhaps most frequently the prohibition against calling attention to textual production. The notions that nineteenth-century novelists ever aspired to perfect "transparency" in language, or that their understanding of reality and of art's power to reproduce it was so simplistically monolithic, are products, according to Gasiorek, of a late-twentieth century condescension: "This view rests on a theory of belatedness symptomatic of much postmodernist thought; it is 'we' who are doubting, ironic, self-reflexive and detached, whereas 'they' are innocent, gullible, benighted, and unable to stand back from the beliefs of the day" (13). In addition, Gasiorek says, such arguments "essentialize" and "homogenize" (10) a vast number of historically different works under a single rubric. Despite the many fallacies of the conventionalist attitude towards real-ism, however, it has become entrenched in Western literary tradition as a "story" whose central theme is a naive credulity in representationalism.

This reductive formulation is crucial to a specific view of modernism, in which realism is used as a background against which the later period is defined. From this perspective, realism is "that with which modernism has had to break, that norm from which modernism is the deviation"; it therefore acts as the "neg-ative or straw term" in a binary in which the representational urge is debunked as a kind of "superstition" (Jameson, "Ideology" 233–34). Rather than assum-ing the existence of a stable world to be objectively copied, "classic" mod-ernism focuses instead on the individual act of artistic creation, a shift that entails a concomitant increase in what Stephen Heath, after J.P. Stern, calls "language-consciousness" (106). Because the modernist text gives unwonted attention to language and structure, it is often seen as negating the value of con-tent, in particular of the social and historical actualities that are the province of realism. In the place of a seemingly ever more incoherent external "reality,"

English writers who are unwilling to abandon lightly the concept of mimesis, for reasons of fidelity both to the realist tradition, and to historical subject matter, as Section Three of this introduction will show. Gasiorek explains that

> [r]ealism continues to be a presence in the post-war period but not as a set of formal techniques. It functions, rather, as a constellation of discursive practices, making it more pertinent to talk of an impulse to represent the social world than of a particular narrative mode. (13–14)

This "impulse" takes the form of a desire which, though never fulfilled, is perceptible in the texts as an unattainable and unforgotten ideal. In conflict with that wish, though, is a counteractive one on the part of authors to extend their immediate predecessors' work, to be "*post*modern" in the sense of improving on that which came before. The towering influence of the modernist period on recent British fiction, especially as embodied by such canonical luminaries as Marcel Proust and James Joyce, is evident in the frequency with which writers such as Carter and Rushdie refer to and clearly pattern their texts after high modernist works; and though these evocations sometimes have a deflationary undertone, they often suggest a stylistic deference coupled with an anxiety about surpassing those prior accomplishments. The contemporary drive to carry on the modernists' legacy most notably involves taking their linguistic concentration and autonomy to a more intensive level through pronounced textual self-reflexivity, while eschewing their "faith in totalizing meaning-systems" (Maltby 520) and exposing their propensity to distance themselves from social and historical realities. What much postmodern British fiction does is attempt to prove that these competing desires—the desire to represent the world, and the desire to celebrate the text as text—are in fact compatible in the manner proposed by Heath:

> "'Language-consciousness' shifts realism *importantly*; it poses central questions for a contemporary realism, with this last term in no way then becoming inappropriate or merely arbitrary. Relations between literary work and world, that is, are not broken, though understanding of those relations and of reality with them may be recast, which recasting indeed might be seen as fundamental for any significant activity of realism. (106)

The effort to move beyond the realism/modernism binary and forge a textuality that is, at the same time, insistently referential yet explicit about the act of

> transcription from "reality" to novel. Implicit in this is the idea that lan-
> guage is transparent, that "reality" creates language and not the reverse
> […]. Finally, there is the notion that there is a common, shared sense of
> both "reality" and "truth." (12)

Owing to this unimpeded intercourse between world and text, the novelist, who is conventionally a person of uncommon sensibility, should be able to convey a picture of reality which is not only mimetically faithful and "true," but also morally edifying.

Among the problems with this conception is the fact that literary realism in the terms outlined above, as Lee makes clear, "does not exist" (8) except as a critical fabrication. All so-called classic realist texts, including the standard English example of George Eliot's *Adam Bede*, lapse from one or more of the listed tenets, perhaps most frequently the prohibition against calling attention to textual production. The notions that nineteenth-century novelists ever aspired to perfect "transparency" in language, or that their understanding of reality and of art's power to reproduce it was so simplistically monolithic, are products, according to Gasiorek, of a late-twentieth century condescension: "This view rests on a theory of belatedness symptomatic of much postmodernist thought; it is 'we' who are doubting, ironic, self-reflexive and detached, whereas 'they' are innocent, gullible, benighted, and unable to stand back from the beliefs of the day" (13). In addition, Gasiorek says, such arguments "essentialize" and "homogenize" (10) a vast number of historically different works under a single rubric. Despite the many fallacies of the conventionalist attitude towards real-ism, however, it has become entrenched in Western literary tradition as a "story" whose central theme is a naive credulity in representationalism.

This reductive formulation is crucial to a specific view of modernism, in which realism is used as a background against which the later period is defined. From this perspective, realism is "that with which modernism has had to break, that norm from which modernism is the deviation"; it therefore acts as the "neg-ative or straw term" in a binary in which the representational urge is debunked as a kind of "superstition" (Jameson, "Ideology" 233–34). Rather than assum-ing the existence of a stable world to be objectively copied, "classic" mod-ernism focuses instead on the individual act of artistic creation, a shift that entails a concomitant increase in what Stephen Heath, after J.P. Stern, calls "language-consciousness" (106). Because the modernist text gives unwonted attention to language and structure, it is often seen as negating the value of con-tent, in particular of the social and historical actualities that are the province of realism. In the place of a seemingly ever more incoherent external "reality,"

English writers who are unwilling to abandon lightly the concept of mimesis, for reasons of fidelity both to the realist tradition, and to historical subject matter, as Section Three of this introduction will show. Gasiorek explains that

> [r]ealism continues to be a presence in the post-war period but not as a set of formal techniques. It functions, rather, as a constellation of discursive practices, making it more pertinent to talk of an impulse to represent the social world than of a particular narrative mode. (13–14)

This "impulse" takes the form of a desire which, though never fulfilled, is perceptible in the texts as an unattainable and unforgotten ideal. In conflict with that wish, though, is a counteractive one on the part of authors to extend their immediate predecessors' work, to be "*post*modern" in the sense of improving on that which came before. The towering influence of the modernist period on recent British fiction, especially as embodied by such canonical luminaries as Marcel Proust and James Joyce, is evident in the frequency with which writers such as Carter and Rushdie refer to and clearly pattern their texts after high modernist works; and though these evocations sometimes have a deflationary undertone, they often suggest a stylistic deference coupled with an anxiety about surpassing those prior accomplishments. The contemporary drive to carry on the modernists' legacy most notably involves taking their linguistic concentration and autonomy to a more intensive level through pronounced textual self-reflexivity, while eschewing their "faith in totalizing meaning-systems" (Maltby 520) and exposing their propensity to distance themselves from social and historical realities. What much postmodern British fiction does is attempt to prove that these competing desires—the desire to represent the world, and the desire to celebrate the text as text—are in fact compatible in the manner proposed by Heath:

> "'Language-consciousness' shifts realism *importantly*; it poses central questions for a contemporary realism, with this last term in no way then becoming inappropriate or merely arbitrary. Relations between literary work and world, that is, are not broken, though understanding of those relations and of reality with them may be recast, which recasting indeed might be seen as fundamental for any significant activity of realism. (106)

The effort to move beyond the realism/modernism binary and forge a textuality that is, at the same time, insistently referential yet explicit about the act of

> transcription from "reality" to novel. Implicit in this is the idea that lan-
> guage is transparent, that "reality" creates language and not the reverse
> [...]. Finally, there is the notion that there is a common, shared sense of
> both "reality" and "truth." (12)

Owing to this unimpeded intercourse between world and text, the novelist, who is conventionally a person of uncommon sensibility, should be able to convey a picture of reality which is not only mimetically faithful and "true," but also morally edifying.

Among the problems with this conception is the fact that literary realism in the terms outlined above, as Lee makes clear, "does not exist" (8) except as a critical fabrication. All so-called classic realist texts, including the standard English example of George Eliot's *Adam Bede*, lapse from one or more of the listed tenets, perhaps most frequently the prohibition against calling attention to textual production. The notions that nineteenth-century novelists ever aspired to perfect "transparency" in language, or that their understanding of reality and of art's power to reproduce it was so simplistically monolithic, are products, according to Gasiorek, of a late-twentieth century condescension: "This view rests on a theory of belatedness symptomatic of much postmodernist thought; it is 'we' who are doubting, ironic, self-reflexive and detached, whereas 'they' are innocent, gullible, benighted, and unable to stand back from the beliefs of the day" (13). In addition, Gasiorek says, such arguments "essentialize" and "homogenize" (10) a vast number of historically different works under a single rubric. Despite the many fallacies of the conventionalist attitude towards realism, however, it has become entrenched in Western literary tradition as a "story" whose central theme is a naive credulity in representationalism.

This reductive formulation is crucial to a specific view of modernism, in which realism is used as a background against which the later period is defined. From this perspective, realism is "that with which modernism has had to break, that norm from which modernism is the deviation"; it therefore acts as the "negative or straw term" in a binary in which the representational urge is debunked as a kind of "superstition" (Jameson, "Ideology" 233–34). Rather than assuming the existence of a stable world to be objectively copied, "classic" modernism focuses instead on the individual act of artistic creation, a shift that entails a concomitant increase in what Stephen Heath, after J.P. Stern, calls "language-consciousness" (106). Because the modernist text gives unwonted attention to language and structure, it is often seen as negating the value of content, in particular of the social and historical actualities that are the province of realism. In the place of a seemingly ever more incoherent external "reality,"

English writers who are unwilling to abandon lightly the concept of mimesis, for reasons of fidelity both to the realist tradition, and to historical subject matter, as Section Three of this introduction will show. Gasiorek explains that

> [r]ealism continues to be a presence in the post-war period but not as a set of formal techniques. It functions, rather, as a constellation of discursive practices, making it more pertinent to talk of an impulse to represent the social world than of a particular narrative mode. (13–14)

This "impulse" takes the form of a desire which, though never fulfilled, is perceptible in the texts as an unattainable and unforgotten ideal. In conflict with that wish, though, is a counteractive one on the part of authors to extend their immediate predecessors' work, to be "*post*modern" in the sense of improving on that which came before. The towering influence of the modernist period on recent British fiction, especially as embodied by such canonical luminaries as Marcel Proust and James Joyce, is evident in the frequency with which writers such as Carter and Rushdie refer to and clearly pattern their texts after high modernist works; and though these evocations sometimes have a deflationary undertone, they often suggest a stylistic deference coupled with an anxiety about surpassing those prior accomplishments. The contemporary drive to carry on the modernists' legacy most notably involves taking their linguistic concentration and autonomy to a more intensive level through pronounced textual self-reflexivity, while eschewing their "faith in totalizing meaning-systems" (Maltby 520) and exposing their propensity to distance themselves from social and historical realities. What much postmodern British fiction does is attempt to prove that these competing desires—the desire to represent the world, and the desire to celebrate the text as text—are in fact compatible in the manner proposed by Heath:

> "'Language-consciousness' shifts realism *importantly*; it poses central questions for a contemporary realism, with this last term in no way then becoming inappropriate or merely arbitrary. Relations between literary work and world, that is, are not broken, though understanding of those relations and of reality with them may be recast, which recasting indeed might be seen as fundamental for any significant activity of realism. (106)

The effort to move beyond the realism/modernism binary and forge a textuality that is, at the same time, insistently referential yet explicit about the act of

> transcription from "reality" to novel. Implicit in this is the idea that lan-
> guage is transparent, that "reality" creates language and not the reverse
> [...]. Finally, there is the notion that there is a common, shared sense of
> both "reality" and "truth." (12)

Owing to this unimpeded intercourse between world and text, the novelist, who is conventionally a person of uncommon sensibility, should be able to convey a picture of reality which is not only mimetically faithful and "true," but also morally edifying.

Among the problems with this conception is the fact that literary realism in the terms outlined above, as Lee makes clear, "does not exist" (8) except as a critical fabrication. All so-called classic realist texts, including the standard English example of George Eliot's *Adam Bede*, lapse from one or more of the listed tenets, perhaps most frequently the prohibition against calling attention to textual production. The notions that nineteenth-century novelists ever aspired to perfect "transparency" in language, or that their understanding of reality and of art's power to reproduce it was so simplistically monolithic, are products, according to Gasiorek, of a late-twentieth century condescension: "This view rests on a theory of belatedness symptomatic of much postmodernist thought; it is 'we' who are doubting, ironic, self-reflexive and detached, whereas 'they' are innocent, gullible, benighted, and unable to stand back from the beliefs of the day" (13). In addition, Gasiorek says, such arguments "essentialize" and "homogenize" (10) a vast number of historically different works under a single rubric. Despite the many fallacies of the conventionalist attitude towards realism, however, it has become entrenched in Western literary tradition as a "story" whose central theme is a naive credulity in representationalism.

This reductive formulation is crucial to a specific view of modernism, in which realism is used as a background against which the later period is defined. From this perspective, realism is "that with which modernism has had to break, that norm from which modernism is the deviation"; it therefore acts as the "negative or straw term" in a binary in which the representational urge is debunked as a kind of "superstition" (Jameson, "Ideology" 233–34). Rather than assuming the existence of a stable world to be objectively copied, "classic" modernism focuses instead on the individual act of artistic creation, a shift that entails a concomitant increase in what Stephen Heath, after J.P. Stern, calls "language-consciousness" (106). Because the modernist text gives unwonted attention to language and structure, it is often seen as negating the value of content, in particular of the social and historical actualities that are the province of realism. In the place of a seemingly ever more incoherent external "reality,"

modernism posits an artistic object that produces provisional order and meaning out of disorder, frequently with the aid of such totalizing discursive structures as myth, symbol, and cultural quotation. This retreat into the autonomous
realm of the text coincides with a movement into the closed sphere of human
consciousness, and a new emphasis on the subjective processes of time, memory, and perception. The subject/object dualism is beset by epistemological
doubt, frequently spawning multiple perspectives on, and retellings of, an event
in the vein of William Faulkner's novels. The modernist text, then, is thought
to be an aesthetic re-creation of the world rather than an unmediated transcription of it; and while there are those who argue persuasively that modernism,
with its sensitivity to the complexities of both experience *and* signification,
achieves a degree of referentiality that nineteenth-century realist fiction never
does (see Heath 108 and Nash 33–36), the period's established impression is
that it is predominantly linguistically-centered and anti-representational.

Realism and modernism have therefore come to occupy successive positions in a diachronic, progressional narrative of literary history, with the primary marker of development being the enlightened step from naïveté into
recognition regarding the unavoidable separateness of world and text.
Following from this logic, British postmodern fiction, to continue the evolution,
would have to extend the modernist project, moving further away from any pretense of representation towards a "pure" textuality along the lines of experimental writing such as the *nouveau roman* or American "surfiction." Yet recent
British novelists have resisted breaking with realism in the way that the modernists supposedly did, choosing instead to reinstall the earlier period in an
authoritative role equal to that of what came afterward. This apparent retrogres-
sion to, and obsession with, realism is one of the defining features of postmodern British fiction as distinct from other contemporary literatures, and it has
been comprehensively studied in terms of influence and parody by Lee and
Gasiorek. My concern here, though, is not how British fiction leapfrogs back
over modernism to take its inspiration, however ambivalently, from realism in
isolation, but how it simultaneously internalizes *both* periods, despite their differences, and attempts, through various intertextual configurations, to arrive at
a reconciliation between them. This is not to imply that the authors under discussion have uncritically acceded to the conventionalist ideas surrounding realism and modernism, nor that they are unaware of the periods' ideological and
aesthetic blind spots; the ubiquity of parodic gestures throughout their texts
belies such an argument. Rather, contemporary British fiction disregards

conventional assumptions, retaining and combining, after scrutiny, those aspects of realism and modernism that it finds to be of lasting significance, without necessarily claiming for itself a status superior to the writing of either period.[4]

As we see in Chapter One, realism's appeal for recent British writing goes beyond its representationalism to include its symbolic connection with the literary past that became especially meaningful in the era of post-war upheaval. Realism's ease of readability and clear presentation of plot and character—what Barthes, in *S/Z*, dubbed "readerly" qualities—held their attraction for the British reading public, which longed for a return to what it perceived as a more socially responsible, less gratuitously "artistic" fiction. Consequently, the interpretive difficulty and linguistic self-consciousness, or "writerliness," popularized by modernism and magnified by experimentalism, was not as well received in post-war England as it was in concurrent literary circles elsewhere in the world, leading to an exclusion of British fiction from international trends. By looking at Sarah in *The French Lieutenant's Woman* as a self-referential model of the transition between writerliness and a renewed form of readerliness—a conversion mirrored by the text's overlaying of a savvy metafictional narration on the structure of a generic nineteenth-century English novel—I contend that Fowles effects an enduring *rapprochement* between the hitherto incompatible aesthetic principles of modernism and realism. This successful synthesis paved the way for subsequent contemporary British fiction writers to portray the periods intertextually such that their contrary representational implications are brought into conjunction.

Although tempered by retrospective reassessment, the representational tendencies of realism and modernism nonetheless remain potent forces in the British literary imagination. Despite the fact that the prospect of mimetic representation has been rendered problematic by twentieth-century linguistic and theoretical discoveries, the urge to reflect the real continues to affect

---

[4]My argument here is in contrast to those of postmodern critics such as Jameson, Terry Eagleton, Hal Foster, and Hutcheon, each of whom promotes either modernism or postmodernism on the grounds that one period is better than the other at exploiting the post-realist decline of representational certainty (see David J. Herman, "Modernism vs. Postmodernism," pp. 159–73). Rather than elevating postmodernism over realism and modernism, I suggest in Chapters Three and Five that recent British fiction is engaged in an unresolved dialogue with those periods, and that its relationship to its antecedents is respectful, sometimes antagonistic, but not based on the necessary progressive superiority of the contemporary.

English writers who are unwilling to abandon lightly the concept of mimesis, for reasons of fidelity both to the realist tradition, and to historical subject matter, as Section Three of this introduction will show. Gasiorek explains that

> [r]ealism continues to be a presence in the post-war period but not as a set of formal techniques. It functions, rather, as a constellation of discursive practices, making it more pertinent to talk of an impulse to represent the social world than of a particular narrative mode. (13–14)

This "impulse" takes the form of a desire which, though never fulfilled, is perceptible in the texts as an unattainable and unforgotten ideal. In conflict with that wish, though, is a counteractive one on the part of authors to extend their immediate predecessors' work, to be "*post*modern" in the sense of improving on that which came before. The towering influence of the modernist period on recent British fiction, especially as embodied by such canonical luminaries as Marcel Proust and James Joyce, is evident in the frequency with which writers such as Carter and Rushdie refer to and clearly pattern their texts after high modernist works; and though these evocations sometimes have a deflationary undertone, they often suggest a stylistic deference coupled with an anxiety about surpassing those prior accomplishments. The contemporary drive to carry on the modernists' legacy most notably involves taking their linguistic concentration and autonomy to a more intensive level through pronounced textual self-reflexivity, while eschewing their "faith in totalizing meaning-systems" (Maltby 520) and exposing their propensity to distance themselves from social and historical realities. What much postmodern British fiction does is attempt to prove that these competing desires—the desire to represent the world, and the desire to celebrate the text as text—are in fact compatible in the manner proposed by Heath:

> "'Language-consciousness' shifts realism *importantly*; it poses central questions for a contemporary realism, with this last term in no way then becoming inappropriate or merely arbitrary. Relations between literary work and world, that is, are not broken, though understanding of those relations and of reality with them may be recast, which recasting indeed might be seen as fundamental for any significant activity of realism. (106)

The effort to move beyond the realism/modernism binary and forge a textuality that is, at the same time, insistently referential yet explicit about the act of

representation—that is, a doubly aware "contemporary realism"[5]—is symbolized in the form of various intertextual interactions in the works of Swift, Byatt and Rushdie.

How this mediatory process is figured in *Waterland, Possession* and *The Satanic Verses* becomes clear through interpretations based on the two methodologies mentioned earlier. With Swift's novel, I first draw on Benjaminian historiography to show how realism and modernism, as typified by the intertextual presences of Charles Dickens's *Great Expectations* and Faulkner's *Absalom, Absalom!*, appear not as polar opposites, but as two modes of "remembering" the external world which, though mutually undermining, are also mutually sustaining. The contemporary text, I contend, brings these two representational forces from the past together in a present moment where their differences are held in equilibrium. The attitude of British postmodern fiction towards its literary precursors is not always conciliatory, however; as I go on to argue with the aid of the Freudian metanarrative of Oedipal progression, *Waterland* represents its ties to its realist and modernist "parents" in order to demonstrate its attempts to struggle with and subsume their authorities.[6] While *Possession* also figures its realist and modernist influences in generational terms, its primary depiction of intertextuality takes the form of what Edward Said, working out of Vico's theoretical vision of human history, calls "affiliative" repetition. In Said's conception, affiliation—which implies a voluntary, co-operative and mutually beneficial relationship rather than an involuntary, conflicted "filiative" one—can

---

[5]Working from Brian McHale's analysis of the "ontological dominant" of postmodern fiction, Amy J. Elias formulates a definition of "postmodern Realism," in which "the world has become textualized." In contrast to the epistemological stability conventionally aspired to by Victorian realism, this postmodern novelistic mode "records the multiple worlds/texts within contemporary culture and recognizes the *inability* to evaluate society's conflicting values; it mimics the multiple selves of characters [...] and recognizes the problem of articulating an essential Self in this social context" (12).

[6]My discussions of intertextual "parental" influence and descent throughout are framed in the language of "fathers" and "sons," largely owing to the consonance of such terms with the psychoanalytic metanarratives I employ, and to the preponderance of male-dominated models of influence in literary circles. For critiques of these models, see Annette Kolodny's "A Map for Rereading: Gender and the Interpretation of Literary Texts," in *The New Feminist Criticism: Essays on Women, Literature, and Theory*, Ed. Elaine Showalter, New York: Pantheon, 1985, pp. 46–62 and Barbara Johnson's chapter "Les Fleurs du Mal Armé: Some Reflections on Intertextuality," pp. 116–33, in her *A World of Difference*, Baltimore and London: Johns Hopkins UP, 1987.

be used to describe the co-existence of a contemporary text with the past discourses that appear in it as densely codified ideological structures. Chapter Four shows how *Possession* internalizes the discursive tenets of realism and modernism in an effort to expose both the negative and the positive aspects of those periods. In particular, we see how, through a mediated rewriting of the garden scene from Jean-Paul Sartre's late modernist novel *Nausea*, Byatt's text performs an act of Heideggerian "destruction," self-consciously challenging tradition while reclaiming from it the representational power of naming the world that has come under scrutiny in the postmodern era. The model of lineal descent is seen in yet another light in Chapter Five, in which I examine a passage from *The Satanic Verses* involving a haunted house as a *mise en abyme* of how the novel conducts a dialogue with its literary ancestors about the future direction of fictional representation by reverentially invoking their intertextual "ghosts" in a synchronous space. Each of these analyses reveals how the text at hand uses embedded intertextual figurations to allegorize its relationship to the literary tradition, and to comment self-reflexively on its internal project of working out the terms of a new representational stance for contemporary narrative that allows for mimetic reference despite textual self-consciousness. This intergenerational compromise, as Section Three makes clear, is of particular importance given the British fascination with the fictional depiction of history.

## 3. History, Representation, and Narrative

Not only do many writers of contemporary British fiction evince a strong allegiance to the canonical literary tradition, but they also have a singular preoccupation with the past *per se*. *The French Lieutenant's Woman*, with its nineteenth-century setting, is once again in the vanguard, preceding by a decade several novels with primarily historical content, including works by Peter Ackroyd (*Hawksmoor*), Julian Barnes (*A History of the World in 10 1/2 Chapters*), and Pat Barker (the *Regeneration* trilogy). Malcolm Bradbury asserts that the 1980s' proclivity for history was still the benchmark for good English fiction in the 1990s (*Modern* 432). As David Leon Higdon points out in *Shadows of the Past in Contemporary British Fiction*, this revival of interest in the past began in the early 1950s and continued into the 1960s, when English writers broke with the modernist mind set, prevalent until World War II, that craved innovation and rejected history as a "nightmare"; the post-war generation instead "emphasized the concept of continuity, an important reversal from the earlier discontinuity, the recognition that the future is vitally related to the past, and an awareness that tradition was not in and of itself a reactionary con-

cept" (7). The recent turn in British fiction towards history, then, hearkens back
to an earlier desire to restore a lost sense of cultural progression and connectedness; and, despite the noticeably more skeptical treatment which representations of the past receive at the hands of postmodern writers, they are nonetheless associated with a persistent referential urge evident, as we have seen, in the
on-going intertextual influence of canonical realism.

Yet the theoretical and critical approaches usually brought to bear on these
novels tend to stress contemporary fiction's capacity to alienate, not to re-establish contact with historical reality. Because novels such as *Waterland*,
*Possession,* and *Midnight's Children* thematize the fact that the past can only be
known through its reconstructions, they are often held up to support a line of
thought maintaining that historical reality has become unrepresentable,
obscured behind a network of conflicting points of view and textual traces, and
that it is therefore both unreachable and unable to have any genuine effects in
the present. As we shall see, this rather negative method of interpreting these
contemporary texts relies on certain debatable premises about the interrelationship between narrative and history.

This typically "postmodern" way of thinking derives in large measure from
theorists such as Louis O. Mink and Hayden White, who have studied the narrativizing processes involved in the recording of history. In "The Historical
Text as Literary Artifact," for example, White explains how, even in accounts
that pretend to "scientific" accuracy, historical facts become organized according to rules of "emplotment" (46) very much like those used to create literary
narratives, with attention to the selection and suppression of details, characterization, overall structure, and so on. The result, White says, is not a reliable picture of the specific occurrences, information which is impossible to verify anyway; instead, the historical record organizes the data into preconceived patterns,
such as tragedy or comedy, already known to both historian and audience.
Historical reality, which is otherwise remote and "mysterious" (49), is thus rendered familiar and culturally relevant: "As a symbolic structure, the historical
narrative does not reproduce the events it describes; it tells us in what direction
to think about the events and charges our thought about the events with different emotional valences" (52). With this process of narrativization, though, the
historian inevitably "translates" (53) fact into fiction, thereby creating the conditions which some believe lead to the estrangement of the referent.

Jameson regards the ramifications of the past's textualization as disturbing,
particularly as they are embraced by postmodern aesthetics. In *The Political
Unconscious*, where he concentrates on realist and modernist fiction, he argues

that history does filter through its representations, though not directly: "history is *not* a text, not a narrative, master or otherwise, but [...] as an absent cause, it is inaccessible to us except in textual form, and [...] our approach to it and to the Real itself necessarily passes through its prior textualization" (35). We therefore need to read narrative "essentially as a *symbolic* act" (76) in which this "absent" reality appears in a manner somewhat like that in which actual events are refigured by dreams. In his later *Postmodernism*, however, Jameson does not impute the same conversionary power to contemporary literature. Instead, as I address in more detail in Chapter Five, Jameson avers in that book that postmodern fiction, like all other cultural productions of the period, disclaims any responsibility for "real" representation, symbolic or otherwise, but instead offers only completely artificialized narrative versions of the past while actual "history [...] itself remains forever out of reach" (25).

Jameson's standpoint has contributed to a widespread view of postmodernism as superficial and ahistorical. Andreas Huyssen, for instance, proposes that "[t]he problem with postmodernism is that it relegates history to the dustbin of an obsolete episteme, arguing gleefully that history does not exist except as text, i.e., as historiography" (35). Critical considerations of postmodern culture, and especially of contemporary fiction, are rife with the presumption that self-conscious textuality acts as a barrier to historical reality. These commentaries rely tacitly on the notions that the purpose of writing about the past is to represent it in a verifiable fashion, and that any challenges to the feasibility of that project, such as those mounted by White, devalue "history" at the same time.

Not all postmodern commentators, though, feel that narrative distances the historical referent and saps its significance. Hutcheon, for example, commends the theoretical highlighting of history's textual nature by White and others for its interrogation of "the implied assumptions" of traditional historiography— "objectivity, neutrality, impersonality, and transparency of representation" (*Poetics* 92)—which, not coincidentally, correspond with those conventionally attributed to realism. When combined with literary self-consciousness, this kind of questioning creates what she calls "historiographic metafiction," one of the premier types of postmodern writing, which induces new awareness of the reality lying behind discursive replications.

As Gasiorek notes, neither is the Jamesonian skepticism about historical narrativization shared by all those who reflect on the practice and background of historiography as a discipline: "Many historians recognize the predominantly textual nature of what constitutes the historical record, but see this as the necessary ground of research into history, not as an insuperable obstacle to knowledge of the past" (148). One historiographer untroubled by the role of textuality is Paul Ricoeur, who, according to Donald E. Polkinghorne, changes the terms of the debate "about historical narrative from its legitimacy as an epistemologically sound method to, more generally, what the use of historical narrative reveals about human beings and their relation to the past" (67). In other words, Ricoeur shifts the emphasis to a different kind of "truth," that which can be discerned by examining the culturally significant patterns chosen to give order to agreed-upon "facts" in the way identified by White. Different from White, however, Ricoeur does not see this meaning-generating activity as distinct from some idealized, though impossible, form of empirically valid representation, but as the very process by which people come to know reality in the first place. Following Ricoeur, Polkinghorne asserts that "[e]xperience does not originally appear as discrete atoms," but rather "forms and presents itself in awareness as narrative"; the historian, therefore, "does not narrate past facts but retells past stories from a present perspective" (68–69). When reshaped as historical narratives, these stories reveal how we deal with past events as they recede in time, and how those events are preserved and constantly reimagined both culturally and individually. Rather than obstructing our access to history, then, narrative mediates and encodes our relationships to it.

This alternative vision of narrative's role in historical representation is allegorized in *Waterland, Possession,* and *Midnight's Children*, in contradiction of their apparently deconstructive intentions. Although these texts seem to insist that history is knowable only as a series of ungrounded and untrustworthy fictions, they latently suggest that even the most self-admittedly textualized structures can lead to renewed understanding of the past, and authentically alter its on-going effects. In all three novels, the surface thematizations of how narrative reconfigures actuality in the manner decried by some postmodern theorists are undermined by subtextual reflections on contemporary fiction's legitimate and effective role as a communicator of historical knowledge.

As mentioned earlier, *Waterland* is frequently cited as a contemporary novel that exemplifies the disappearance of the historical referent behind a web of discursive reproductions. The narrator, a history teacher confronting the termination of both his post and his discipline, seems to confirm through his overtly fictionalized account of actual events that the past is indeed irretrievable. By extrapolating *Waterland*'s intimations of both profound psychic trauma and miraculous recovery, however, I use revisionist Freudian psychoanalysis and the Benjaminian concept of redemptive history to expose how the text actually demonstrates narrative's ability to function as a medium in which otherwise irreversible personal and cultural losses can be reconstructed and accepted in the present. These complementary readings bear out Bradbury's conclusion that *Waterland* is "essentially about recuperation, about rediscovering what the past and memory have left for us to use" (*Modern* 433).

*Possession* apparently laments the inability of postmodern society, with its anxieties over the failing referential power of language, to reclaim those elements that supposedly granted meaning and vitality to those living in earlier periods, especially the Victorian predecessors of the twentieth-century main characters. Although the novel seems to nostalgically celebrate the past while condemning the present, it in fact provides a fictional blueprint for the restoration of postmodernity. Using Vico's theory of the *ricorso* as a metanarrative basis, Byatt shows how a culture on the verge of collapse can regain provisional stability through the reading of historical documents with a view to recapturing lost values that are still desired, regardless of contemporary skepticism. This act of beneficial cultural reflection can take place despite, and largely because of, the very linguistic self-consciousness that seems to render the past inaccessible.

While *Midnight's Children* openly acknowledges the fallibility and biases to which memory is susceptible, particularly when transferred into written form, it too concerns the process of salutary cultural recollection. *Midnight's Children* is not, as Jameson would have it, itself an adulteration of the historical referent, but instead is a subtle endorsement of postmodern fiction as a conduit to the reality that lies outside its fictional borders, in this case the history of modern India around the time of British decolonization. Through the embedded model of the "Midnight's Children's Conference" which comes into being at the moment of Indian independence from colonial rule, Rushdie enacts a sort of "virtual realism" (analogous to the recent technology) which reconciles representation and artifice in the way envisaged by the intertextual paradigms described above. Unlike the technology, however, *Midnight's Children* calls attention to its artificiality, engaging the self-conscious reader such that she or he recognizes the potential of so-called objective, empirical accounts to distort the past.

What the following chapters illustrate, then, is that these novels, which appear to be so candid and straightforward about their fictional statuses and designs, are in fact deceptively complex. The self-referential material uncovered by these interpretations militates against the perception that contemporary literary narrative is merely anti-representational, self-indulgent linguistic play. On the contrary, all of these texts contain indications of their efforts to relate meaningfully to their readers and the phenomenal world. Nonetheless, these relations are consistently worked out in the expressly literary, uniquely British, context of realist and modernist influences which, rather than being remote from extratextual concerns, is intimately tied to them. It is with Fowles's allegorical treatment of this dual heritage in *The French Lieutenant's Woman* that we shall begin.

# Chapter One
## Narrative as Seduction:
## John Fowles's *The French Lieutenant's Woman*

According to Malcolm Bradbury, *The French Lieutenant's Woman* is one
of two "exemplary" (*Modern* 351) novels that epitomized a fundamental shift
in the course of British fiction in the 1960s (the other is Doris Lessing's *The
Golden Notebook*). Fowles's text is singled out for this special status because it
came to be seen as the creative resolution of a lengthy and anxious critical con-
troversy over the state of the post-war British novel. As Bernard Bergonzi's
famous proclamation that the novel "is no longer novel" (*Situation* 25) suggests, the debate arose from a perception that the fiction being written in
England in the 1950s and 1960s had lost any sense of originality, and particularly that it had turned its back on the formal advances of modernism and experimentalism in favour of reinstating nineteenth-century style realism as the dominant fictional mode. This apparently retrograde inclination made British novelists seem inferior, it was thought, to their international counterparts, who at
the same time were reacting to the ideas being generated by structuralist and
post-structuralist theory and trying out new narrative forms (such as the *nouveau roman*) that departed from conventional notions of representation, characterization, and plotting. Although the use of realist conventions ostracized their
fiction from the international mainstream of the time, domestic writers persisted in the practice, demonstrating an attachment to tradition and an awareness of
a specific reading taste, both of which are peculiarly British. With its conscious
imitation of a Victorian novel circumscribed by an unconventional twentieth-
century metafictional narrative, *The French Lieutenant's Woman* satisfied the
realist urge of the time while bringing the British novel in line with international developments. Consequently, Fowles helped to initiate what Bradbury, borrowing from David Lodge, calls the "aesthetics of compromise" (*Modern* 378)
that has characterized much of British writing since the late 1960s, bringing
realism and innovation into mutually illuminating co-existence.

As the culmination of the critical debate between realism and experimentalism, *The French Lieutenant's Woman* not only reflects the cultural moment

in which it was produced; it also actively facilitated its contemporary reader-ship's acceptance of the transition to this new kind of hybrid fiction. Ross Chambers argues that all "literary narrative [...] includes as part of its self-ref-erence system specific indications of the narrative situation appropriate to it" (4); that is, each narrative has embedded within it signs of the context in which it will most likely be understood, encompassing the audience which will read/hear the story and the story's intended effect on that audience. In the case of *The French Lieutenant's Woman*, these embedded indications of narrative sit-uation take the form of scenes of storytelling and seduction that mirror the text's enticement of contemporary readers to accept a recasting of the realist novel, along with all of the "readerly" qualities it entails, in terms of aesthetic thought and practice after modernism. Before looking in detail at how Fowles's text internally represents this extratextual narrative seduction, we need first to clar-ify the cultural context in which *The French Lieutenant's Woman* could most successfully manipulate its readers' desires and expectations to its own ends.

-i-

Recent commentators on the intense discussion surrounding the plight of the post-war novel describe the debate as having been prone to broad general-izations linking literary and cultural decline. In their Preface to *The Contemporary English Novel*, Bradbury and David Palmer, for example, take issue with the "prevailing folklore" of the time, which claimed that, by return-ing to realism, British novels such as William Cooper's *Scenes from Provincial Life*[1] had become isolationist and had sunk into a "relative stagnation" (9) com-parable to that of Britain's diminished post-imperialist state after the war, which included a destabilized class-system, an unsteady economy, and a deflated sense of nationhood. In this climate, the inward-looking textual self-conscious-ness associated with the high modernist experiments of James Joyce and Virginia Woolf was considered inappropriately frivolous; the novel had a responsibility, it was felt, to address collective rather than individual concerns, an attitude reinforced by the prevailing critical current of Leavisite moralism. Whether entirely defensible or not, such nationalistic lines of thought dominat-ed the contemporary critical scene for several years, giving rise to a series of

---

[1]For a comprehensive overview of post-war realist fiction, see Bradbury's *The Modern British Novel*, Chapter 5, "The Novel No Longer Novel: 1945–1960."

books devoted exclusively to the subject, including James Gindin's *Postwar British Fiction: New Accents and Attitudes*, Rubin Rabinovitz's *The Reaction Against Experiment in the English Novel, 1950-1960*, Bergonzi's *The Situation of the Novel*, and Lodge's *The Novelist at the Crossroads*.[2] With the benefit of hindsight, Bradbury and Palmer, Andrzej Gasiorek, Richard Todd, and others now challenge the views promoted in these canonical critical works on the grounds that they assume a unity of purpose in a heterogeneous field of authors with little reference to artistic priorities, and that they tend to overlook exceptions for the sake of tidy generalization.

Indisputably, though, post-war critics focused on the realist revival, largely neglecting writers such as Christine Brooke-Rose and B.S. Johnson who, in the 1960s and early 1970s, sought to popularize the tenets of internationally-influenced experimentalism through their work. Both Brooke-Rose and Johnson used non-linear narratives and various printing anomalies (such as the holes cut in the pages of Johnson's novel *Albert Angelo*) to disrupt the realist illusion and draw attention to their fiction's textuality. Following the anti-humanist ideas of the *nouveau romanistes*, Johnson was particularly vocal in his belief that the English novel had to pick up where Joyce and Samuel Beckett had left off, and abandon the impulses for rounded characters and coherent stories that belonged properly to the "exhausted, clapped out" (13) form of nineteenth-century fiction. Much of Johnson's frustration was directed at the English reading public, general readers and reviewers alike, who ignored attempts at change while indulgently welcoming a seemingly endless and uninventive selection of "genre" novels written in the realist vein (for example, university novels) on which they "gorge[d] [...] to surfeit" (15). The critical response towards experimentalism was so negative that, according to Rabinovitz, authors became too timid to try anything new:

---

[2]Creative writers of the time also weighed in with their opinions about the state of the post-war novel. In her essay "The Small Personal Voice," Doris Lessing laments: "We are not living in an exciting literary period but in a dull one. We are not producing masterpieces, but large numbers of small, quite lively, intelligent novels. Above all, current British literature is provincial" (22). Iris Murdoch, in a polemic entitled "Against Dryness" that became one of the touchstones of the debate, divided contemporary prose fiction works between the "crystalline"—"a small quasi-allegorical object portraying the human condition and not containing 'characters' in the nineteenth-century sense"—and the "journalistic"—"a large shapeless quasi-documentary object, the degenerate descendant of the nineteenth-century novel, telling, with pale conventional characters, some straightforward story enlivened with empirical facts" (20). Neither kind, she makes clear, lives up to the harmonization of the individual and the social that characterizes the Victorian novel.

> The greatest fear of the English contemporary novelist is to commit a *faux pas*; every step is taken within prescribed limits; and the result is intelligent, technically competent, but ultimately mediocre. When a novelist goes outside the set limits, he can expect no help from the critics, no matter how good his work. (169)

Unlike contemporaneous trends on the Continent and in the United States, then, the experimentalist strain in British writing in the 1960s, although active, was relegated to obscurity.

The reasons behind the widespread rejection of experimentalism and simultaneous embracing of realism are various, and can be categorized, as Gasiorek points out, into those related to "external events" (1) and those related to literature itself. As we have seen, the "folklore" of the time equated the realist resurgence primarily with a domestically-centered, liberal humanist cultural mindset. In her essay "People in Paper Houses: Attitudes to 'Realism' and 'Experiment' in English Post-War Fiction," Byatt suggests why the socially-conscious humanism that flourished in the 1950s and 1960s (begun, arguably, with W.H. Auden's movement in the 1930s) turned to the Victorians for its expression: "Respect for the tradition of the realist novel is apparently a very rooted fact, and is inextricably involved in a very complex set of responses to the decline of religion and the substitution of a Religion of Humanity" (*Passions* 149). While English cultural traditionalism and nativism clearly figured prominently in the preference for realism over modernism, though, this retrospection also had its basis in some purely literary motivations. Rabinovitz cites the shared observation of Raymond Williams and Walter Allen that the realist writers of the 1950s had come full circle, reacting against the modernists just as they, in their turn, had reacted against the Victorians (10–11). As Johnson complained, however, it was not only authors who broke with modernism, but readers as well, who were alienated by the elimination of conventional storytelling, a direction they saw furthered by experimentalism. As Neil McEwan proposes in *The Survival of the Novel: British Fiction in the Later Twentieth Century*, English readers have a special attachment to the narrative style of realist fiction:

> In Britain, most of us seem to be nineteenth-century readers in part when we come to contemporary fiction, because we still read the Victorians, and because our society is in many respects anachronistic. (We may also feel that what Johnson calls our 'nineteenth-century reading' corresponds to a basic human need for stories and characters.) (6)

With his invocation of the "basic human need for stories," McEwan is echoing the view, widely held by critics and writers of the time,[3] that the post-war British public longed for the return of the classic Barthesian "readerly" text: the text that can be passively and pleasurably "consumed" with a minimum of interpretation, in contrast to the "writerly" text that demands the reader's active participation. In defiance of the spirit of what Fowles's narrator refers to as "the age of Alain Robbe-Grillet and Roland Barthes" (80), which disdained realism for its supposedly soporific effects and bourgeois sensibilities, the British reading public eschewed the "writerly" textual attributes descended from modernism in favour of the readability characteristic of the Victorian novel. By responding to this demonstrated penchant for realism, British writers consequently isolated themselves and their work from the directions fiction was taking internationally.

The challenge that faced British novelists in the 1960s was therefore how to meet the readership's demands without being left behind by their contemporaries. In his famous 1971 metaphor, Lodge portrays this dilemma as a "crossroads," with realism as the main road, and the non-fiction novel and self-consciously fantasy-oriented fiction or "fabulation" (as defined by Robert Scholes in *The Fabulators*) as the two possible deviations from it (*Novelist* 19).[4] To continue along the road seemingly oblivious to "the pressure of scepticism on the aesthetic and epistemological premises of literary realism" (19), Lodge contends, would be foolhardy; on the other hand, to diverge from the road to pursue exclusively one of the two alternatives could "lead all too easily into desert or bog self-defeating banality or self-indulgent excess" (22). The solution lies, he suggests, in what he calls the "'problematic novel' [which] clearly has affinities with both the non-fiction novel and fabulation, but remains distinct precisely because it brings both into play" (22). In the writing of problematic novels, authors recognize the limitations of the realist mode yet still use it, after stopping at the crossroads, appreciating its implications for representation, and "*build[ing] their hesitation into the novel itself*" (22). This "hesitation" takes the form of metafictional self-awareness and overt intertextuality, remnants, as Randall Stevenson points out, from the experimentalist period (29). With the

---

[3] For example, Rabinovitz cites Pamela Hansford Johnson and William Cooper's calls for a return to plot, character and narrative intelligibility (5–7).

[4] Lodge later regretted his "crossroads" metaphor, feeling that it was "inadequate" because it presented the novelist's choices in absolute terms without leaving open the possibility of pluralist "mixing of genres and styles within a single text" ("Novelist" 207–08).

adoption of this compromise, British novelists could preserve the realist tradition while bringing it into step with the developments in the rest of the literary world.

In essence, the conjoining of realism with experiment in the manner described by Lodge made it possible for the "readerly" novel—reformulated, British-style—to assume a place of respectability on the international stage. Lodge reminds us in his 1992 update of the "crossroads" essay that the novel, as a product of bourgeois capitalistic society, has always "had an equivocal status somewhere between a work of art and a commodity" (211). With the advent of modernism, the novel as a commodity was split between two distinct readerships: the "mass audience," which bought popular fiction; and a much smaller "discriminating elite," which patronized "the highbrow novel of aesthetic ambition" (211). The latter kind of writing had to entice its audience with far different attractions than the former, which relied on the readability inherited from nineteenth-century fiction. As Barthes argues in *The Pleasure of the Text*, the modernist limit-text, estranged from the mainstream, had become a "fetish object" (27), appealing to those specialist readers who enjoy engaging themselves beyond the initial difficulties of interpretation. Despite having attained the "highest degree of reified objectivity" (13), as Chambers explains, the "writerly" text was thus able to find its niche; with the ascendancy of experimental writing worldwide, it eventually dominated the specifically "literary" corner of the market-place so completely that "readerly" texts that had pretensions beyond the category of popular fiction were dismissed as obsolete. In order for the "readerly" novel to assert itself in this context, it had to incorporate some of the qualities of the "writerly" text which were held to be valuable, while using the conventional realist features of readability and interpretability to its advantage.

It was at this moment in the history of modern British fiction that *The French Lieutenant's Woman* appeared, putting paid to the debate about how the novel could survive if it persisted in its present outmoded state. With its revamping of traditional realism in light of current innovations,[5] Fowles's book was highly successful not only abroad but also at home, where it made textual self-consciousness and the intrusion of new theoretical ideas into fiction

---

[5]Linda Hutcheon makes clear that recent realism has been irreversibly altered by contemporary theory and practice, an evolution that Fowles demonstrates in his novel: "While remaining faithful to the moral and social concerns of Henry James and the English novel tradition, Fowles knows that a new form must emerge from its antiquated conventions. If he self-consciously imitates George Eliot, it is as a way to Roland Barthes" ("Real Worlds" 121).

palatable to a reading public that had previously disapproved of them.[6] *The French Lieutenant's Woman* thus helped to bring about a shift in the taste of consumers of "serious" domestic literature, a shift that was accomplished by using the on-going English fascination with the realist novel and the ease of readerliness to convince reluctant readers of the virtues of some unconventional practices. This subtle deception is self-referentially figured in the novel as a form of seduction, a *mise en abyme* of the negotiation for acceptance that the text was carrying out with its contemporary British readership.

-ii-

In *The Pleasure of the Text*, Barthes claims that seduction scenes in fiction produce an inferior kind of reading pleasure; "such desire," he says, "never leaves the frame, the picture; it circulates among the characters; if it has a recipient, that recipient remains interior to the fiction" (57). As Chambers points out in *Story and Situation*, however, the desire reproduced in such scenes does exceed the textual frame, since they function as models of the text's own narrative situation. With their tendency to include acts of verbal solicitation, seduction scenes are examples of what Chambers calls "narrational embedding," which means the "representation, internally to the fictional framework, of a situation involving the major components of a communicational act (emitter-discourse-recipient)—and very frequently the mirroring within a story of the storytelling relationship itself: narrator-narration-narratee" (33). Whether couched in overtly sexual terms or not, this relationship always naturally entails a form of "seduction": a narrator, who desires to tell a particular story, engages the attention of a listener or reader who is willing to hear it. Under the terms of this mutual desire, the story is told; if the "transaction" is successful, the audience is persuaded by the tale in the way the teller hoped, and leaves the encounter altered. When this sort of influential exchange takes place in an embedded fictional depiction of either specifically romantic seduction or storytelling *per se*, its implications reach beyond the scenes themselves to the actual context of

---

[6]Ronald Binns compares the popularity of Fowles's work to that of pulp fiction generally, with which it is often found on "the station bookstall" and from which, "[a]t first sight," it "seems indistinguishable" (19) owing to its basis in the romance genre. Binns also argues that Fowles makes use of the "exotic distance" (22) afforded by romance to critique contemporary English society in a way that realism cannot do without seeming churlish.

reading, with the internal "narrators" and "narratees" standing in as "fictive entities" (23) respectively for the text and the readers whom it wishes to sway. Chambers suggests that we can discover "the circumstances *in* which, and *on* which, [a given narrative] may have an impact" (8) by thinking of these scenes as internalized "markers [...] of historical situation" (10)—that is, as indications of the context in which that narrative is bound to have its maximum effect on its readership.

In his analyses, Chambers examines what he designates "art stories" (51): short pre-modernist or early modernist prose pieces that are suggestive of a transition from the "readerly" to the "writerly" as the primary source of textual appeal. This change in emphasis he attributes to the evolution in the modern age of the literary text as a *"specialized"* form of communication outside the "more normal, or dominant, systems of communication and exchange" (11–12). To continue to have value in this isolated state, the literary text had to be able to attract an audience, to satisfy its "desire to narrate" by "arous[ing] some corresponding desire for narration" (11) in the public, an undertaking it initially achieved through readability. As literature became increasingly "alienated" from mainstream culture, however, its methods of securing a readership altered accordingly, so that "textual seductiveness relie[d] in growing measure on techniques and conceptions of art that today we associate rather with the notion of the 'writerly'" (12–13), techniques that bind the reader in a pact based on the desire to become part of the text's exclusivity, to revel in its interpretive multiplicity and difficulty. Chambers charts this development by looking at scenes of seduction and storytelling in these stories as "markers" of the shifting bases of textual interest at the turn-of-the-century from accessibility to abstruseness, and of readerly engagement from passivity to activity.

While the art stories studied by Chambers reveal the movement in the late nineteenth century and early twentieth from the "readerly" to the "writerly," *The French Lieutenant's Woman* has embedded within itself signs of the reverse transition, from the lionization of the "writerly" back to a renewed appreciation of the "readerly," for the reasons having to do with the British distaste for experimentalism and the concomitant stagnation of post-war realism outlined above. It is this "narrative situation" that is represented by the notorious sexual liaison of Sarah Woodruff and Charles Smithson in *The French Lieutenant's Woman*, a relationship conducted largely through the medium of storytelling. With Charles as her voluntary target, Sarah sets out to seduce using an unorthodox combination of candour and complexity in the telling of her tales, a scheme that internally figures the work's own intercourse with its readers.

The success of Sarah's seductive activities is predicated upon two contradictory desires on Charles's part: his fascination with her telling of her unconventional story, which he feels well-equipped to interpret; and his willingness to be deceived by her tales again and again. Charles is seduced, then, by Sarah's narrative itself; yet the novel's readers, as characterized in Chapter 13 and elsewhere, seemingly should be able to share Charles's pleasurable fascination with Sarah's story while avoiding the deception to which he falls prey. Like Charles, these characterized readers or "narratees" have attributed to them by the narrator a high degree of interpretive acumen, enhanced, in their case, by an awareness of contemporary literary theoretical issues (such as those spearheaded by Barthes and Robbe-Grillet) as well as an extensive reading background. Most significantly, though, the narratees have an advantage that Charles does not: they receive their information directly from the narrator, who obligingly gives them clues to Sarah's duplicity to which Charles is not privy. The embedded narrative relationship between Charles and Sarah, with its effective coercion of one party by the other, would thus seem not to reflect outward to that between Fowles's novel and its readership, acted out on the textual level between narrator and narratees.

Nonetheless, the narrative seduction of Charles does indeed act as a model for how the characterized readers, regardless of the metanarrational perspective from which they view the action, are taken in by Fowles's text. This second stage of seduction involves a literary sleight of hand: the narrator, using his forthrightness as a ruse, plays on his narratees' contemporary "sophistication" to trick them into enjoying a metafictional text designed to evoke, then frustrate their conventional desires as readers. Just as Charles lets himself be tantalized by Sarah's stories despite his unflagging confidence in his skills as a "reader" and powers of resistance, so too do the text's characterized readers unwittingly allow their desires to be enlisted for a specifically postmodern agenda—that is, to be swayed by a text that is both "readerly" and "writerly" at the same time.

Although the characterized readers are delineated such that they cannot help but be seduced by the narrator's tactics, the implied or ideal reader theorized by the text is both more actively hermeneutically engaged and more aware of the novel's overall workings. Unlike the narratees, who are internal to the work itself, the implied reader can consider, from an external perspective, how Sarah and Charles's interactions cast light on the duplicity behind the narrator's supposed honesty. By seeing through these instances of self-referential narrational embedding, the implied reader discovers the novel's shrewd plan to change the reading tastes of its contemporary British audience. This more self-conscious position provides the basis from which the following analysis is argued, with the "readers" referred to being those characterized entities who both form part of the text under interpretation and stand for the generalized contemporary readership which it constructs for itself.

In order to demonstrate how *The French Lieutenant's Woman* perpetrates this subterfuge on its readers, let us begin by focusing on two scenes. First, we will look at an exchange between Charles and his fiancée, Ernestina Freeman, which functions as what Chambers describes as an "antimodel" (29) of the novel's narrative situation. Second, we will turn to Sarah's storytelling interlude with Charles, and examine how it artfully mirrors the narrator-narratee relationship which, in turn, reflects the novel's seduction of its readers.

When Ernestina reads to Charles one evening the narrative poem *The Lady of La Garaye*, she does so ostensibly for the purposes of entertainment, to fill the hours when, as the narrator puts it, Victorians "must be bored in company" (94). The real impetus behind Ernestina's reading is soon apparent, however: she wants the poem to inspire thoughts of love in Charles. The poem itself is an "insipid" (95) Victorian romance, overly metrical and full of clichés about duty. In the passage read by Ernestina, the Lady has just suffered an accident, and is being attended anxiously by her lover. Charles, meantime, has assumed a posture in which he seemingly is giving the recitation his full attention: sprawled on the sofa with his eyes closed. Only when Ernestina pauses to note the effect of the "tragic scene" on Charles does she detect that he is shamming; she thus concludes her reading:

> "Oh! Claud—the pain!" "Oh! Gertrude, my beloved!"
> Then faintly o'er her lips a wan smile moved,
> Which dumbly spoke of comfort from his tone—
> You've gone to sleep, you hateful mutton-bone! (96)

Charles receives a blow from the hurled book for his indiscretion. Rather than resulting in anything even vaguely sexual, the episode therefore ends with dissension: as a narrative seduction, it is a flop, the complete opposite of its literary antecedent, the "Paolo and Francesca" story in Canto Five of Dante's *The Inferno*, in which the reading of poetry produces lust.

Ernestina's attempt fails so miserably because the poem she recites—one of her favourites, which moves her to feel both virtuous and titillated—is not the sort of text likely to captivate Charles. Because the poem is a conventional romance, he can guess what will happen: it does not engage his imagination; it bores him in the way Barthes describes being bored by texts that "prattle"

(*Pleasure* 4). The poem is therefore readable but not pleasurable, very much like Ernestina herself. Charles inwardly complains that he understands everything about her while she understands him not at all. Of course, Ernestina's relationship with Charles is based not on love or pleasure, but on monetary exchange: like the "best seller" (94) she reads, she is a commodity in trade—the standard, dowered Victorian bride. Although she has moments of self-conscious irony, Ernestina remains fundamentally conventional, predictable, and dull. As "texts," then, both Ernestina and the poem she reads represent an exhausted nineteenth-century "genre" that Charles ultimately rejects, a break symbolized finally by the contract formalizing the demise of their engagement.

How does this poetry reading scene clarify the narrative situation of Fowles's novel? Certainly, the companionable narrator does not wish his readers to drop off to sleep in response to his story. Instead, this scene marks a complicity between narrator and readers, a shared view that the stuff of conventional romance is not worth either telling or hearing. What is worth their mutual attention, however, is the scene itself. "Listen" (96) says the narrator conspiratorially to his narratees, and they do, to their amusement rather than their boredom. With this metanarrative twist, the scene settles one of the novel's terms with its readership: while conventional texts in and of themselves may be tedious, they can instill pleasure when they are looked at from a self-consciously ironic point of view. Extrapolated, though, the poetry scene becomes a model for how readerly desire should be properly invested in a more unconventional—and necessarily more modern—sort of text.

The novel immediately provides its readers with just such an alternative text. Right after the poetry scene, the narrator turns to Charles's fossil-hunting the next day on the Common, where he accidentally meets Sarah alone for the second time. His previous encounters with Sarah have already established her as an inscrutable character. Unlike the narrator's treatment of the other characters, his presentation of Sarah does not give us access to her thoughts; he never "*unfold[s]*" her "*true state of mind*" (81) as he says he meant to do in Chapter 13. Instead, the narrator presents a "portrait of a lady" (if you will) from the outside only, a depiction reminiscent of the "flattened" characterization popularized by the *nouveau roman*. Sarah is a roving story, told over and again by the townspeople like one of Dr. Grogan's yarns; she is a solitary "black figure" (13) inviting interpretation, having a face cryptic yet strangely open, seemingly without "artifice" (14). When Charles meets Sarah this second time, he associates her face first with his sexual experiences in "foreign beds" (99), and then with a foreign text which he had to read "very much in private" (99), the scandalous *Madame Bovary*. Gustave Flaubert's novel is not a romance *per se* but an unconventional romance about the *reading* of romances, exhibiting a proto-modernist textual self-consciousness. If Ernestina, then, resembles the conventional romance, bland but suitable for public entertainment, Sarah is like a new kind of text that emerged in the nineteenth-century: innovative, daring, to be enjoyed in private by a reader of cosmopolitan sensibility who is prepared to take a more active role in the reading process. The initial impression given of Sarah, therefore, is that she is somewhat akin to what Barthes would call a "writerly" text, a text whose meaningfulness depends upon the reader's partic-ipation. Such a text, as Chambers argues, "tends [...] to realize itself as a seduc-tive *object*" (13–14); that is, it entices readers by its recondite quality, its very inaccessibility to the common reader.

Charles does not consider himself a common reader. While Ernestina, as a "text," bores him, Sarah intrigues him. As a broad-minded man of worldly sophistication, Charles believes himself uniquely qualified to interpret this enigmatic figure who baffles the unrefined townspeople. He prides himself on his ability to penetrate dissimulation: he has a keen eye for acting, in Sarah and in others, and is convinced that she is essentially honest and therefore eventu-ally understandable, interpretable. It is by appealing to Charles's superior skills as a "traveled" and "educated" listener (116) that Sarah secures his agreement to hear her unusual story.

In doing so, she initiates what Chambers calls a narrative "*contract*," "an understanding between the participants in the exchange as to the purposes served by the narrative" (8). Similar to the narrative contract between the Vicar and Mrs. Poulteney, in which he tells Sarah's story as part of a trade—employ-ment for celestial credit—this narrative contract is sealed in symbolically eco-nomic terms: by the sand dollars or "tests" given to Charles by Sarah in exchange for his time. When Charles offers to pay for the tests, he offends her and finds himself suddenly flustered and overmatched, much like Gabriel Conroy with Lily in Joyce's "The Dead." Charles consequently loses the mix-ture of sympathy and ironic "distance" (134) with which he had planned to mas-ter the situation. Instead, it is Sarah who takes control: just as she initiates the contract, she sets the terms whereby her story will be told. She leads him to a "secluded place" (134), and deliberately delays until Charles "surrender[s]" (136) and asks her to speak. The narrative scene therefore begins with an implicit agreement as to the nature of the exchange: it has the mystique of the forbidden, since it must be held in private; and it requires a yielding of author-ity by its listener.

Charles's reception of her tale noticeably changes during the course of her telling of it. Although he still is a pursuer of meaning, he lets his desire to hear more dominate his critical faculties. Sarah anticipates and directs his desire, so that her narration performs what Chambers would describe as the "*active* seductive maneuver" (14) of the "readerly" text. While Ernestina's poem can also be said to be "readerly," it delivers none of the pleasure (at least to Charles) that the Barthesian concept of readerliness often implies. Sarah's narrative, on the other hand, holds its listener in rapt attention. Sarah knows exactly what sort of story will mesmerize Charles. As we have seen, Charles has no truck with conventional romance; but as we have also seen, this so-called "despiser of novels" (15) does enjoy romance when it is reworked in new ways. Because Sarah's affair with Varguennes is supposedly lived experience, her description of it does not conform to traditional narrative patterns: her tale of deception is idiosyncratic, "modern" in its emphasis on psychology and motivation, bold in its personal and sexual frankness. Charles listens, passively engrossed; yet both the teller and the tale actively solicit his uncommon capacity for understanding. Sarah's narration, therefore, fuses the pleasure of the "readerly" text with the interpretive allure of the "writerly" text. This proves to be an irresistible combination for Charles: he imagines, the narrator tells us, "the scene she had not detailed: her giving herself. He was at one and the same time Varguennes enjoying her and the man who sprang forward and struck him down" (143).[7] With this imaginative engagement, Charles's seduction by Sarah's narrative is complete.

From this point on in the novel, Charles opens himself to continual deception. He loses all sense of ironic distance, and his desire overcomes his powers of discernment. Despite the reasonable warnings of Dr. Grogan, who acts as an alternate "reader" of Sarah, Charles is persuaded by her stories again and again. His later sexual capitulation merely re-enacts the seduction which takes place with Sarah's initial storytelling.

If Charles is seduced by Sarah's narrative because he gives in to his desire, how does this scene work as a model of the readers' situation? Undoubtedly, they share Charles's fascination with Sarah's story—they too want to find out why she "gave herself" to Varguennes—but they also enjoy the scene in another way. Like Sarah, the narrator knows what sort of story will capture his listeners' interest, and he supplies not one but two unconventional romances: the story of the French Lieutenant, and that of Charles and Sarah, whose dalliance

---

[7]As Hutcheon points out, Charles later becomes the "real" Varguennes by receiving her request for an assignation written in French, and later "enjoying" her in the fashion he imagines during her narration ("Real Worlds" 127).

is watched voyeuristically here, as they watch Sam and Mary's from behind the foliage. Although readers are thus doubly intrigued, they nevertheless believe that, like the crusty old bachelor Dr. Grogan, they can withstand seduction, responding to narrative enticement imaginatively yet rationally. Given the metanarrational vantage point from which they receive their information, readers regard this scene with the same ironic detachment with which they do the poetry scene. The narrator gives multiple clues that Sarah's story is more fiction than truth: the hollow in which she tells it is described as an "amphitheatre" (135), she pricks her finger on a "hawthorn[e]" (146) bush, and so on.[8] Readers may be attracted by Sarah's narrative, but they need not be fooled by it; similarly, they should be able to take pleasure in her romance with Charles without losing sight of its fictionality.

The scene of Sarah's storytelling contains a suggestion, however, that the internalized readers of Fowles's narrative are being tricked on an entirely different level. Just after Sarah admits that she was deceived by Varguennes because she allowed herself to be, the narrator says: "That might have been a warning to Charles; but he was too absorbed in her story to think of his own" (140). This narratorial caution about Charles is also a signal that takes on larger significance when the embedded scene of Sarah's tale is reinterpreted in the context of the novel's narrative situation: readers, too, may be so "absorbed" in the story they are reading that they are unaware of a narrative seduction being practised on them. As in the case of Charles, the self-conscious irony on which they pride themselves as readers may fail them in one crucial respect. Indeed, if we attribute to the narrator Charles's love of bad puns, we see that what he is really doing is *test*-ing his readers. For while they congratulate themselves on seeing through Sarah's duplicity, they may overlook that of the narrator himself, who seems to be the personification of a new kind of textual honesty, much as Sarah does to Charles. Yet the narrator, like Sarah, creates the illusion that he is giving a truthful outlook on events, when in fact he is deliberately using that false appearance as a way of drawing in his audience.

---

[8]If the hints provided in Sarah's storytelling scene are insufficient to provoke our suspicion, those in the document given to Charles to read by Dr. Grogan about the trial of La Roncière should twig us retrospectively. As Simon Loveday indicates (49–50), from this inset narrative concerning deceptive women, we learn that the first name of the wronged French Lieutenant (Emile) is cognate with Sarah's middle name (Emily); and his last name translates to "bramble bush," the very thing on which Sarah intentionally pricks herself (releasing a drop of blood suggesting her hidden virginity). Tarbox cites the La Roncière episode as "the most extreme case of maladroit judgment in the book" (69), illuminating other instances of misreading, including Charles' of Sarah.

The narrator's interruptions and metanarrational hints, with their promise of privileged information that should obviate deception, divert readers from seeing how their relationship to the novel is actually reflected in the seductive dealings of Sarah and Charles. Chambers contends that such a correspondence between an inner scene of storytelling and the text itself is standard in what he classifies as "self-designating narratives" (i.e., those "that focus on their own status as narration" [32]), in which "the presence of 'narrational' embedding provides an immediate clue to the situational model the text is producing" (34). We must consider, then, why Fowles has his narrator go out of his way to conceal this correlation in a text that otherwise forthrightly proclaims its diegetic intentions.

According to Chambers, one of the purposes of the type of "situational self-reflexivity" (26) provided by narrational embedding is to give readers an example of how the narrative should be interpreted, and thereby to exert control over the reading process. This internalized effort at limiting the production of meaning is what characterizes the readability of the "readerly" text, in contrast to "the more radical semantic indeterminacy" (26) of the "writerly." Fowles's narrator takes pains, however, to differentiate himself from his Victorian predecessors with their God-like omniscience and ubiquitous power:

> If I have pretended until now to know my characters' minds and inner-most thoughts, it is because I am writing in [...] a convention universal-ly accepted at the time of my story: that the novelist stands next to God. He may not know all, yet he tries to pretend that he does. (80)

Instead, he aligns himself in Chapter 13 with contemporary literary theory's promotion of abdicating authorial and narratorial control in favour of greater liberty for both characters (in terms of action) and readers (in terms of interpretation). As Elizabeth Rankin argues, though, "the narrator's repudiation of control [...] is actually only a smokescreen, under cover of which he intends to continue a quite traditional sort of narrative" (196); in other words, the narrator pretends that he is appearing as an interested observer in the freely developing world of a "writerly" text while he is actually presiding over the presentation of a closely restricted "readerly" one, centered on the love story of Sarah and Charles. While Rankin goes too far in her polarization of the novel into unconventional surface and conventional depth, she is right to point out that *The French Lieutenant's Woman* self-consciously adopts characteristics of the *nouveau roman* and Barthesian theory as a means of "blend[ing] with its literary environment in order to survive" (196). By having his narrator make clear that "novelists write for countless different reasons" including "money," "fame," and "reviewers" (81), Fowles reminds us that his text is, among other things, a commodity in the literary marketplace and, as such, it must acquire a readership. In order to do so, it makes use of the aesthetic devices in vogue at the time, as well as the same traditional novelistic properties (coherent development of characters and plot, omniscient description, creation of suspense) that Robbe-Grillet and Barthes rejected. To make this updated "readerly" narrative saleable, however, Fowles uses his narrator's intrusions to give the impression that his text is conforming with the qualities of interpretive freedom required for a novel to succeed in the contemporary literary environment. Rather than making it plain that the text's readers, too, are being seduced by a combination of "readerly" and "writerly" features, the narrator thus disguises the similarities between the embedded model of Sarah and Charles and the text's narrative situation as conducted between the narrator and narratees.

Just as Sarah's genius as a storyteller depends on her own brand of intelligence, described as "an uncanny [...] ability to understand people's worth: to understand them, in the fullest sense of that word" (47), the narrator's persuasiveness comes from his skill in sizing up his audience and telling it what it wants to hear. He assumes an attitude of familiarity with his narratees, an intimacy born from shared erudition and experience. With the many explicit and implicit intertextual references in his narration, he takes for granted his narratees' high degree of literacy—"Of course to us," he says, "any Cockney servant called Sam evokes immediately the immortal Weller" (39)—and he often refers confidentially to twentieth-century events and ideas of which the characters are ignorant. As we have seen, an aspect of this congenial relationship is that he downplays his authority, extending to characters and readers alike a seemingly revolutionary textual freedom, designed to satisfy his readers' sophisticated demands. By affecting an interest in the narratees' preferences in terms of how the novel should proceed, Fowles's narrator cajoles them into thinking that he is putting them in a position of superiority (think of how often Charles stands above Sarah and looks down at her).[9] Nevertheless, this fraternizing conceals an agenda on the narrator's part, an agenda worked out subtly over the course

---

[9]By providing his readers with both Charles's "superior" position and Sarah's "debased" one, the narrator creates the opportunity for them to identify with both activity and passivity, the subject and object of the gaze, a situation which Teresa de Lauretis cites as the norm for female film viewers. The purpose of eliciting this "double identification," according to de Lauretis, is to "solicit the spectators' consent and seduce women into femininity" (143); in the case of Fowles's narrator, his seductive intentions are geared to a more specifically literary agenda.

of the novel. Like Charles, readers are beguiled by flattery of their readerly talents; and like Charles, they permit a storyteller to coax them into wanting a specific outcome, and then accepting that decision as their own.

Like Sarah, Fowles's narrator regulates readerly desires by knowing how to capitalize on some very traditional narrative techniques in order to grab his audience. For example, they both employ the romance convention of coincidence to their benefit: Sarah turns her ankle at convenient moments, and the narrator has coal fall from a grate when it is most likely to bring Sarah and Charles into physical contact. But more importantly, both storytellers are adept at managing information. As Katherine Tarbox suggests, Sarah makes clever use of the quite sexual devices of "frustration and tension" (76) to sustain Charles's curiosity, breaking off her confession at points of startling revelation, such as her admission that Varguennes is already married. Further, Sarah can continue to interest Charles in her story because it is always changing; only she knows what its final version will be. Likewise, the narrator has ultimate authority over what will happen to the characters, regardless of their supposed independence. In each case, the audience involved has to exchange its faithful attention for the missing information: that is, it has to submit to a kind of "blackmail" similar to that carried out by Sam on his employer. And while Charles does not, at first, take Sam's threat seriously, readers should not make the same mistake with the narrator. In spite of the ironic distance that the novel affords them, the narrator holds his readers in thrall until every variable is disclosed, just as Sarah puts Charles "totally in her power" (278) with her spellbinding tales. The desire invested in the story of Charles and Sarah, aroused by the pleasure of narrative suspense, is exploited by the narrator to the last.

The withholding of information is not, however, the only method of retaining readers' interest that the narrator has at his command. Chambers distinguishes between two kinds of authority, equally seductive, that a narrator can exercise. "Narrative authority" (51) involves a gradual diminishment of power as the narrator reveals the details of plot that readers want to know. With "narratorial authority" (51), on the other hand, the narrator shifts the focus away from the conventional "readerly" stratagem of suspense and revelation to the text's production of itself as a "narrating instance" (51). In self-conscious narrative, this emphasis on the act of storytelling "compensates for the divulgence of (fictional) information and [...] has as its object the gaining of a new kind of authority (in the form of the reader's attention, respect, and indeed fascination)" (51). With his interventions on the subject of the art of writing fiction, and especially with his insistence on textual freedom, Fowles's narrator would seem to be willingly abandoning his narrative authority (which necessitates the sort of omniscience he has abjured) for the sake of increasing his narratorial authority, a tactic in keeping with his stated devotion to the "writerly" cause. Nevertheless, the narrator goes on masterminding the plot at the same time that he most vocally declares the merits of a freer and more self-reflexive narrative process, a ruse that is evident in his preamble to the novel's famous multiple endings. Even though he claims to have sworn off the "fight-fixing" (317) prac- tised by traditional novelists in determining how their narratives conclude, he betrays the duplicity behind his apparent liberality: "And we judge writers of fiction […] by the skill they show in fixing the fights (in other words, in per- suading us that they were not fixed)" (317). By engaging in metanarrational dis- cussions while continuing to reserve and control information to the very end of the novel, the narrator uses both types of authority to direct the reader towards a text fusing "readerly" and "writerly" tendencies.

Of the three possible conclusions made available by the narrator, the third is the least likely to fulfill conventional readerly expectations. The most likely to do so, of course, is the one in which Charles and Ernestina marry; but the nar- rator makes this ending ridiculously ungratifying by pushing past the happy wedding to the unhappy marriage. The first ending, and the vapid sort of pleas- ure associated with it, is therefore debunked by the narrator in the same way conventional romance is in the poetry scene. The second ending promises to be more to the taste of both narrator and narratees, since Sarah has been held out all along as the proper object of both Charles's and their interest. Surely, read- ers think (as does Charles), some compromise can be found between conven- tional desire and newfangled, enigmatic pleasures. But the reconciliation of Charles and Sarah, with its built-in test of his conversion to the "modern," is quickly disappointing: Sarah's mysteriousness is reduced to moralistic "para- bles" (360), and the whole scene becomes a sappy reworking of Charles's expe- rience with the prostitute, complete with bathos and adorable infant. The sec- ond ending, we soon see, is no more than a tawdry melodrama got up by a the- atrical "impresario" (362), as the narrator fancies himself in his second cameo. It is only after providing his readers with these two obviously inadequate choic- es that the narrator "offers" a third, Sarah's rejection of Charles—the least palatable from a traditional viewpoint, since it denies any reassuring romantic closure. Paradoxically, this last ending becomes the most satisfying of the three, but precisely because the narrator tenders it as the only reasonable alternative to the other two. Also, because of the order in which the endings are presented, the third one seems, as the narrator confesses in advance will be the case, to be "the final, the 'real' version" (318). In his terms, he "fixes the fight," making up readers' minds for them at the same time that he is complimenting their self-aware and independent abilities to choose for themselves. Just as Sarah "manipulates" Charles "[f]rom the first [...] to the end" (364), so too, then, does the narrator manipulate his readers: he reorients their desires so that they cannot help but actually prefer what would normally frustrate them.[10]

Some commentators see in this parallel manipulation an essentially altruistic motive on the part of both Sarah and the narrator with regard to their respective narratees. Tarbox, for instance, excuses Sarah's game-playing on the grounds that she does it because she is deliberately "training Charles away from contradictions, appearances, superficies, and conventions" (70); further, she asserts that the "methods of instruction" used by Sarah and the narrator are "virtually identical," and that "everything Sarah does to Charles, the narrator does to his reader, and for the same reason" (83). Rankin echoes this view by stating that "both Charles and the reader are manipulated towards ends that are ultimately advantageous to both" (197). Charles's solitary wandering away from the final estrangement thus serves as a figuration of the readers' exhilarated perplexity with the new-found liberty given by this postmodern narrative. To argue that Sarah and the narrator mutually perform their deceptions for the sole reason of liberating their victims from Victorian constraints would be to overlook the means for the end, however.

Although Charles and readers may eventually profit from their victimization, it is important to remember that their ostensible "freedom" derives from machinations carried out as much for the seducers' benefit as for theirs. Rankin contends that, while both Sarah and the narrator produce good results, the latter's intentions in doing so are fundamentally more benign:

---

[10]Loveday gives another reason for the third ending's unavoidable superiority: he says that, in this conclusion, the narrator returns to the "non-omniscient" voice that he used in Chapter 13, which readers have been trained up to this point in the novel to respect more than the "ridiculous" and openly "manipulative" voice he uses elsewhere (59–60). Rankin interestingly matches up the three endings with Sarah's three "stories": her narrative seduction of Charles which, like the narrator's "Ernestina" ending, is a "deliberate lie"; her post-coital retraction, which is a "melodramatic confession" directed at her audience's "romantic sensibilities," just as the first "Sarah" ending is aimed at ours; and her final claim to have changed from her days in Lyme, when she was afflicted by a "madness" (351), which corresponds with her rejection of Charles. As Rankin deduces, only this last option is plausible, because it, like the third ending, "is the missing piece which completes the puzzle" (206).

> Whatever Sarah's motives were, they were basically selfish; Charles's
> best interest was not her concern, although his best interest was finally
> served by her actions. The narrator's motives are more apparent: he has
> been manipulating his audience not out of any selfish need, but simply
> for the purpose of constructing a meaningful world. (206)

That "meaningful world," of course, is constructed for the appreciation of the readership, whose captivation it is the narrator's business to secure. The narrator, then, also has a self-interested stake in his deceptive gambit, and like Sarah, he is not above calling on a variety of conventional and unconventional practices to achieve his aim.

As Fowles's intratextual surrogate, the narrator comes up with a number of ploys designed to appeal to readers, including using aspects of the classic "readerly" narrative to sell them on the virtues of the current international trends in writing. This narrative strategy, which was designed to have had the greatest impact contextually on the text's contemporary English audience, anticipates the reaction to the doubled sort of postmodern narrative of which Fowles's novel is representative. Successors to Fowles's effort—among which number postmodern works by Rushdie, Byatt, and others—form a particular strain within recent British fiction, combining the "writerly" sophistication characteristic of modernism and experimentalism with the "readerly" attractions of postwar realism. *The French Lieutenant's Woman* is about seduction—the readers' seduction—by the pleasure of the postmodern text.

An analysis of the embedded scenes of storytelling and seduction in Fowles's novel yields an implied reader whose features include an alertness to self-referential narrative material and a refusal to identify unreservedly with the position characterized for him or her by the metafictional text. Chapter Two will show how this sort of hermeneutic self-consciousness is advocated as the basis of the ideal reader's role in an allegory devoted specifically to the act of reading postmodern fiction.

# Chapter Two
# A Postmodern Allegory of Reading: Angela Carter's
## *The Infernal Desire Machines of Doctor Hoffman*

When Desiderio, the hero of Carter's *The Infernal Desire Machines of Doctor Hoffman*, finally penetrates the Doctor's defences and enters the Castle, he not only succeeds in his mission to defeat his enemy, but he also acts out the movement from modernism to postmodernism. Gone is the epistemological uncertainty that gave Franz Kafka's modernist edifice its mystery; instead, what Desiderio finds are the inner workings of the Doctor's warfare, the gizmos responsible for the fabulous apparitions and unsettling timescape that have taken over the world, and his immediate response is one of disappointment: "My disillusionment was profound. I was not in the domain of the marvellous at all. I had gone far beyond that and at last I had reached the power-house of the marvellous, where all its clanking, dull, stage machinery was kept" (201). While this anticlimax might seem to be a pointed indictment of postmodern textual self-consciousness—an attitude that would conflict strangely with the substance of the foregoing narrative and Carter's general *modus operandi*—it is not. For, as Desiderio goes on to clarify, it is not the magical entities themselves which are disappointing, but their source: "Indeed, I knew from my own experience that, once liberated, those desires it seemed to me he cheapened as he talked of them were far greater than their liberator and could shine more brightly than a thousand suns and yet I did not think that he knew what desire was" (213). With his discovery of the laboratory, Desiderio confirms what he has suspected all along: the Doctor has used the animated reflections of Desiderio's own unconscious desires, rigged in advance and controlled throughout his adventures, to lure him so that he can be coerced into fulfilling the Doctor's nefarious plan. Despite his pretences as an emancipator, then, the Doctor ultimately is no more than a "totalitarian" and a "hypocrite" (207–08). Only when Desiderio realizes that his own narcissism has been used against him does he truly gain freedom, a deliverance achieved after a painstaking, if unorthodox, undercover operation within the Doctor's dream-like "reality," ending with the decisive confrontation in the Castle.

This espionage, whose aim is to determine the truth behind the Doctor's system, dramatizes readers' efforts to piece together the text's meaning, as they make connections among the multivalent figures and symbols repeated across its episodic structure. By setting up Desiderio's experiences as an allegorical paradigm for the reading process, Carter creates a characterized reader's position that we can analyze, with the aid of various kinds of extratextual knowledge, to reconstruct the implied readers which the text theorizes for itself. These ideal readers are prompted to a realization analogous to Desiderio's; that is, just as he becomes cognizant of the Doctor's manipulation of his unconscious wishes, they should make themselves aware of how readerly desires are mobilized and directed by the external force of narrative. Through this awareness, readers can break subjective identification with the text, and especially with Desiderio as their surrogate, and instead objectively consider how and why those desires are being projected. The novel's debunking of the Doctor's "machinery" is therefore not a condemnation of overt textual artifice, which in fact helps to disrupt identification, but rather a gesture highlighting the potential for ideal readers of postmodern fiction to move beyond conventionally passive roles and self-consciously consider their participation in the act of reading.

One of the ways in which *The Infernal Desire Machines of Doctor Hoffman* evokes readerly self-scrutiny is by openly reworking exemplary modernist intertexts which are themselves allegorical representations of reading. Both Kafka's *The Castle* and Marcel Proust's *Remembrance of Things Past* deal with the subject's search for meaning amidst indeterminacy. This search involves the attempt to bridge, as Alan Wilde suggests, the "omnipresent separation of self and world" by sending outward from individual consciousness the "value and meaning" (15) that the world itself lacks. In the modernist context, this reconciliation is tentatively accomplished, if at all, through aestheticization. Brian McHale points out that the modernist novel, through its disjointed narrative composition, frequently "transfers the epistemological difficulties of its characters to its readers" (9); the act of reading thus parallels the characters' hermeneutical drive for understanding as the reader strives, as they do, to impose a coherent interpretation on inchoate data. While *The Infernal Desire Machines of Doctor Hoffman* continues the practice of internally figuring readers' epistemological encounters with the text, it also, as we have seen, conspicuously goes beyond the modernist undertaking, since it exposes the mechanics of how the textual world is created. In what McHale would describe as a typically postmodern development, Carter's novel transforms the epistemological activity associated with reading into an ontological one, positioning its central character within a state of being where self literally *becomes* world—whatever Desiderio subconsciously wishes comes to life—rather than merely casting meaning onto it across an interpretive distance. This postmodern emphasis on ontology makes it possible to re-examine the modernist problematic in terms of desire: when one attempts to give "value and meaning" to a text, to what extent does one also project one's subconscious desires onto it? By taking the episte-mological confrontation represented in her modernist predecessors, and restag-ing it as a fantasy in which an allegorical figure's desires are instantaneously realized, Carter renders visible the process of subjective projection latent in the act of reading.

To clarify how *The Infernal Desire Machines of Doctor Hoffman* both internalizes and reframes the concerns of its modernist precursors, we will look first at one of the novel's primary intertexts, Proust's *Remembrance of Things Past*, and particularly at Paul de Man's treatment of it in *Allegories of Reading*. Through his narrator Marcel's obsessive pursuit of Albertine (who appears in revised form in Carter's novel), Proust combines the epistemological search for truth with the frustrations arising from the limitations of subjective externaliza-tion. While Marcel's eventual turn to writing is generally regarded as the reso-lution of his estrangement from life, de Man argues instead that the narrative of Marcel's experiences (the novel itself) in fact reveals the unbridgeable disjunc-tion between self and world, and thus symbolizes "reading" as an endless "flight of meaning" (78), perceptible in the text's tropological preference for metonymy over metaphor. This review of the Proustian intertext via de Man will illuminate desire as the invisible energy that propels the reading process.

-i-

The idealized love object pursued by Marcel throughout *Remembrance of Things Past* begins as a vague notion connected with the visions of distant lands summoned by his childhood reading:

> Thus for two consecutive summers I sat in the heat of our Combray gar-den, sick with a longing inspired by the book I was then reading for a land of mountains and rivers […]. And since there was always lurking in my mind the dream of a woman who would enrich me with her love, that dream in those two summers was quickened by the fresh coolness of running water […]. (1.92)

De Man contends that the frequent impulses for both love and travel in Proust's work relate to his overall thematization of the reading process; they signify "an irresistible motion that forces any text beyond its limits and projects it towards an exterior referent. The movement coincides with a need for a meaning" (70). Marcel's search for meaning through love entails his considering a series of prototypes—Swann's liaison with the unfaithful Odette, his own relationship with Gilberte—before he happens, in late adolescence, upon Albertine among a group of girls at a seaside resort.

From the outset, Albertine is associated with birds and flight, and it is her elusiveness that Marcel finds most appealing. He at first believes that the pleasure in getting to know her will come from having to abandon solipsism to encounter something new. This movement outside the self to understand the beloved, according to Gilles Deleuze in *Proust and Signs*, is in effect an act of reading: "The beloved appears as a sign, a 'soul': the beloved expresses a possible world unknown to us, implying, enveloping, imprisoning a world which must be deciphered, that is, interpreted" (7). As time passes, however, Marcel loses interest in Albertine's differences, and starts to reimagine her through the lens of his own fantasies, gradually displacing her individuality:

> That Albertine was scarcely more than a silhouette, all that had been superimposed upon her being of my own invention, to such an extent when we love does the contribution that we ourselves make outweigh— even in terms of quality alone—those that come to us from the beloved object. (1.917–18)

Even at this early stage, Albertine is, as Nicholas Kostis points out, "predominantly a projection of Marcel's desires" (70); she becomes for Marcel, as Germaine Brée notes Odette did for Swann, "simply a pretext for this indirect narcissism" (150). When Marcel finally meets Albertine, his expectations are thwarted, for she does not live up to the image he has created of her. Nonetheless, he perseveres with the courtship, though this process is also discouraging, for two reasons. First, Albertine seems always to be changing—she has, for instance, a beauty spot that seems to be in a different place each time Marcel sees her—making it difficult for him to grasp her nature. After describing how her looks could alter from one day to the next, he says: "each of these Albertines was different, as is each appearance of the dancer whose colours, form, character, are transmuted according to the endlessly varied play of a projected limelight" (1.1010). Second, Marcel cannot stop himself from wanting Albertine to conform to his vision of her as his perfect lover, a wish complicated by the possibility that she is a lesbian. Marcel's need to know about and control Albertine's daily activities develops into an obsession, until she almost becomes his captive. Only when she is asleep does Marcel feel that she reflects back to him his desires: "I had an impression of possessing her entirely which I never had when she was awake" (3.64). To the end of their unconsummated relationship, Albertine continues to evade Marcel's increasingly frantic attempts at possession. In Deleuze's terms, Marcel's failure to decipher Albertine as a "sign," to fathom the "unknown world" she represents, illustrates his inability to use love as a way of moving beyond narcissism to satisfy his general yearning for meaning.

Marcel's unsuccessful career with Albertine exemplifies the "subjective idealism" (Brée 160) that influences all of his dealings with the outside world, making him anticipate that his desires will be faithfully realized there, and resulting in an inevitable succession of disappointments:

> We try to discover in things, which become precious to us on that account, the reflection of what our soul has projected on them; we are disillusioned when we find that they are devoid of the charm which they owed, in our minds, to the association of certain ideas [...]. (1.93)

De Man calls attention to this passage as an indication that what Marcel seeks, in the rhetorical sense derived from the work of Roman Jakobson,[1] is "the complementary and totalizing power of metaphor" (71); that is, Marcel hopes to experience truth by locating the resemblance between his preconceptions and actuality. In the last book of *Remembrance of Things Past*, Marcel believes that he finds this truth, which life could not produce, in art. Through his writing, Marcel aspires to preserve the essence of his flashes of involuntary memory, which disclose a meaningfulness to experiences and objects transcending their mere objective reality. Writing should therefore obviate his disillusionment by uncovering retrospectively the correspondences between the world and his perceptions of it.

According to de Man, Proust sets out in the passage about Marcel's childhood reading from Book One to show how that activity, like writing, should reconcile Marcel's internal life with the external world. Although the passage

---

[1]For Jakobson's seminal discussion of metaphor and metonymy, see his "Two Aspects of Language and Two Types of Aphasic Disturbances," in Fundamentals of Language, The Hague: Mouton, 1956, especially pp. 76–82.

apparently relies on metaphors to establish reading as a method of rendering Marcel's introversion compatible with active life, de Man demonstrates through a detailed rhetorical analysis that its subtle use of metonymy undoes its totalizing effect.[2] Owing to the undermining presence of metonymy, which links ideas according to contiguous association rather than inherent similarity, de Man concludes that the passage does not harmonize Marcel's inner and outer lives, but rather shows up their disparity.

De Man analyzes this passage to suggest how "reading"—in both the senses of engagement with the world at large, and engagement with a written text—is allegorized in *Remembrance of Things Past*. Just as Marcel's rationalizing of his seclusion only *seems* to work on the basis of metaphoric resemblance, so too does Proust's novel only *seem* to bring about a final aesthetic unification between perception and object, self and other. Instead, the narrative as a whole betrays the fact that the subject's relation to the "inner book of unknown symbols" (3.913) that is the world is always contingent, and that satisfactory interpretation of that "book" is as elusive as Albertine's true character is to Marcel. Consequently, de Man argues, as an "allegory of reading," *Remembrance of Things Past* "narrates the impossibility of reading" (77); regardless of its integrative modernist ending, it depicts the individual in a never-ending and constantly disillusioned quest for meaning that is fugitive and forever out of reach.

---

[2]As a justification of the narrator's decision to remain inside on summer's days in defiance of his family's wishes, the passage presents reading, de Man suggests, "as a defensive motion [...] it is an inner, sheltered place [...] that has to defend itself against the invasion of an outside world, but that nevertheless has to borrow from this world some of its properties" (59). To wage his defence, Marcel describes how the buzzing of the flies in his room evoke summertime, not through random association as "human music" might, but rather "by a more compelling tie—born of the sunny days, and not to be reborn but with them, containing something of their essential nature" (1.89). Hence, Marcel believes that he experiences summer more fully by staying indoors reading than by venturing out. With this trope (the synecdoche of the flies for the entire season), de Man says, Proust brings the outside in, taking the first step towards exposing the hidden similarities between Marcel's reclusive reading and participation in the world. This is not enough, however, to generate the truth that comes with metaphoric correspondence; for "totalization" to occur, de Man asserts, "the inwardness of the sheltered reader must also acquire the power of a concrete action" (63)—that is, the inside must also be seen reciprocally to move outward. The passage's final simile—"my state of repose [...] sustained, like a hand reposing in a stream of running water, the shock and animation of a torrent of activity" (1.90)—intends to attribute to Marcel's leisurely entertainment the energy of real action; thus, de Man states, "[t]he guilty pleasures of solitude are made legitimate because they allow for a possession of the world at least as virile and complete as that of the hero whose adventures he is reading" (64). Yet this final step toward reconciliation takes place through the chance verbal linkages between "torrent" and water, and "torrent" and heat ("torride")—a metonymic connection.

What de Man's exegesis ignores, however, is the element of desire that pervades this quest, as is evident in Marcel's relationship with Albertine. When Marcel attempts to interpret Albertine as an unknown phenomenon, he uses her as a means of realizing an already formed desire from his own subconscious, rather than coming to terms with her as a separate being. Since she does not fulfill that desire, he must proceed to the next "object" in search of success. As we have seen, this action is futile, for the external world can never fully reflect the inner one; Marcel, as a "reading subject," is left in a perpetual motion of projection and failure.

This combination of projected desire and restless reaching after meaning, which Carter adapts from *Remembrance of Things Past*, corresponds to metonymy as reconceptualized in psychoanalytic terms by Jacques Lacan. According to Lacan, the (male) subject is forced to repress his desires and sever himself from blissful unity with his mother, entering instead the world of language in which words are detached from their signifieds, and meaning can only be generated provisionally through the contiguity of signifiers. The subject travels through this "symbolic order," projecting his repressed desire in the hope of recovering it, yet is always disappointed. Since no one signifier can ever adequately capture what is lost, he can only keep moving along the chain of signification. Lacan describes this process as "that of being caught in the rails—eternally stretching forth towards the *desire for something else*—of metonymy" (*Ecrits* 167). Working from the Lacanian definition of metonymy as a simultaneous movement and projection of desire, we can see how Carter both builds on her modernist intertexts and makes use of psychoanalytic theory to create a postmodern allegory of reading.

-ii-

Like Marcel, Desiderio is a "reader" of the world he inhabits, interpreting what he sees around him in an effort to divine the meaning behind the Doctor's scheme; he recalls: "Now I know that the manifestations of those days were [...] a language of signs which utterly bemused me because I could not read them. Each phantom was a symbol palpitating with appalling significance" (25). Unlike Marcel, though, Desiderio lives in a world in which the phenomena are not empirically real, but rather are "personified ideas" (18) actualized from the subconscious. While Marcel can only try to make Albertine into a reflection of himself, Desiderio can actually create Albertina in the forms of his fantasies. In keeping with his allegorical sobriquet—and the Doctor's revised *cogito*: "I DESIRE THEREFORE I EXIST" (211)—Desiderio is impelled only by desire, and specifically by desires that apparently emanate from himself and not others. These desires are projected across the landscape through which he travels, taking the forms of various displaced and condensed figures and situations, repeated, with differences, from episode to episode like dream-images. Desiderio follows these contiguous "signs," able to make some loose connections among them owing to his "facility in the processes of analogical thought" (40), developed through his hobby of doing crossword puzzles; and while each of them seems to bring him nearer to his destination, none truly embodies his desires. In effect, the Doctor's altered "reality" through which Desiderio moves is a fantastical version of Lacan's metonymic chain, a zone in which "nothing" is "identical with itself any more" (12), where progress takes place by means of the casting forward of unappeased desire from materialized signifier to signifier. In contrast, the purview of the Minister of Determination, who believes that "the identity of a thing lay only in the extent to which it resembled itself" (23), is closer to the tropological stability of metaphor, though in this case without the gratification characteristic of Lacan's Imaginary union. We can chart Desiderio's journey in search of meaning and fulfillment from a "metaphoric" condition bereft of desire, through a "metonymic" one set into motion by his fantasy of Albertina, then back to the dull "metaphoric" mode. He arrives at this final stage after the disheartening discovery that what the Doctor's equipment manufactures are not genuine objectifications of his deepest wishes, but merely simulations of them intended to deceive him through his own narcissism.

Desiderio's trajectory approximates readers' engagement with literary narrative as they traverse its semantic field, tracing its underlying movement of desire with a view to eventually obtaining the text's withheld meaning. Using Sigmund Freud's *Beyond the Pleasure Principle* as a model for this kind of textual interaction, Peter Brooks theorizes in *Reading for the Plot* that narrative has embedded within it "a system of energy which the reader activates" (112). This system has as its primary motivation the attainment, by the shortest route possible, of an ending that notionally precedes the narrative's beginning, just as all basic organisms, according to Freud, instinctually wish "to restore an earlier state of things" (47), to return to original non-being through death. Between the two poles of initial and final "quiescence" (103) that mark the boundaries of the reading act, the reader is swept along the narrative's metonymic sequence, yearning for the significance that flickers through the links of the discursive chain but cannot be fully expressed in any one of them. For the terminus towards which the narrative relentlessly presses to deliver maximum revelation and satisfaction, it "must be," Brooks says, "the right death, the correct end" (103), which will allow the reader to "understand end in relation to beginning" (139). This stipulation requires the plot to undertake delays and detours involving various forms of internal resemblance—"repetition, repeat, recall, symmetry"—which help to "master" and "bind" the textual energy in preparation for the concluding "discharge" (101). Brooks refers to these textual components as "the motors [...] that drive and consume" narratives, but that also "implicate" (61) the reader in the dynamics of the plot; the reader invests his or her interest in the working-through of details, which reciprocally arouse and shape readerly desires. As D.W. Harding points out, while narrative may seem to realize pre-existent wishes, it also actively instills fantasies in readers' minds:

> It seems nearer the truth, therefore, to say that fictions contribute to defining the reader's or spectator's values, and perhaps stimulating his desires, rather than to suppose that they gratify desire by some mechanism of vicarious experience. (144)

In other words, when readers project desires onto a text, they do so in response to certain narrative cues rather than spontaneously. It is an awareness of the directive and formative influences that narrative exerts over desires that readers should reach in their parallel recognition to Desiderio's discovery of the Doctor's machinery, not so that literary texts will be denounced as totalitarian, but so that new attention will be focused on the process and results of projection.

Although Desiderio typifies *a* reader, he is not meant to be adopted unreservedly by individual readers as *their* representative; that is, readers should not identify with him and live his adventures vicariously without considering their implications. To do so would be to grant tacit approval to his often unsavory activities, particularly those with misogynistic overtones. By expressly making her allegorical figure male, Carter gives readers an opportunity to examine dispassionately the sexist attitudes emanating from Desiderio, which entail the projection of his masculine fantasies onto women without regard for their "otherness," reducing them to his negative and positive conceptions of them. Desiderio's "reading" habits thus consistently cast women into passive, objectified positions; but Carter's text, by reproducing those habits in exaggeratedly fantastic forms which are readily perceptible, makes it possible for its ideal audience to assume a level of self-conscious involvement appropriate to female readers (and writers) as they actively attempt to understand and change how women are conventionally constructed in the discourses of male-dominated cultures—a construction typified by Desiderio's fantasies.

In this respect, Desiderio's sexual relations have much in common with the text's motif of colonization. As McHale argues, the African society that appears in the sixth episode is made up "wholly from European fantasy," with "tribesmen straight out of party jokes, comic-strips, and slapstick comedy"; the purpose of this caricature, he says, is to "foreground" the "imperialism of the imagination" practised by Westerners, both generally and within their literature, and "expose it for what it is"—that is, the use of another culture as "a particularly inviting blank space" on which to realize their "dreams and wish-fulfillments" (55). McHale's analysis can equally apply to the novel's portrayals of the Arab acrobats, with their "slippery viciousness of manner" (112), and the vengeful black pimp. While Desiderio's maleness intentionally gives readers (of either sex) a conventionalized position against which to evaluate cultural objectifications of women, his membership in a marginalized group—the indigenous society massacred by the Europeans—provides an intratextual minority position from which these racial stereotypes can be seen "for what they are." The fact that these Eurocentric fantasies also emerge from Desiderio's unconscious in response to the Doctor's provocations demonstrates the extent to which his imagination has been infiltrated by others, just as he, in turn, colonizes women.

As a figure with whom readers should identify critically rather than subjectively, then, Desiderio makes evident the dangers of projecting cultural wishes onto the "blank spaces" of texts without taking into account either the ideological bases of those fantasies, or how they are being formed, as Harding suggests, by the texts themselves, reified in the same way that Desiderio's desires are reified by the Doctor's tableaux. What *The Infernal Desire Machines of Doctor Hoffman* proposes is that readers react to Desiderio with the detachment of what Harding calls the "onlooker" (134), seeing in him an image, not necessarily of themselves, but of the possibilities of their own reading processes. In a novel populated by often deceptive twins and *Doppelgängers*, Desiderio does not exist as a "projective other" (168) for readers as the pimp does for the Count, but rather as a characterized figure or "foil" calculated to turn readers' scrutiny back onto themselves. This agenda is emphasized by Carter's having the Count ironically invoke the last line of Charles Baudelaire's poem, "To the Reader": "You altered my compass so that it would point only to you, my hypocritical shadow, my double, my brother" (159). Carter fosters readerly distance by setting her allegory within a world whose textuality is openly signalled in several ways: frequent intertextual references, not only to the modernist period but also to Jonathan Swift's *Gulliver's Travels*, E.T.A. Hoffmann's *Tales*, etc.; constant literary stylizations, such that everything in the novel, like the Count, has "scarcely an element of realism" (123); the thematization of artifice and simulacra through the Doctor's creations; and metanarrational devices such as the opening and closing frames. With the aid of this postmodern textual self-consciousness, readers can recognize Desiderio as a constructed "alter ego," and his entire career as an allegory of how their own desires can be manipulated.

Owing to the advantage of extratextual knowledge, readers are cognizant, in ways that the character cannot be, of how Desiderio's desires are used to trick him. While he acknowledges his attraction to Albertina, he does not have the readers' intertextual access to *Remembrance of Things Past* to help him perceive how the Doctor capitalizes on his latent tendency to impose his ego onto others, especially love objects. In addition to projecting Albertina as a romantic ideal, the Doctor exploits the repressed contents of Desiderio's unconscious about his dead mother and missing father, both figurations of an originary loss which, in Freudian terms, formulates desire as lack. Desiderio does not realize the significance of many of the phenomena he encounters, and therefore cannot interpret them correctly, being led on unwittingly towards a goal predetermined by the Doctor. The unmastered material from Desiderio's infantile memory is repeated throughout the transferential medium of the Doctor's altered timescape, where the past continues to exist as if still present. When Desiderio quotes Freud's *The Interpretation of Dreams* to Albertina— "In the unconscious, nothing can be treated or destroyed" (186)—he chances momentarily upon the metanarrative that readers can bring to clarify practically all that happens to him. Drawing on psychoanalysis, readers can discern the interrelations among Desiderio's experiences, in particular how they combine to form an archetypal pattern that ultimately fails to restore the originary loss and bring the metonymic slippage of desire to a meaningful stop. Carter clearly overlays her narrative with psychoanalytic theory as a means of what Brooks calls plotting "with irony and bad conscience," the intent of which is "to expose the artifices of formal structure" (113). By making visible the metanarrative underpinnings of her narrative's structure, Carter allows readers to make connections among the intertextual references and repetitions, to "bind" the textual energy in such a way that the novel's ending seems to be "the right death, the correct end." That is, by piecing together how the central character is nearly swept to his doom because of his narcissistic projections, readers come to understand why Desiderio reaches the decision that he does, choosing regretful self-awareness over illusory fulfillment.

-iii-

The need for objective self-reflection is suggested by the opening frame, in which Desiderio comments from the vantage-point of old age on the memoirs of his youth, which he is writing for posterity's sake. Unlike *Remembrance of Things Past* in which past and present, "Marcel" and "Proust," eventually merge, *The Infernal Desire Machines of Doctor Hoffman* insists on an initial separation between character and narrator which reappears intermittently throughout the narrative. With his acknowledgement that "I am an old man now and no longer the 'I' of my own story" (14), Desiderio sets up a split position from which he can look back critically on his experiences at the same time that he relives them through writing. From this perspective, he can retrospectively examine how the Doctor almost succeeds in trapping him with his own narcissism, despite his belief in his own immunity from desire.

In the introductory frame, Desiderio claims that, like his leader the Minister whose impassive rationality he admires, he withstood the Doctor's "spooks":

> I survived because I could not surrender to the flux of mirages. I could not merge and blend with them; I could not abnegate my reality and lose myself [...]. I was too sardonic. I was too disaffected [...]. I believed perfection was, per se, impossible and so the most seductive phantoms could not allure me because I knew they were not true. (11–122)

This bravado is an act of retroactive embellishment, however, as is his later statement that he "knew [him]self to be a man without passion" (97). (The discrepancy between Desiderio's post-war recall and the "actual" events is evident in the first sentences of the frame and main narrative respectively: "I remember everything" [11] and "I cannot remember exactly how it began" [15].) In the main narrative, Desiderio's disaffection holds out only until certain manifestations from his own unconscious start to materialize. He then gradually loses his resistance to the Doctor's simulated phenomena and becomes susceptible to their temptation.

Until the arrival of Albertina in his dreams, Desiderio is equally bored with both sides of the war; only the prospect of finding and possessing her piques his interest in his assignment to leave the City in search of the Doctor. Although

Desiderio first meets Albertina in the semblance of the androgynous ambassador, his vision of her, nurtured by his dreams of her as a glass woman and a swan, is of a conventionally feminine love object: "I was nourishing an ambition—to rip away that ruffled shirt and find out whether the breasts of an authentic woman swelled beneath it [...]. And then? I would fall on my knees in worship" (41). Notwithstanding his expression of humble adoration, Desiderio wants Albertina to be consistent with this "ambition," which places the woman in an inferior position. That Desiderio, like Marcel, thinks of his lover as the objectification of his fantasies is clear in his statement in the Introduction: "I see her as a series of marvellous shapes formed at random in the kaleidoscope of desire" (13). With the assistance of the Doctor's magic, Desiderio experiences his fantasy in various forms, each of them involving submission, before meeting Albertina herself. The first of these prototypes, Mary Anne, is a composite of suicidal literary female figures, including Alfred Lord Tennyson's Mariana and William Shakespeare's Ophelia. Virtually alone in her mansion, Mary Anne is the exemplary Gothic heroine; and like Marcel with Albertine, Desiderio can make love to her only when she is asleep, seeing himself reflected by her mirror image the next morning in a symbol of narcissistic fulfillment. The child Aoi among the River People is similarly passively innocent as a partner, though she stops short of delivering complete sexual satisfaction. When Desiderio finally comes into contact with Albertina herself, she appears to him first as the abused slave Lafleur, and then as "herself" as the beautiful woman Desiderio first envisioned, though this turns out to be another disguise designed to entice him into the Doctor's clutches. By allowing Desiderio to externalize his erotic ideal of feminine compliance, the Doctor is able to lure him away from the Minister's dispassionate influence.

The movement from the Minister's realm into the maelstrom of desire is replayed in "The River People" episode, which also serves as an internalized allegory of reading. Like the Minister, the River People believe in a consistently stable reality, and thus are immune, like him, to the generated illusions. After narrowly escaping his first solo encounter with the Doctor's apparitions, Desiderio thinks that he has found a refuge from his own subconscious. (The possibility that the Indians themselves are projections does not seem to occur to him.) It is Desiderio, though, who disrupts this paradise by introducing the ability to read. Through his negotiation with a seed-broker over a contract, Desiderio shows himself to be a "magician" (79) along the lines of the Doctor. The capacity of written language to have meaning without its referents' being physically present threatens to sever the bond between signifier and signified that constitutes the Indians' understanding of the world. In response to Desiderio's attempt to teach him to write "the cat sat on the mat," his adopted father Nao-Kurai says: "'But, Kiku! [...] The cat sits there, on your knee, and though she is not the only cat in the world, she is for me the very essence of cat'" (79). When the lessons prove futile, the Indians conspire to eat him to gain his knowledge, a plot betrayed by Nao-Kurai's drunken tale about the snake eaten by his ancestors to acquire its Promethean skill of fire-making. Desiderio saves himself by interpreting Nao-Kurai's story with information gleaned from "an old book" (90)—likely by Claude Lévi-Strauss—which had, on a previous occasion, helped him to solve "a difficult crossword puzzle" (91).

This embedded scene, complete with its illuminatory parable, reasserts several key points that are made by the novel as a whole. First, reading has great power, and it is important to control that power self-consciously. Second, reading inevitably entails desire because it exposes the lack of "presence" in the individual sign and the necessity to produce meaning through contiguity. Third, once desire has been set into motion, there is no going back: Desiderio cannot return to "metaphoric" stability, either with the Minister or the River People, whose system he would have eventually destroyed. As a "reader," Desiderio can only keep moving along the metonymic field, a fact emphasized by his glimpse of Albertina as a gipsy girl, a reminder of the initiatory fantasy exploited by the Doctor.

This section of the text also encapsulates the repressed material concerning Desiderio's lack of a home and family which the Doctor taps into and projects along with Desiderio's romantic idealism. These archetypal desires for pre-Symbolic oneness, which Desiderio wants desperately to recapture but cannot, take various forms in each episode as the Doctor uses them as a means of leading his quarry to the Castle. Despite having a job in the City, Desiderio is always an outsider there owing to his paternal Indian background. While the River People's warm reception seems to provide the inclusiveness of a common heritage, their offer of asylum is fraught with danger, a pattern which continues in other instances where Desiderio is extended hospitality. For instance, when the Acrobats of Desire invite him to their caravan, they do so with the intention of raping him; Desiderio's suspicions should be raised by the presence of a stove, a recurring symbol from the "The River People" where it is associated with the plan to eat him. As the experience with Nao-Kurai suggests, Desiderio's inability to find a safe home is intimately connected with his disastrous relationships with father-figures.

In Nao-Kurai, Desiderio hopes to find a replacement for his unknown father, someone who will allow him to assume his place in the social order as both son and lover. As Lacan has theorized following Freud, the father plays two symbolic functions in the male child's psyche. First, he is the "Imaginary father [...] to whom is related the whole dialectic of aggressivity and identification" (*Language* 271); the child wishes to *be* the father in the sense that he wants to enjoy the father's sexual privileges with the mother. This Oedipal dilemma is usually cleared up by the second function, the Symbolic father, who, through the menace of castration, forces the child to repress his incestuous desires and instead await his chance to take over the father's role with a woman of his own. With the River People, however, Desiderio's Oedipal struggle is complicated and its resolution is blocked. Although Nao-Kurai appears to supply the missing paternal authority, with Aoi as the promised future bride, Desiderio is not prevented from having sex with the maternal figure, here represented by Nao-Kurai's own mother, "Mama." When the danger of castration eventually arises in Nao-Kurai's story (the snake is threatened with death when it sticks its head out of the girl's vagina), it does so in the context of cannibalism, since the snake is consumed for its power, as Desiderio nearly is also. In keeping with the primal myth of patricide told by Freud in *Totem and Taboo*, cannibalism should imply the son's rightful usurpation of the father; but here, it is the "father" who intends to eat the "son." Because of this basic reversal of the Oedipal process, Desiderio departs from the River People with his need for a proper paternal figure unsatisfied.

Because of his failure to find a substitute in Nao-Kurai, Desiderio continues to manifest his desire for a father in different ways throughout his journey. In later episodes, he tries unsuccessfully to fill this lack by projecting positions for himself as "son" in relation to various "fathers" or "masters"—for example, as the peep-show proprietor's "nephew" and the Count's "secretary." His foiled aspiration to identify with and surpass a paternal authority is clear in his exasperated statement among the Centaurs: "[P]erhaps the whole history of my adventure could be titled 'Desiderio in Search of a Master'. But I only wanted to find a master, the Minister, the Count, the bay, so that I could lean on him at first and then, after a while, jeer" (190).

Since Desiderio does not have the opportunity to finish his Oedipal passage properly, though, one means by which he deals with his incomplete genital organization is through sexual passivity, which, according to Juliet Mitchell, circumvents the possibility of castration: "[m]asochism and passivity of a man

before a woman imply no danger of loss of manhood as it is in that very role
that the mother accepted him" (52). Several of Desiderio's liaisons with women
are essentially passive—Mary Anne seduces him and Aoi fondles him, as do
the Centaur women—but it is when he is with the circus performers that this
fantasy is most fully realized. Madame La Barbe calls him "Désiré" (106)—
desired one—emphasizing his movement from erotic subject to object. Just
after recording the peep-show proprietor's castratory threat to "cut [his] hands
off" (108), Desiderio recounts how Mamie Buckskin, despite her lesbian orientation, liked having sex with him for she "admired passivity in a man more than
anything" (109). Desiderio's relationship with Mamie, "a fully phallic female
with the bosom of a nursing mother and a gun, death-dealing erectile tissue,
perpetually at her thigh" (108), also suggests the homosexual tendency that he
develops in reaction to his interrupted Oedipal progression. Mitchell notes that,
by accepting "the supposed *actual* castration (in phantasy) that is the mark of
femininity" (86), the male child can prolong his identification with the father
and imagine himself receiving the sexual attentions that had been lavished on
the mother.

In Freud's famous "Wolfman" case (*From the History of an Infantile
Neurosis*), the patient, who has also had pleasurable experiences being touched
by his sister, secretly wants to be used by his father *a tergo* as his mother had
been. Desiderio's homosexual wishes are set loose from his unconscious in his
sodomitical rape by the Acrobats of Desire, though in a particularly masochis-
tic manner. Both kinds of submissive sexuality are in conflict with his fundamental masculine narcissism and, like the Wolfman, Desiderio gradually learns
to suppress the impulses associated with them in favour of a more active attitude which transfers women into the passive position. He accomplishes this
shift first by displacing his homosexual urges onto Albertina in the form of the
boy Lafleur, who is violated "*in anum*" (168) by the Count, and then by recasting his ordeal with the Acrobats in heterosexual terms when Albertina is raped
by the Centaurs. Desiderio's unresolved feelings about his father therefore
underlie many of his fantasies, sexual and otherwise, which are brought to life
through the Doctor's machinations.

Desiderio also leaves the River People without having worked through his
repressed desires about his dead mother. In Freudian terms, we will recall, the
infant's separation from the mother marks the movement into a state of irreversible absence; the effort to regain maternal plenitude is central to
*Remembrance of Things Past*. In Carter's novel, Desiderio believes that he has

achieved this impossible feat when he is rescued by an Indian woman speaking what seems to be a pre-Symbolic language: "I recall the touch of fresh linen against my cheek and the sound of a woman's voice speaking a liquid and melodious language which took me back to my earliest childhood, before the time of the nuns" (66). In Mama, Desiderio appears to recover the nurturing he lost when his mother died, as well as fulfill his incestuous sexual drive; he says of her, "Indeed, I was growing almost reconciled to mothers" (85). Nonetheless, Desiderio's attitude towards his actual mother is too complex to be resolved so easily and pleasantly.

Following from his Oedipal jealousy of his father, Desiderio blames his mother for having had sex, as a prostitute, with other men. The depth of Desiderio's hostility towards his mother is evident in the fact that, in the first days of the Doctor's phantasms, she appears to him in diverse shapes, always expressing penitence for her "sins" (12).[3] Yet Desiderio is unwilling to grant her bid for atonement, and he consistently relates maternity with cruel and profligate sexuality, such as when he describes the Count as having "cursed the womb that bore him" (125) at the climax of his rape of Lafleur/Albertina.

Desiderio's unconscious image of his mother as heartless is inflated, in "The Coast of Africa," into an army of cold-blooded Amazons who defy all "the traditional notions of the figure of the female" and who collectively signify a ruthless version of motherhood, as described by their Chief to Desiderio and the Count:

> Tear this [traditional] notion of the mother from your hearts. Vengeful as nature herself, she loves her children only in order to devour them better [...]. Not one of my callipygian soldiery but has not earned her rank by devouring alive, first gnawing limb from limb and sucking the marrow from its bones, her first-born child. (160)

Along with their cannibalism, which inverts the natural order in the same way that Nao-Kurai's attempted "infanticide" does, these mothers are symbolically menacing because of their association with castration. The clitorises of the women in the tribe are removed, the Chief explains, because "[his] early researches soon showed [him] that the extent of a woman's feelings was directly related to her capacity for feeling during the sexual act" (160). This practice, in contrast to the more benevolent policies of the River People who extend

---

[3]The obvious modernist intertext here is Joyce's Ulysses, in which Stephen Dedalus is guiltily haunted by his "beastly dead" mother for whom he refused to kneel down and pray.

girls' clitorises in order to enhance their enjoyment, connects Desiderio's mother's emotionless sexuality as a prostitute with his buried resentment towards her. Desiderio's ambivalence about his own mother is thus projected as a series of fantasy and nightmare scenarios involving mothers in general.

Desiderio's animosity towards his mother also reveals itself in the numerous manifestations produced from his unconscious in which women are violently subjugated, especially sexually, and/or presented in some dehumanized manner. The Doctor plays on Desiderio's negative feelings about women by presenting to him, near the beginning of his mission, exhibits and "samples" which inculcate certain ideas into his mind for later realization and guide him in the direction of his final entrapment. The first of these collections, the peep-show's "SEVEN WONDERS OF THE WORLD" (42), uses automata to depict women, including Albertina, in various positions of sexual submission and mutilation. While women are related throughout the novel to machinery and dolls, in the early adventures these associations are not particularly malevolent; Desiderio thinks of the River People's women, for instance, as "benign automata" (73). Similarly, female characters in the opening episodes are frequently portrayed in relatively innocuous terms that blend the human with other characteristics, such as Mary Anne, who is like "a plant bred in a cupboard" (53); this hybridization is made possible by the dream-like conditions created by the war, in which the usual classifications and categories of empirical reality give way to fusion and condensation.

As Desiderio progresses, however, and especially as his desires are given freer rein following the temporary suspension of the Doctor's control with the loss of the samples, these references take on more pernicious connotations, leading up to the Count's ruthless orgy in the "House of Anonymity." Not only do the brothel's occupants bring to mind Desiderio's mother's profession, but the scene is also redolent of how he remembers being terrified by her sexual activities as a child: "I would lie awake at night and hear my mother panting and grunting like a tiger in the darkness beyond the curtain and I thought she had changed into a beast" (30). The impression left by this traumatic memory literally materializes in the bordello in several forms: the libidinous Count, whose "emblem" (124) is the tiger, and who chooses for his pleasure a flagellated whore, "my striped tiger woman [...] a cannibal feast" (135); the live animal furniture in the Bestial Room; and the prostitutes themselves, "the wax mannequins of love," who are "the only beings kept in cages" (131). Bringing together the previous images of women both as mechanisms and hybrids, Desiderio describes the prostitutes as "sinister, abominable, inverted mutations, part clockwork, part vegetable and part brute" (132). Through the absolute dehumanization of women in a setting of sexual debasement, the scene in the House of Anonymity culminates the externalization of Desiderio's repressed maternal hatred.

Although Desiderio, who spends most of his time in the brothel in a romantic interlude with Albertina, may appear to be innocent of the brutality towards women that occurs there, it is important to recall that everything that he encounters, including the Count, is a product of his own subconscious. Just as the Count believes himself to be a "dream of the black pimp" (148) while, as Albertina points out to him, the opposite is the case, so too does Desiderio mistakenly think that his existence is superseded by that of the Count, with his superior will and extreme narcissism. Rather, as the pimp is for him, the Count is for Desiderio an "icon of his own destructive potential"; and Desiderio is not only the Count's "audience" but also his "dramatist" (168), conducting by proxy the sexual atrocities to which he seems only to be a passive witness. When Desiderio apathetically agrees to join the Count's search for lustful escapades, he is therefore actually advancing his own aims.

Throughout Desiderio's journey, he is attracted to communities that offer him self-effacement, such as the River People and the circus; yet, as the brothel's ironic name makes clear, what he ends up achieving instead of anonymity is a total imposition of ego onto the world around him, a process of which the Count's sadistic treatment of the prostitutes is the most acute example. While Desiderio is so tenderly engaged with Albertina, then, another part of his "self" is acting out his more violently oppressive attitude towards women, a split that reveals the dark underside of the conventional reverence of femininity that he builds up around his various love objects.

In the episode before Desiderio's arrival at the Castle, both his romantic and repressed desires take the form of a cumulative, narcissistic self-expression that is paradoxically the final stage of his surrender to the Doctor. The tropical forest of "Nebulous Time" through which Desiderio and Albertina pass in Edenic unity reflects the mixture of horrors and fantasies in Desiderio's unconscious: while some plants are "cannibal and full of perils" (166), others with nipples give milk in response to his wish for maternal care. The earlier oneiric collapsing of categories results here in floral-faunal hybrids, as well as the Centaurs themselves, who spring, with modifications, from Desiderio's recollections of *Gulliver's Travels*.

His archetypal feelings about his mother and father are recapitulated through the belief system that he projects for the Centaurs. The myth of the

Sacred Stallion, who is betrayed by the Bridal Mare with the Dark Archer, continues Desiderio's antagonism towards maternal infidelity; the Centaur women are punished for this crime with severe suffering and additional penance, a magnified version of Desiderio's mother's ghostly atonement. The Centaurs' general degradation of women based on this myth provides the vicarious circumstances in which Desiderio can remorsefully perform his rape of Albertina, bringing to fruition the picture implanted in his mind by the peep-show operator's photographs of horses trampling a young woman to death.

In terms of paternal anxiety, the Centaurs' mythology reiterates the canni-balistic death of the Symbolic father introduced with Nao-Kurai: the Sacred Stallion, eaten by the Bridal Mare and her lover to conceal their murder of him, returns eternally as his own foal, preventing the son from ever taking his prop-er place in the hierarchy. While in "The River People" Desiderio's crossword puzzle acumen enables him to escape from the danger posed by a father-figure, in this case that skill simply allows him to understand the Centaurs' books (the first ones to appear since the disastrous reading lesson); he is cut off from the power of writing, the sole preserve of the Scrivener, and at the mercy of his host, the bay. Instead, it is Desiderio and Albertina who become the objects of "reading," a "sign from heaven" (184) to be deciphered, a passive condition that leads to their nearly being sacrificed by the Centaurs.

Desiderio thus becomes the prisoner of creatures generated from his mem-ory of a book, and he gradually cedes his own identity to that of a fictional char-acter; like Gulliver, he questions his own humanity: "If I was a man, what was a man?" (189). Unlike in earlier episodes, he can no longer escape on his own, but must wait for the Doctor's troops to rescue him and Albertina. In effect, Desiderio becomes a complacent victim of his own externalized desires, suc-cumbing to the apparitions he was so certain he could withstand.

Although the Castle holds out the hope of supreme fulfillment for Desiderio—of his wishes to possess Albertina and to learn the Doctor's secret—there are indications en route that it will only give disappointment. Once in the helicopter, Albertina immediately loses her Eve-like splendor, don-ning combat fatigues and answering to "Generalissimo Hoffman" (192). Desiderio notes that "she put away all her romanticism," and that he conse-quently "felt an inexplicable indifference towards her" (193). By assuming a role of masculine superiority, Albertina conflicts with Desiderio's fantasy of her as his romantic partner, placing him unexpectedly in a position of passivity which he no longer craves; she also exposes herself as a separate being, one who has been working to ensnare him. With his growing awareness of Albertina's treachery, Desiderio can extricate himself from her and recover some of his immunity to passion, reaffirming his commitment to the Minister's side. Concomitantly, he begins once again to be aware of the inherent artificiality of everything connected with the Doctor, a fact to which he had been blinded while under the influence of his own unconscious manifestations. Both the Doctor's troops and the Castle itself seem to him like images from films, and he doubts the authenticity of all that he sees: "Although it was real, I knew the perfection around me was impossible" (197). As a potential haven where Desiderio might overcome his persistent feeling of being an outsider, the Castle threatens to be a letdown: "I waited expectantly for a sense of homecoming but I experienced nothing [...]. I thought that perhaps now I was a stranger everywhere" (195). Rather than acting as a "home," a potent signifer that would bring to rest his search for satisfaction and answers, the Castle, Desiderio suspects, will only leave him discontented.

Desiderio's suspicion that his quest has brought him to a false destination is borne out by his experience within the Doctor's domain. Instead of adequate replacements for his absent mother and father, Desiderio finds only reminders of their lack: Albertina's mother is a corpse, and the Indian graveyard on the Castle grounds betokens the demise of his paternal ancestors. Further, the Doctor is shown to be the last in the series of failed masters. Unimpressed by the prosaic nature of the Doctor's technical innovations and the dryness of his methods, Desiderio thinks of him as a poor "Prometheus" (209) in comparison with the Count, who, as a figment of Desiderio's own imagination, better suits his notion of a mad genius with desire as his creative medium. Unlike the snake in Nao-Kurai's story, the Doctor does not have any new magic to share, only pre-formulated phenomena derived from the external world and others' minds, then scientifically reproduced as a form of mass domination.

Using an established "sample" from Desiderio's unconscious, the Doctor attempts to exercise control over him one last time by transforming Albertina into the "romantic heroine" (201) of his reverie. In doing so, the Doctor animates Desiderio's narcissistic vision; Albertina becomes his female mirror image, an incarnation of the "model of eternal regression" (45) prefigured by the exhibit of the reflecting eyes among the Seven Wonders. Desiderio follows Proust's Marcel, however, in being skeptical about the ability of reality to measure up to the original fantasy; looking at Albertina in her Victorian garb, he thinks: "Even if it is the dream made flesh, the real, once it becomes real, can be no more than real [...]. I was already wondering whether the fleshly posses-sion of Albertina would not be the greatest disillusionment of all" (201). Because Albertina as an individual necessarily differs from Desiderio's ideal, she will inevitably disappoint him, regardless of the persuasiveness of the Doctor's mirages.

When Albertina sheds her disguise as a hermaphrodite and reveals, as promised, her "true" identity in the laboratory, Desiderio is no longer fooled by her romanticized exterior:

> She wiped the silver from her eyes and the purple dress dropped away from the goddess of the cornfields, more savagely and triumphantly beautiful than any imagining, my Platonic other, my necessary extinc-tion, my dream made flesh.
>
> 'No!' I cried. 'No, Generalissimo! No!' (215)

Remembering Albertina's previous departure from conventional femininity, Desiderio is able to resist her overtures and thereby save himself from being turned into an automaton in the same way that he has been allowed to objecti-fy women throughout his travels. Although Desiderio kills the Doctor as father-figure, finally completing his Oedipal passage, he must also kill Albertina to protect himself, so he is still blocked from consummating their union and assuming his place in the sexual order. After leaving the Castle, Desiderio is taken in briefly by Indians, yet remains "homeless,"[4] since neither his archetyp-al nor his erotic desires have been fulfilled by his journey.

While Desiderio succeeds in crossing the phantasmagoric landscape and attaining his goal, what he finds when he gets there is that his arrival has been prearranged, and that everything he has experienced along the way has been purposely concocted to make him believe that his unconscious urges could actually come to life. The Doctor comes close to prevailing with his deception by taking advantage of Desiderio's hidden narcissistic yearning to see himself reflected in the phenomena around him, including in others. The Doctor's plot is defeated through Desiderio's realization that wishes can never be given sat-isfactory concrete form; in his closing remarks to his manuscript, he notes that his predominant post-war feeling has been "that insatiable regret with which we

---

[4]The theme of homelessness, a powerful reminder of the modernist era, is emphasized by Carter's references to Oz-like scarecrows, particularly near the beginning and at the end of Desiderio's journey (see pages 41, 221), and by the Doctor's failure as a wizard-figure to send Desiderio "home."

acknowledge that the impossible is, *per se*, impossible" (221). At the end of his travails, he knows that there can be no metaphoric correspondence between self and other, because the world as a "text" is incapable of fully embodying desire.

Nonetheless, the stasis of the closing frame, penned from the drab safety of the City, is only temporary, for Desiderio's longing persists, despite its ultimate unattainability. With the return of his dream of Albertina—"Unbidden, she comes" (221)—the motion of Desiderio's desire recommences, actuating the narrative that he writes to enliven his old age, and that readers encounter as Carter's text.

-iv-

After following Desiderio's oblivious progression through the terrain of his own objectified unconscious to the recognition that saves him, readers can "understand end in relation to beginning," appreciating why the text's conclusion denies fulfillment and insists on self-perception at the expense of gratification. Through an active engagement with Desiderio's predicament, readers become aware of the process of subjective projection involved in reading, and of how their narcissistic wishes and cultural fantasies can be elicited and materialized by narrative without their knowledge, just as Desiderio finds that his desires have been deliberately managed by the Doctor. Readers are enjoined to practise "persistence of vision" (107), in the peep-show proprietor's phrase, to keep a clear view of their own capacity to expect the text-as-world to conform to their preconceptions.

Using self-conscious techniques that inhibit easy identification, and giving vivid textual form to psychoanalytic theories of desire and narrative, Carter puts the emphasis directly on readers' participatory role, thereby extending the work of her modernist predecessors such as Proust. Near the end of *Remembrance of Things Past*, Marcel reflects on the readers who will one day peruse his narrative:

> For it seemed to me that they would not be "my" readers but the readers of their own selves, my book being merely a sort of magnifying glass ...
> it would be my book, but with its help I would furnish them with the means of reading what lay inside themselves. (3.1089)

With her postmodern allegory, Carter provides her readers with just such an introspective device.

Psychoanalytic theory usefully illuminates the hidden meaning behind Carter's allegory, revealing how desire, the motivating force in narrative, can mislead readers if they relinquish their awareness of the process in which they are engaged. In the next chapter, we shall see that psychoanalysis is one of two metanarratives that can be used to interpret Swift's *Waterland* such that the novel's self-referential theorizing about fictional narrative's ability to influence our relationship to history becomes apparent.

# Chapter Three
## The Whole Story: Graham Swift's *Waterland*

Swift's *Waterland* epitomizes what Linda Hutcheon defines as "historiographic metafiction," one of the most prevalent types of postmodern literature. Texts of this variety use self-reflexive techniques to insist on their own status as fictions and, through the recounting of made-up pasts, disclose the generic similarities between literary narrative and history, which is traditionally assumed to record the "truth" in contradistinction to literature's "lies." Historiographic metafiction does not set out to deny that the events recorded in history really did occur, nor to claim, as Price taunts in *Waterland*, that they "only happened in the imagination" (121); rather, Hutcheon says, it "reminds us that [...] we name and constitute those events as historical facts by selection and narrative positioning" (*Poetics* 97). As Hayden White has pointed out, history is a discourse which, like fiction, refashions events in keeping with narrative conventions, endowing them with continuity that they did not originally have. The meaning of past events thus resides not in themselves, Hutcheon argues, but in the "*systems*" that give them "meaning and shape" (*Poetics* 89). It is these ordering principles that historiographic metafiction brings to our attention, disabusing us of our notions that the past can ever be reproduced completely accurately or "naturally"—that is, from a neutral ideological perspective. According to Hutcheon, novels such as *Waterland* instill in their readers an awareness of the tacit structures underlying all historical accounts, and point up the inaccessibility of the "real" past except through its "discursive inscription" (*Poetics* 97).

With its overt emphases on the fictionalizing processes involved in the telling of history, *Waterland* clearly produces the general deconstructive effects outlined by Hutcheon. Yet Swift's novel goes beyond exposing the affinities of literature and historiography to suggest that some of the narratives these discourses use in their reshaping of events can formulate and change human relationships to the past in authentic and measurable ways. In other words, the "systems" or stories with which we order historical experience, while themselves only reminders of that which is forever out of our reach, nonetheless act as means whereby we can genuinely alter our understandings of that unattainable reality. By examining how two such systems—psychoanalysis and Benjaminian historiography—function in *Waterland*, we can see that these metanarratives make possible, respectively, the mastery of trauma and the retrieval of incidents that had seemingly passed permanently from remembrance. These readings will clarify *Waterland*'s specific postmodern thematization of how narrative not only replaces the "truth" by constituting the basis of our historical knowledge, but also facilitates our reconciliation with that truth by providing us with a medium through which we can self-consciously reconstruct the past and consequently mitigate its loss.

-i-

Alison Lee identifies two points at which *Waterland*'s narrator, Tom Crick, contradicts something that he has said earlier. The first of these inconsistencies seems trivial: Tom says that he is unaware of the prevailing weather at an ancestor's funeral (70), yet later refers to "the unbefitting sunshine" (84) on the same day. The second case also has to do with death, but more seriously: Tom claims early on never to have seen a corpse (25), but then, near the end of the novel, divulges the childhood scene in which he was taken to see his mother's dead body (245). Lee argues that both versions of the events are equally "true" in the context of the narrative; she concludes that "narrating *makes* things real. There is no way to know 'facts' outside the telling/writing of them" (45). While this deduction is in keeping with *Waterland*'s historiographic concerns, it does not explain why Swift chooses these particular passages to cast doubt on the reliability of his narrator's memory, nor why the conflicting details appear in the orders that they do.

The weather becomes more precise rather than less so, but more importantly, Tom alludes to a vivid experience of his mother's death that he seemed somehow to have forgotten. Tom's belated reference to his mother's body could be not merely a contradiction but also a sign that he is confronting a memory that was previously too painful to recall. We could therefore regard the intervening text, comprising the greater portion of Tom's address to his history students, as the medium that enables him finally to master that repressed trauma. In this way, the contradictory elements *are* equally true, not just because they prove the relative discursivity of all historical accounts, but because they represent distinct points in a sort of progressive psychoanalytic encounter, with the reader playing the part of analyst to Tom's analysand.[1]

Yet it would seem incongruous to relate basic Freudian analysis, with its confidence in the total and unambiguous recoverability of memories, to *Waterland*, with its postmodern emphasis on the precarious nature of historical representation. Tom repeatedly expresses his belief that the past is endlessly interpretable and therefore never entirely knowable. He extends this attitude to psychoanalysis, which he ironically describes as part of his wife's treatment for madness: "They're trying it on Mary [...]. First you tell your dreams [...]. Then all the rest follows—the whole story" (135). Despite this skepticism about therapy's ability to bring out "the whole story" and thereby achieve a cure, the narrative betrays itself in strikingly psychoanalytic terms. The quotation about the treatment continues, "Even back to when you were a little—" (135), significantly breaking off at the word "baby," connected with an incident that has been temporarily repressed, the abortion of Mary's child. The novel's seemingly disjointed narrative revolves around a series of interrelated, fundamentally Oedipal traumas: Mary's loss of her child, Tom's brother Dick's loss of his paternity, and Tom's own loss of his mother, which is also the "primal scene" latent behind the others. In narrating these traumas, Tom interweaves recent occurrences with two earlier sequences—one from his youth, and one reviewing the lineage of his matrilineal ancestors. Tom's narration juxtaposes current and past events in the associative manner of analytic narrative, in which everything co-exists in a continuous present as the analysand compulsively repeats repressed material in an effort to work through and beyond it.[2] In order to reconcile the novel's psychoanalytic preoccupations and its dismissal of that

---

[1]The similarity between Tom's narration and standard psychoanalytic transference has also been noted by Jakob Winnberg in "'What won't go away': *Waterland* and Traditional Psychotherapy," <http://landow.stg.brown.edu/post/uk/gswift/wl/ winnberg.html>.

[2]Freud most extensively discusses the "compulsion to repeat" in *Beyond the Pleasure Principle*, in which he considers the terrifying dreams of those suffering from war neuroses, as well as an infant's intentional stagings of painful absence (the *fort da* game). Further, he hypothesizes that this compulsion—which is "more primitive, more elementary, more instinctual than the pleasure principle" (26)—explains the desire of all organic beings to "restore an earlier state of things" (47), even if the restoration means their own deaths. This last idea is echoed in Tom's disquisition on the eel and the arduous efforts it undertakes to breed, only to die immediately thereafter. After pondering aloud about such "natural" history, Tom returns to the finale of the swimming contest scene, at which point he cites his facility to "escape[s] to his story-books" (179) whenever life becomes unbearable. The distinction drawn here between "natural" and "artificial" history points

system's exaggerated claims, we need to identify those aspects of Freudian thought that acknowledge the improbability of the past's ever being truly and unconditionally retrieved.

In his later career, Freud suggested that the narrative formed during analysis, while based on traumatic experiences in the analysand's life, does not necessarily impart what "really" took place; rather, it remakes memories into stories, which may bear little resemblance to actual occurrences. A consideration of how the psychoanalytic narrative *creates*—and not simply communicates— its own versions of the past will provide us with a more sophisticated model that we can apply to *Waterland* in a way that suits the novel's representational skepticism.

The radical shift away from the standard Freudian "archeological" approach, which maintains that real traumas must be uncovered for a successful cure, comes with Freud's famous concession in the "Wolfman" case study that fidelity to the truth of the past is not crucial to the therapeutic effect of the transference. This document records the sequence of events mutually constructed by Freud and his patient over several years of therapy focusing on neurotic symptoms suffered by the patient as a child. In an effort to explain this infirmity, Freud moves steadily (if circuitously) back into the Wolfman's past, deciphering various "screen memories" and, through the interpretation of a revelatory dream, gradually arriving at a repressed "primal scene"—the child's witnessing of his parents' coitus *a tergo*. While Freud's entire diagnosis depends upon the reality of this traumatic incident, he first asks only for the reader's

---

to narrative's role in allowing human beings to master the effects of the basic, repetitive drives completely regulating the lives of lesser creatures. According to Freud, when repressed trauma surfaces in the form of compulsive repetition, it can be mastered through the narrative created during transference (see "Remembering, Repeating, Working Through").

Several of Tom's musings could be read as reflections on how the analytic narrative functions. His description of the fens as "reclaimed land [...] that is not quite solid" with "simultaneous accretion and erosion" (7) resembles the provisionality of the "past" that is recovered through therapy. Like the fens, history is characterized as a product of double movements—"Forwards to go backwards? Backwards to go forwards?" (81)—similar to those involved in the working through of trauma. The closest analogue is Tom's meditation on the Ouse, a river which he describes as prone to "short-cuts, long loops" (125) and resistances much like the analytic narrative; he also says that whatever is thrown into the river will inevitably "return" (127). The "repressed" does indeed return in the Ouse in the forms of Freddie's corpse and the "willythewisp" (200) seen by Henry the same day that the chest containing the secret of Dick's origin is brought into the house.

"*provisional* belief" (*History* 39), then introduces the possibility that what the child had seen was actually the copulation of some sheep-dogs, and that he has retrospectively and unconsciously created the scene with his parents. Finally, Freud resolves that whether the primal scene as described in his case study is "phantasy or a real experience ... is not a matter of very great importance" (97). As Peter Brooks points out, Freud's admission here invalidates his previous insistence on authentic causality, "substituting for a founding event a phantasy or fiction on which is conferred all the authority of prime mover" (276); the Wolfman's pathology can be the effect of a story, just as the fairy tales he knew as a child can be as significant to his present formation as any real past experience. What *is* important, from Freud's viewpoint, is that the primal scene forms part of a persuasive narrative that accounts for the onset of his patient's illness and thus allows him to overcome the neurosis.

How the psychoanalytic encounter re-creates the past in the form of coherent stories has been elaborated more recently by Donald Spence in *Narrative Truth and Historical Truth: Meaning and Interpretation in Psychoanalysis*. Taking issue with Freud's early contention that there is always a "kernel of truth" (27) in every interpretation made by the analyst, Spence argues that the information disclosed in the sessions is subject to two forces that preclude such confidence. First, language as a medium can never precisely convey the memory or dream that the analysand wishes to share; it is prone, as Robert S. Wallerstein makes clear in his Foreword to Spence's book, to "inevitable slippages" (11), especially where visual images are concerned. Second, the analyst and the analysand are under the sway of a "narrative tradition" (21) that leads them to organize data into seamless accounts without gaps or contradictions. With these influences in mind, Spence recharacterizes the psychoanalytic process by asserting that it deals not in "historical truth"—what the younger Freud believes is "unearthed" during transference—but in "narrative truth." Unlike historical truth, which presupposes that the past can be faithfully portrayed, narrative truth rejects such veracity as implausible and embraces instead the principles of good storytelling, as Spence explains:

> Narrative truth can be defined as the criterion we use to decide when a certain experience has been captured to our satisfaction; it depends on continuity and closure and the extent to which the fit of the pieces takes on an aesthetic finality [...]. Once a given construction has acquired narrative truth, it becomes just as real as any other kind of truth; this new reality becomes a significant part of the psychoanalytic cure. (31)

Despite its unavoidable difference from the history that it purports to depict, the narrative that arises from analysis is "true" in the sense that it is compelling to both the analysand and the analyst. The identification of narrative truth as the basis of psychoanalysis therefore builds on Freud's recognition in the Wolfman case that direct access to a patient's real history is not needed for successful treatment—and is, in Spence's more decisive formulation, impossible anyway. Rather, the past can be a retroactively constructed "fiction" that assists the analysand in his or her mastery of trauma.

We can examine *Waterland* from this revisionist Freudian perspective as a kind of psychoanalytic "text" while respecting its postmodern suspicion of the difficulties involved in historical representation. We do not have to accept Tom's tales as reconstructions of a "real" past; instead, we can read them as constructions *in the present*, with their own contextual truth, which facilitate the working through of traumatic loss. *Waterland* shows that, as in analysis, telling stories—even stories that we know to be historically untrue—can allow us to come to terms with the past. In what follows, we shall see how *Waterland* figuratively enacts this process through its narrative, which repeats and gradually masters repressed events, and through its characters, who symbolize various ways of responding to loss.

To understand how *Waterland* demonstrates the therapeutic potential of narrative, we need first to look at why the novel tells the stories that it does. The text opens with an incident from Tom's adolescence: the discovery of Freddie Parr's body. Tom ostensibly recounts this event to explain the present-day actions of his wife, who has stolen an infant, leading to her institutionalization. In order to answer the question of why Mary took the baby, however, Tom must simultaneously answer the related questions of who killed Freddie and why, necessitating that he fill in information from the past, including his youthful sexual adventures and, though its relevance is not immediately apparent, his ancestral history. While the theft of the child occurs chronologically *after* the events in these other sequences, it nevertheless acts in Tom's address to his students as the impetus for the telling of them all, a "founding event" with fairy-tale overtones reminiscent of the "Wolfman" case study.[3] Tom thus begins his account

---

[3]In response to one of Price's taunts about history, Tom thinks about the theft of the baby as a "fairy-tale" (5) in which he and Mary are actants. The theft itself is seemingly instigated by the feelings aroused in Mary after hearing about the "homeless-looking" (109) Price; the stolen baby can be seen as a fairy-tale "foundling" similarly abandoned by its parents. Tom clearly narrates the event which causes Mary's infertility in the first place—the abortion—as a fairy-tale, with Martha as the witch and him as "little Hansel" (264) to Mary's Gretel.

as a somewhat convoluted attempt to provide cause and effect for a seemingly inexplicable action, exposing the "real" motivation behind the babynapping just as he divines the true meaning of the concealed bruise on Freddie's head.

Tom's narration quickly becomes something else as well, though: a response to his students, who grow intrigued with the mystery and demand to hear more, refusing his effort to cut the matter short. This arousal of narrative desire is figured within the text by the game of striptease[4] played by Tom and the others the day of the swimming contest at the Hockwell Lode, which Freddie tries to rush prematurely to its ending by having Mary remove all her clothes at once. The game is based on the male and female players' mutual wish to see each others' genitals, but especially on the boys' fascination with Mary's "hole," a secret that only she can reveal. Similarly, the novel manipulates readers' attention, withholding the solutions to the mysteries and compelling us to read on. The deliberate prolongation of readerly pleasure is evident in Swift's carefully placed interruptions, just at the crucial moment when Mary's hole has supposedly been infiltrated at last by the substitute phallus—the eel which Freddie puts in her knickers. First, there are Tom's remarks, addressed to Price, on how curiosity not only moves history forward but also slows it down, followed by a seemingly irrelevant digression (along the lines of the cetology section in Herman Melville's *Moby-Dick*) on past scientific attempts to demystify the breeding habits of eels. These interventions produce the resistance to onward movement that Brooks contends is one of the formative impulses of all narrative. Such delays, he states, work against the "drive toward the end" (102) activated by readerly desire, preventing "the danger of short-circuit" (103–04) through the accumulation of plot in the form of repetitions that "bind" (101) the text's motile energies. The eel digression not only demonstrates this counterforce by breaking off the scene at the Hockwell Lode; it also thematizes the double impulses of narrative through the scientists' inquisitiveness, which both propels their investigations and detains their interest in the manner that Tom attributes to historical curiosity generally: "Hey, that's interesting, let's stop awhile [...] What's the hurry? What's the rush? Let's *explore*" (168–69). (Further, with its theme of sexual reproduction in connection with the search for

---

[4]In *The Pleasure of the Text*, Roland Barthes rejects the "corporeal striptease" of "narrative suspense" (10) as the basis of the reader's true pleasure. As I discussed in Chapter One, the postmodern novels under consideration here seek to reinstate readability, to which narrative suspense greatly contributes, after its depreciation during the modernist period. Robert K. Irish, in "'Let Me Tell You': About Desire and Narrativity in Graham Swift's *Waterland*" (*MFS* 44.4 [Winter 1998]: 917–34) considers how Swift's novel carries out a "flirtation" with its readers through selective strategies of arousing and frustrating curiosity.

lost origins, this chapter repeats, in the form of an alternative "story," the overall narrative's repressed concerns and assists in its mastery of them.) Complete
with interruptions, then, the anecdote of the swimming contest's sexual ten-
sions, which Tom relates as part of his response to his students' request for him
to "keep telling" (95), represents intratextually the dynamic operation of narrative desire.

In addition, the sexual history that follows from Tom's explanation of
Freddie's murder also works as a figuration of narrative as a counteractant to
nothingness. Mary's "hole" not only represents the object of readerly curiosity,
but is also a site of negativity which, when filled with a "thing," is transformed
into a new potentiality, as Tom describes: "Children, women are equipped with
a miniature model of reality: an empty but fillable vessel. A vessel in which
much can be made to happen, and to issue in consequence" (35–36). Sexual creation here becomes an analogue of narrative: it is initiated by desire, and it
posits presence against absence, just as stories, throughout *Waterland*, are identified as the only means to ward off the "Nothing" (11) that lies at the heart of
reality.[5] Tom's reminiscence about his sexual past, one of the novel's central
plot lines, therefore acts as a metanarrative commentary on how storytelling can
mitigate emptiness and loss.

Within the narrative itself, this creative power is associated most authentically with Tom's dead mother, who possessed a "knack" (2) for telling bedtime
stories. Tom recalls how his mother relieved his vague fears of "something vast
and void" (15); like young Marcel's maternal bedtime kiss in *Remembrance of
Things Past*, Helen's tales restored a feeling of unconditional well-being. We
can relate Tom's sense of contentment after hearing these stories to the period
of infantile development before the child becomes aware of its own difference
from its mother. In psychoanalytic terms, this blissful oneness is exemplified by
the baby's attachment to the breast, to the "mother's milk" (1) which, significantly, is mentioned in *Waterland*'s opening sentence. Though generalized, this
immediate reference in Tom's narrative to the unity between mother and infant
signals the depth of the trauma inflicted by the death of his own mother, a trauma that included the loss of a primordial storytelling that dispelled anxiety and
imbued reality with plenitude.

The stage in Tom's life when he must learn to cope with his mother's death
parallels the infant's transition from dyadic unity with the mother to its position
in the symbolic order, characterized by the awareness of difference and lack.

---

[5]As with "holes and things," the novel's paradoxical title brings together "Nothing," as Tom
describes water (11), and "something" (land) to make a new creation.

This shift occurs because of the figurative intervention of the father, represented by the phallus, who forces the male child to repress his incestuous desire for the mother or face the punishment of castration. After this Oedipal struggle, the son takes his place in the hierarchy at the proper time, eventually assuming the father's authority; he can never return, however, to the meaningful presence of the pre-symbolic state, which he seeks constantly to replace through a series of substitutes.[6]

In Tom's case, this phase of substitution begins just before his mother's death. He remembers imagining, through the delirium of influenza, that her bedside tales were foreshadowing her death: "they seemed [...] to be rising up to envelop and overwhelm her, casting round her their menacing miasmas, so that through his hours of fever he strove to cleave a passage to a mother who was becoming less and less real, more and more besieged by fiction" (235). By gradually changing the mother into "fiction," the hallucinated stories mediate her disappearance and make it bearable, acting as symbolic replacements like the wooden reel thrown by the baby in the *fort da* game described by Freud in *Beyond the Pleasure Principle*. Yet this imaginary transfiguration is insufficient to alleviate Tom's loss,[7] as is his father's storytelling, which Henry Crick increases after Helen's death as he attempts in his own way to adjust to her loss. Although Henry also has the "knack" (1), his stories do not have the soothing power of his wife's; he is beset by "nocturnal restlessness" (2) after her death, and paces and rubs his knee repeatedly, suggesting that he is troubled by his own hidden trauma, by the repressed "story yet to be told" (2) about Dick's true parentage.[8] Rather, Tom must go beyond his father and fashion his own response to his mother's absence.

Once Henry pronounces the ambiguous word "Gone," marking the irreversible separation from the mother, Tom begins his search for an

---

[6]Owing to the abstruseness of his prose, Jacques Lacan's concepts are notoriously difficult to cite precisely, but the key points in this paragraph can be found in "On the possible treatment of psychosis" (in *Ecrits*, 179–225), especially pp. 197–99. For a summary of the mother-father-child Oedipal dynamic in general terms, see Chapter 4, "The Different Self, the Phallus and the Father" (382–98) in Juliet Mitchell's *Psychoanalysis and Feminism*.

[7]We can read Tom's story of how George and Alfred Atkinson could not get over their "Mother Fixation" (76) as a retroactive construction of his own inability to overcome his own desire for his lost mother.

[8]Henry's pacing and knee-rubbing are among the many compulsively repeated actions in the novel; others include Tom's weekly walks with Mary to Greenwich Park and Paddy's games of fetch. Henry is described as pacing "up and down like a tethered dog" (131) pages after Paddy is "lashed" (128) to the park bench, an image that relates these different instances of repetition.

"Explanation" (244), something that will make sense of her loss. This pursuit, he says, "made him set out, in ways of which he was scarcely conscious and over which he had scarcely any control, to find again, at least to revive in some new form (ah, bashful, yearning railway journeys...) the image of his departed Mummy" (244–45). In his youthful affair with Mary, Tom finds one new "image" of his mother, while he looks for another in books, and particularly in the study of history, as he tells his students: "So I began to demand of history an Explanation. [...] And can I deny that what I wanted all along was not some golden nugget that history would at last yield up, but History itself, the Grand Narrative, the filler of vacuums, the dispeller of fears of the dark?" (53). Tom hopes to acquire a substitute for his mother's storytelling, a consolation for the void opened by her death. And though Tom does not locate in history a satis-factory "Explanation," by speaking to his class he fulfills a need to narrate, with the students as the "children" to whom he confides the "bedtime story" which all adults long to tell, "those most unbelievable yet haunting of fairy-tales, their own lives" (6). During his last days as a teacher, Tom discovers a symbolic medium that allows him to deal with his trauma: the narrative of his own past.

In the process of symbolically working out loss, Tom's narrative internal-izes others' traumas, most importantly Mary's and Dick's from their youth. These embedded stories are told in ways meant to sustain the curiosity aroused by the novel's beginning: the crucial information is withheld until nearly the end in each case. Tom's accounts of both events thus conform to the rules of effective storytelling that distinguish narrative truth from historical truth. Regardless of the factual basis of these incidents in his personal history, Tom unconsciously reshapes them in his narrative *as he tells them* so that they repeat key elements of his own trauma. Consequently, they function as intermediary repetitions or "screen memories" preparing for the eventual disclosure of the "primal scene," the mother's death.

The story of Mary's trauma—a mother's loss of her child, an inversion of the "primal scene"—provides a female version of Tom's Oedipal trajectory, as well as a metanarrative allegory about how stories themselves can become repressed. If Mary's teenaged affair with Tom had ultimately been only between the two of them, it would not have involved repression in any way. Despite their youth, Mary and Tom faced no opposition to their love, nor to an ensuing preg-nancy. About their trysts in the windmill, Tom remembers musing: "everything is open, everything is plain; there are no secrets, here, now" (44). What disrupts this concord, turning its openness to concealment, is the introduction of a third party, Dick, who draws Mary's vaguely incestuous attentions, given her legitimate relationship with his brother. Characteristically curious, Mary is attracted to Dick's "penis of fabulous dimensions" (42), and, with Tom's forbearance, conducts the half-witted boy's sexual education, though without consummation. When Dick wants to claim paternity of Mary's expected baby, she cannot bring herself to admit that the rival is his own brother, so she names Freddie as the father, thereby giving Dick a motive for murder. The baby becomes a "clue" that will implicate Dick, and its abortion, the only action that will reverse the chain of cause and effect. Therefore, like the "father" in the archetypal Freudian family, Dick's phallus is simultaneously a symbol of desire and of repression, of the "law" that forces what was open into secrecy, in this case the "story" of Mary's lost baby.

Whereas Tom's response to phallic repression—the creation of replacements—allows him to continue in his Oedipal progression, Mary's reaction leads to neurotic arrest at the traumatic moment. Rather than resolving her desire for a child that would, in Freud's thinking, fill her lack as a "castrated" being (Mitchell 101–04), Mary rejects all substitutes, including adoption, which Tom feels she dismisses as "make-believe" (110). Although the aborted child was also Tom's, he compensates through his students, especially Price, who becomes almost a "son" (209). Mary, though, believes that she can do the impossible: replace the lost baby, which she believes God delivers to her as the infant at the supermarket. As with Dick's doomed effort to see in Mary his "resurrected mother" (215), Mary's attempt literally to revive what has been lost ends in failure. Her insanity results from an inability to relinquish the actual past, as Tom explains· "First there is nothing; then there is happening; a state of emergency. And after the happening, only the telling of it. But sometimes the happening won't stop and let itself be turned into memory" (284). Through his recounting of Mary's ordeal, including the repressed story of the aborted child, Tom deals with that trauma at the same time that he repeats, with a difference, the experience of his mother's loss.

Further, by relating to his class the recent crisis of his wife's theft, Tom completes a narrative process that recasts Mary as the new "image" of the absent mother, so that her madness represents a double loss. Mary is also suddenly inexplicably "gone" (101), yet her removal to the asylum is prefigured by Tom's stories of the Atkinsons. Although the Atkinsons are Tom's mother's forebears, the women's lives resemble Mary's in several respects, indicating that these ancestral tales are unconscious retroactive reconstructions on Tom's part as he repeats figuratively the loss of Mary as symbolic mother and builds gradually to the narration of her estrangement from him.

Through his description of Sarah Atkinson, one of his mother's distant ancestors, Tom anticipates Mary's mental breakdown. The wife of a jealous older man who unjustly accuses her of infidelity, Sarah receives a blow at his hands that leaves her permanently autistic. Like Mary after the abortion, Sarah continues to live after her life, in effect, has already ended; and, like Mary, who retreats to celibacy for a period before marrying Tom, Sarah develops in her isolated condition the martyred aura of a saint. Sarah's predictions of the future are earlier versions of Mary's ability to hear the voice of God, and both "gifts" lead to the women's commitment to asylums. About Mary's visionary power, Tom says: "In another age, in olden times, they might have called her holy (or else have burnt her as a witch)" (286); along with Sarah, then, Tom uses the local figures of the anchorite St. Gunnhilda and the witch Martha Clay as proleptic recreations of Mary at the point of insanity. Even as a ghost, Sarah signifies the source of Mary's madness; Tom concludes: "Ah, do not ghosts prove [...] that the past clings, that we are always going back ...?" (89).

With another Atkinson woman, his mother Helen, Tom presents the possibility of moving beyond the past through narrative. Helen too is in an asylum, though as a nurse. There she meets Henry Crick, who is convalescing from an injury suffered in WWI, though his more serious wound is psychological; Tom imagines his father's feelings: "it's oblivion he'd like to forget, it's that sense of the dizzy void he can't get away from" (193). Like the war neuroses discussed in *Beyond the Pleasure Principle*, Henry's trauma repeats unabated until Helen's love persuades him to tell of his painful experiences and thereby transform them into memories; Tom extrapolates her thoughts:

> Like frightened children, what [the inmates] most want is to be told stories. And out of this discovery she evolves a precept: No, don't forget. Don't erase it. You can't erase it. But make it into a story. Just a story. Yes, everything's crazy. What's real? All a story. Only a story .... (194)

In Tom's narrative, Helen stands for an alternative to the neurotic repetition binding Mary to the past: storytelling as seduction and therapy, the same storytelling that later soothes Tom as a boy. In contrast to Sarah, in whom Tom reproduces Mary's madness, Helen as a young woman embodies the means by which he can overcome Mary's loss, which is, in turn, the means of overcoming the loss of Helen as his mother.

Nonetheless, Helen's sexual history, particularly as it relates to Dick's paternity, also repeats the process through which Tom assumes his own narrative authority.[9] Similar to the three-way affair of Tom, Mary and Dick, the relationship of Helen, her father Ernest, and Henry replays the metanarrative of Oedipal progression. As with Mary and Tom, if Helen and Henry had confined their affections to one another, the offspring of Helen's youthful pregnancy would have been legitimate. Because of Ernest and Helen's incestuous desire,[10] however, the child is born retarded, and, like Mary's baby, becomes subject to repression. The truth about Dick's birth, in the form of a letter, is literally locked away, with Tom in pursuit of the "key" to the mystery just as the boys wish to see Mary's "hole" the day of the swimming contest. Like the repressed story of Mary's baby, this story inevitably returns: in the aftermath of Freddie Parr's murder, Dick demands to know the full contents of his grandfather's chest. Since Dick cannot read, he is unable on his own to make sense of his origins, as Tom makes clear: "He's made things happen. Things have happened because of him. He can't understand. He's stuck in the past" (275). By explaining the letter to Dick, Tom tries to move Dick beyond the traumatic moment, to help him to convert that loss into memory. In other words, Tom attempts to introduce Dick into the symbolic order from which he has been excluded by his inability to read, to allow him to negotiate a place for himself in the Oedipal hierarchy. But just as Dick is forbidden to have children, he is unable to move into the future symbolically[11]; despite Tom's efforts at "analysis," Dick remains "stuck in the past," and, like Mary, goes "barmy" (304) as a result. He cannot accept Henry as his substitute father, so he commits suicide.

While Dick's story, like Mary's, ends tragically, it also represents a stage in Tom's own development. The fear of dealing with Dick's secret brings back to

---

[9]I am using the phrase "narrative authority" here in the sense of having the authority to tell stories, not in Chambers' sense (see Chapter One).

[10]Helen's incestuous past is subtly connected, through an intertextual reference, to her dislike of eels with their "subtle and versatile flesh" (130). In Günter Grass's *The Tin Drum*, Oskar's mother is coaxed by her husband, whom she detests, to eat eels after she has witnessed the nauseating manner in which they are caught, and becomes violently angry, only calming down after she has made love with her cousin, with whom she is having an affair (141–54). While in the Grass novel the hatred of eels is associated with the imposition of marital sex in a situation where incest is warmly welcomed, in *Waterland* it seems to be connected more loosely with Helen's ambiguous, simultaneous relationships with both her father and Henry. (*The Tin Drum* is also invoked intertextually by the "series of underskirts" [260] worn by Martha Clay, recalling the miraculous "wide skirt" [11] of Oskar's grandmother.)

[11]In *Beyond the Pleasure Principle*, Freud cites the child's realization that he has failed to "make a baby" (22) with his mother as one of the deepest traumas incurred by the male along the Oedipal trajectory.

Tom his as yet unmastered desire for his mother's storytelling; significantly, at this point in his narrative, he recalls thinking as a child: "It's the past! What stops but remains. Mummy, Mummy, tell me a—" (273). Yet during the critical events of Dick's suicide, Tom responds to Henry's plea that *he* tell the others what is happening: "You tell him, Tom, you tell him for God's sake" (303). The tale of Dick's lost paternity therefore signals Tom's acquisition of phallic authority as he takes over from his father as storyteller. Since this symbolic incident concludes Tom's narrative to his students, it suggests that he has reached a point of acceptance of the past, that he has moved beyond the trauma of his mother's death with its attendant loss of meaningful stories.

Does *Waterland*, then, demonstrate that narrative, even narrative that shamelessly refashions real events, can lead to successful mastery of repressed trauma? In other words, can we look at the novel as proof that postmodern fiction's historiographic intentions extend beyond the deconstruction of generic boundaries to a more genuinely therapeutic confrontation with the past? The text gives several indications that its psychoanalytic metanarrative finishes with full resolution: the mysteries of why Mary took the baby and why Dick killed Freddie Parr are cleared up, and the secret in the chest is unlocked for the reader. The three central moments of loss—the mother's death, the abortion and the revelation of Dick's parentage—are each narrated in turn and mastered toward the novel's ending. With Henry's passing on of authority in the final scene, Tom brings his Oedipal passage to a close and claims his right as storyteller. In Brooks's terms, the "[t]extual energy" would seem to be entirely "bound" (101) and the repressed material all brought out into the open. Yet the last reported action—Dick's fatal plunge into the water, with the hint of his possible resurrection in the future—reveals the presence in the novel of unresolved and incredible occurrences that would elude the narrativizing process of psychoanalysis and its alignment of plausible events (whether "true" or otherwise) construed as already irreversibly "completed." This impulse toward the marvellous makes the text's relationship with history more complex still: *Waterland* intimates how we can come to terms with the past by reconstructing it as narrative, but also how the past can exist in ways which exceed our rationalistic efforts to understand them. But that is another story.

-ii-

Among the many "improvised" definitions for history that Tom gives to his students is the following:

> [H]istory is that impossible thing: the attempt to give an account, with
> incomplete knowledge, of actions themselves undertaken with incom-
> plete knowledge. So that it teaches us no short-cuts to Salvation [...]. I
> taught you that by for ever attempting to explain we may come, not to
> an Explanation, but to a knowledge of the limits of our power to explain.
> [...] [A]bove all, what history teaches us is to avoid illusion and make-
> believe, to lay aside dreams, moonshine, cure-alls, wonder-workings,
> pie-in-the-sky—to be realistic. (94)

Yet beneath its surface of logical explication and cynical realism, Tom's own
saga abounds with "illusion and make-believe," with "wonder-workings" of
many kinds: clairvoyance, witchcraft, and the return of the dead. Among the
regenerations are the narrated events themselves, which are given new life, as
if the telling of them obliterates the time elapsed since the actual experiences.
"There's something about this scene," Tom says when recounting the day of the
swimming contest; "It's tense with the present tense. It's fraught with the here
and now" (179). The spontaneous revival in Tom's narrative of bygone occurrences parallels Walter Benjamin's epiphanic conception of history, in which
the forgotten past unexpectedly resurges in the present through involuntary recollection, a happenstance that produces that past's previously unformed, and
therefore unrecognized, meaning. With this revelatory effect, described by
Benjamin as "hymnic," we catch sight of "the unheard-of, the unprecedented"
(204), which would otherwise pass unnoticed from human remembrance.
Despite the practical restraints on our attempts at historical reconstruction, then,
Benjamin speculates that we can recover the evanescent past through aleatory
bursts of memory that are beyond our conscious control.

An examination of some of Benjamin's theories will thus help us to clarify the metaphysical approach to history underlying the "realistic" in *Waterland*.
While Tom's definition presupposes that the past can only be regarded in set
and unalterable terms, the novel's "miraculous" subtext subtly works against
this historicist view by suggesting that any event may be seen in a new light
through its later reanimation in conjunction with other, perhaps seemingly unrelated, events. Just as *Waterland* both performs and allegorizes narrative's ability to facilitate the working through of trauma, it also has embedded within its
structure and storylines a self-conscious model of how narrative can reclaim the
lost past in ways analogous to those proposed by Benjaminian historiography.

Benjamin builds on an idea, inspired by the writings of Marcel Proust, designated "involuntary memory." As John McCole explains, involuntary memory
entails a "fleeting correspondence through which a present sensation evokes an

earlier, lost experience" (259): the narrator of Proust's *Remembrance of Things Past* chances to eat a *madeleine*, and certain events from his childhood spring immediately and vividly to his memory, transporting him to an idealized realm of pure nostalgic contentment. Benjamin describes Proust's attraction to involuntary memory as being based on its "elegiac" quality, on its power to restore "the original, the first happiness" (204). For his part, however, Benjamin resituates the involuntarily recollected moment within the process of collective history.

In his "Theses on the Philosophy of History," Benjamin posits a vision of history that depends upon sudden, radical disruptions of the temporal continuum in the form of "dialectical images." While the traditional historian tells "the sequence of events like the beads of a rosary" (*Illuminations* 263), tracing inevitable progress in a line from one great event to the next, Benjamin sees the truth of history revealed by those instances when the past "flashes up at a moment of danger" (255), sparked like an involuntary memory by some spontaneous connection between it and the present. The past event summoned, and the present in which it arises, do not necessarily resemble one another in a clearly logical way; rather, as Benjamin describes it, they may be "opaquely similar" (204) in the peculiar manner of dream images—apparently different, yet alike on a level that can only be grasped by the unconscious mind. In the resulting "constellation" (263) made by this chance encounter between divergent moments in time, the material from the past does not appear as it literally took place, but changed, as McCole puts it, by the "filter of similarity" (271), just as the day's events are modified by the process of dreaming. This altered version, created through recollection in the present, is "[t]he true picture of the past," Benjamin suggests, that "flits by" and must be recognized in its ephemeral appearance (255) or be forever lost.

What this "true picture" "develops," in the photographic sense, Benjamin says, are "images that we never saw before remembering them" (qtd. in McCole 273)—that is, images that never entered consciousness but have remained latent in the unconscious until their instantaneous emergence. Slavoj Žižek points out that there are affinities between Benjamin's ideas and Freud's "return of the repressed" (141): the dialectical image brings to the surface aspects of the past that have been repressed, effaced from the conscious memory of a culture through the official history written by its "ruling classes" (*Illuminations* 255). In the sudden confluence between past and present, the hitherto suppressed and forgotten struggles of the downtrodden can be rescued from oblivion, made visible for the first time, and reinvested with significance.

This restorative effect is especially important to Benjamin's understanding of "redemptive history." While a revolution or other political movement may fail in its own era, that failed action may be salvaged through its successful "repetition" in a later action; the past is therefore never "finished" in the traditional historicist sense:

> The past carries with it a temporal index by which it is referred to redemption. There is a secret agreement between past generations and the present one. Our coming was expected on earth. Like every generation that preceded us, we have been endowed with a weak Messianic power [...]. (*Illuminations* 254)

This passive force can only make itself felt through the dialectical image, conjured by the opaque similarity between two events, when history "crystallizes into a monad" wherein the "[historical subject] recognizes the sign of a Messianic cessation of happening, or, put differently, a revolutionary chance to fight for the oppressed past" (262-63). As Žižek explains, the monad represents a historical "short-circuit" (141) in which disparate events from the past and present are joined and their unseen correspondences reciprocally made perceptible. As a result of this linkage, the failed revolutionary moment is "retroactively" (141) granted the meaning it did not possess at the time it occurred, and which it could not have had before its "repetition" in the present. These individual events form part of an ongoing sequence of defeat and eventual accomplishment having its own continuity despite its deviation from the standard historical record.

Along the course of this sequence, each sporadic temporal rupture—each "tiger's leap into the past," in Benjamin's phrase (261)—represents a stage at which some elements are reclaimed, while others await their redemption at an unknown point in the future. Without the fortuitous occurrence of the dialectical image, however, the true meaning of such lost events would not be recognized, and history would proceed lacking the cumulative illumination of the past needed to make final sense of it all; that is, it would go forward without really progressing. Benjamin believes that "Judgment Day" will only bring salvation if "the fullness of [mankind's] past" is "citable in all its moments" (254); otherwise, all of human history will be forfeit. The "apocalypse" therefore represents the opposite extreme to redemption: if history does not tend towards an ending which will vindicate past sacrifices by showing them to be necessary steps in a greater progression, as Žižek points out, then "even the dead will again be lost and will suffer a second death" (144). The potential, even if only dormant, of dialectical images to preserve the past in our collective memory thus resists the apocalyptic telos. Regardless of the seeming irrevocability of any specific lost or failed action, hope for its restitution is never closed off in Benjamin's Messianic concept of history.

With Benjamin's ideas of the dialectical image and redemptive history in mind, we can re-examine *Waterland* to consider how it suggests that the past always has the possibility of being recovered through narrative. The novel is primarily concerned with stories from the distant and recent past about irredeemable personal losses and the apparently futile efforts undertaken to replace them. While each of these tales individually seems to preclude any chance of reclamation, their combined revival in Tom's address to his class reveals their hidden potentials for renewal. With its interweaving of occurrences from several different time periods, Tom's narration is the "present" in which these past incidents suddenly "flash up" and are seen in their "true" form for the first time. According to Žižek, the fusion of past and present that characterizes the dialectical image cannot be conceptualized as literally occurring in "real time," but rather must be thought of as taking place "outside time" in the ahistorical realm of signification:

> The monad is thus the moment of discontinuity, of rupture, at which the linear 'flow of time' is suspended, arrested, 'coagulated', because in it resounds directly—that is to say: bypassing the linear succession of continuous time—the past which was repressed, pushed out of the continuity established by the prevailing history. It is literally the point of 'suspended dialectics', of pure repetition where historical movement is placed within parentheses. And the only field in which we can speak of such an appropriation of the past that the present itself 'redeems' it retroactively—where the past is thus included in the present—is that of the signifier: the suspension of movement is possible only as signifier's synchrony, as the synchronization of the past with the present. (140–41)

This suspension of linear causality, in which temporally distant events are taken out of order and brought together, is made possible by the medium of narrative, which can represent in textual form the kind of temporal "leaps" hypothesized by Benjamin.

Retrieved from the obscurity to which "the prevailing history" has consigned them, Tom's individual and familial memories are put into narrative constellations such that their latent resemblances are exposed. They are then further endowed with retroactive meaning by being integrated into a sequence of linked events that would never have been visible without his narration. This sequence centers particularly on the stories Tom tells about Mary and Dick, which conjoin to form a pattern based on Christian typology, a tropological cycle of universal salvation in which children are born, sacrificed, and then promised to return. With its series of interrelated repetitions and open-ended hope for regeneration, this Messianic pattern figures the possibility of that which is seemingly irrevocably lost being replaced through symbolic means. On both the structural and thematic levels, then, *Waterland* enacts and thematizes the salvational power of narrative to reproduce textually the conditions required for the redemption of forgotten history.

Through its overt discussions of historical method, though, the novel promotes a view of human experience that forecloses the likelihood of such retrospective enlightenment. In his discussions about the French Revolution, Tom insinuates that this supposedly "progressive leap into the future" was not a "new beginning," but actually a nostalgic "return," a "reaffirmation of what is pure and fundamental" (119) from an earlier era. Accordingly, he says, the revolutionaries of the day masqueraded in "Arcadian simplicity" (119) in an attempt to recapture a lost "Golden Age" (118). This description clearly echoes Benjamin's Thesis XIV:

> [T]o Robespierre ancient Rome was a past charged with the time of the now which he blasted out of the continuum of history. The French Revolution viewed itself as Rome reincarnate. It evoked ancient Rome the way fashion evokes costumes of the past. (261)

Whereas Benjamin cites the example of the French Revolution in order to show how a dialectical "leap" into the past can inspire change in the present, the parallel passage in *Waterland* indicates that such retrograde gestures may lead to a fundamental conservatism, and therefore set back the revolutionary cause. Tom explains that, "in order to satisfy its insistence on first principles," the revolution was "forced" to reassert its newly-acquired supremacy over the old order, "to renew itself again and again, with ever more ruthless zeal" (120). Rather than moving ahead, then, history becomes caught in a "loop" (117) in which it endlessly and compulsively repeats the past, like the sufferer of a traumatic neurosis: each revolution simply replays the cycle of freedom and brutality without producing any real advance.

In Tom's bleakly pragmatic perspective, history is ultimately static; like the silt that formed the Fens, it "demolishes as it builds" (7), and any apparent progress is only illusory. There is no prospect of regaining the "Paradise" sought by the nostalgic, of "return[ing] to that time [...] before things went wrong" (118); nor is there any chance of reaching "the oasis of the yet-to-come" (118) in which old injustices will be requited and misdeeds rectified. Since Tom thinks of history as circular rather than truly progressive, he rejects the possibility of any forward movement whatsoever; he cannot satisfy Price's demands for a "future" (6) in the face of threatened nuclear holocaust, nor offer any optimism for a coming revelation that will justify humanity's barbaric history. As it holds out no hope for repristination, this *Weltanschauung* essentially rules out historical redemption.

Yet Tom's narrowly pessimistic attitude toward history as a whole is at odds with the remarkable potentialities that emerge from his narrative about his own and his family's past. Although the first anecdote that Tom chooses to tell concerns the irreversibility of death—a theme in keeping with his realism in historical matters—the incident introduces into his narrative a supernatural strain that is counter to such practical thinking. Remembering the morning when Freddie Parr's body washed up against the sluice, Tom says: "I see us, grouped silently on the concrete tow-path, while Dad labours to refute reality, labours against the law of nature, that a dead thing does not live again" (27). Even though Henry knows that Freddie cannot be revived, he persists in his attempts to resuscitate him, according to Tom, because "being superstitious, [he] would never exclude the possibility of a miracle" (26). Tom reports his father's paradoxical stance uncritically, for he recalls that he too was secretly "praying and hoping" (27) for Freddie's miraculous reanimation—for his death, in effect, never to have happened in the first place. Similarly, after Henry has impressed upon his children that their mother is "gone," never to return, he is seen speaking to her gravesite as if she is not "really dead at all" (245), an opinion shared, though to different degrees, by both Tom and Dick. Tom's tale thus accommodates two seemingly contradictory existential points of view: on the one hand, death is final, but on the other, the dead *may* come back to life in ways that defy ordinary comprehension.

Just as the beginning of Tom's narration hints that death can be overcome, so too does it imply that the pernicious effects of history can be reversed. Tom starts off by quoting one of his father's sayings: "And don't forget [...] whatever you learn about people, however bad they turn out, each one of them has a heart, and each one of them was once a tiny baby sucking his mother's milk..." (1). In a general sense, Henry's maxim makes it possible to "eliminate" all wrongdoing by magically transporting those who commit the evil back to their original innocence, to that time "before things went wrong." More specifically, though, his advice to his sons, given for the first time around 1940,[12] helps Tom to perceive the horrors of World War II in such a way that they lose

---

[12]When talking about the night in 1943 when Freddie Parr's body washed up, Tom says that it was "two or three [years] since [his father] began to speak of hearts and mother's milk" (4).

some of their overwhelming historical immediacy. Recollecting hearing squadrons of bombers overhead in 1943, Tom muses: "And all the brave pilots and navigators and gunners and bomb-aimers had hearts and had once sucked mothers' milk, and all the citizens of Hamburg and Nuremberg had hearts also and once sucked mothers' milk too" (259). By imaginatively taking the participants, military and civilian, back through time to a point before the violence, Tom mitigates the war's arbitrary power to claim their lives. The idea expressed in Henry's aphorism therefore provides a means of counteracting the negative interpretation of history as relentless, with its victims' suffering inevitable and unchangeable.

What occurs in each case is that the literally impossible becomes conceivable through an imagined breach of the normal temporal and physical order. Because Tom intimates that the dead can be revived and evil deeds undone—even if only imaginatively—he also suggests that the past can be seen from a perspective that acknowledges its undeniable historical reality as well as its potential to be altered through reconceptualization. The processes of turning back time and reviving the dead are key to the symbolically interrelated stories of Mary and Dick, which undermine Tom's negative view of history by raising the possibility of figurative redemption.

Through the descriptions of her recent adult experiences, Mary initially seems to be a figure of the same kind of repetitive stasis that Tom ascribes to history at large. Unable to move beyond the loss of her child and subsequent infertility, she exists, at least up to the point of the baby-napping, without expectation of any positive change, one of "those whose lives have stopped though they must go on living" (102). Since her voluntary retreat into religious solitude in 1943, Mary has endured this living death[13] without benefit of her earlier curiosity; she no longer believes in "Salvation" (105), and maintains no hope for the "miracle" (106) that would give her and Tom another child. Past menopause and resigned to her plight, Mary apparently settles into a mature

[13]Beyond the obvious ghosts, the novel's depictions of the "living dead" also include the Revolution's victims, whose corpses "wriggled, kicked" (233) after they were guillotined, and Price, who is described early on as wearing white make-up that gives him the pallor of a corpse" (5), and who is later associated with vampirism as he sips the "blood" of his "Bloody *Mary*" (206, italics mine). Price's existential ambiguity prefigures the state he and his friends imagine in their nightmares about nuclear holocaust, in which they survive the end of human history (256). The paradox of appearing to live beyond life's "end" is one of those elements which the "miraculous" subtext of which I speak here converts into a positive principle: rather than merely resulting in the nihilistic torpor which afflicts Mary and Price, figurative life after death becomes connected with reanimation and redemption, the effects which narrative can have on seemingly "dead" history.

realism, having already rejected all "make-believe" solutions such as adoption:

> [S]he made do (so he thought) with nothing. Not believing either in looking back or looking forward, she learnt how to mark time. [...] And whereas he had to keep going back every day to school, there was always this grown-up woman to return to, who was stronger than him (he believed) at facing the way things must be [...]. (110)

When Mary's superficial pragmatism at last fails her and she wants to substitute the child from the supermarket for the one who was aborted, her effort—the desperate act of a middle-aged woman trying to turn back the clock—would appear merely to confirm the impossibility of redressing the loss.

Traumatized by having had her child taken away "again," Mary ends up in the asylum in a state of psychological paralysis even more intense than that in which she lived prior to her unanticipated "annunciation" from God. Mary's institutionalization, then, could simply be the inevitable conclusion of the personal cataclysm that began the day of the abortion, when, according to Tom, "everything [came] to an end" (256) for him, and especially for Mary. (Swift's placement of the Holocaust Club's nightmares about nuclear attack directly after Tom's observation stresses the "apocalyptic" nature of the situation.)

The dream that Tom had while Mary was undergoing the abortion, however, implies that these events were being reshaped at the time by his unconscious mind in more positive ways than his summary comment would indicate. The dream begins when Martha sends Tom outside to wait, with orders to "pluck a duck" (265). As he slips into sleep, the duck remains in his thoughts; it functions as an example of what Freud calls in *The Interpretation of Dreams* the "day's residues" that follow us into our dreams and to which our unconscious wishes "link" themselves in an effort to break free from internal "censorship" and emerge into consciousness (573). In Tom's case, this "residue" becomes linked to his repressed desire for his dead mother.

Just prior to falling asleep, Tom remembers an incident, from before his mother's death, when she taught him how to pluck, using an "old hen that had ceased to lay" (265) and whose neck had been wrung by Henry. Tom sees himself, in his dream, "sitting in the sunny space between the chicken coop and the kitchen door" (265) where this lesson had really taken place, with his mother standing nearby. In the dream, though, the same hen (into which the duck has metamorphosed), is not only alive, but begins energetically laying eggs. The hen's productivity recalls a conversation, overheard by Tom, between his father and the doctor who was attending his ailing mother; the doctor asks about

Henry's chickens: "'Do they keep laying then, even in this weather?' Dad: 'Yes, they lays. Not much. But they lays. Bless 'em'" (238). During the last days of his mother's illness, Tom was charged with looking after the hens in his father's stead, and collecting their eggs. His mother—who, like the old hen, is miraculously "still alive" (265)—helps him with this duty in the dream, gathering the eggs which turn into "fallen stars" at her suggestion, and lie "twinkling and winking on the ground" (266). The description of the stars as having fallen all the way to the ground refers to something else that Tom has heard his father say in the past, in this case to his explanation of what stars are. According to Henry, the stars are "the silver dust of God's blessing" (1), which were showered on the earth, but which God stopped in mid-descent when He saw humanity's wickedness. That is why, Henry says, "they hang in the sky but seem as though at any time they might drop…" (1). With its symbolism of fallen stars, Tom's dream therefore fulfills God's withheld blessing (in connection with his father's "blessing" of the hens). The chicken coop to which Tom and Helen take the eggs changes, in an unconscious movement between opaquely similar places, into the old windmill where he and Mary have conducted their lovemaking, and his mother is likewise superseded by his young lover. Just as Mary begins to repeat her earlier education of Tom about her own "eggs," he hears her scream and say that "she's the mother of god" (266). On waking, Tom finds that what he's heard are actually Mary's prayers to the Virgin ("HolyMaryMotherofGod" [266]) as the abortion nears its painful end.

While the dream stops at a moment when life is being destroyed, it has already reworked this horrific occurrence such that the loss does not seem absolute. By melding Tom's memories with elements from the present circumstance, the dream acts as a synthesis of images and symbols in which grace intercedes to overturn death. Not only is Tom's mother brought back to life, but there is also an intimation that Mary's baby can come back too. The completion of God's interrupted benediction should mean that humanity's evil has been forgiven, a divine act indicating the presence of a Saviour who has atoned for our sins through self-sacrifice. Mary, associated in the dream with both Helen and the Virgin (after whom she was named), becomes the mother-figure to a sacrificial child who has the potential to reappear one day and redeem the world. Thus Tom's reflection when carrying out the aborted fetus to dump it in the river—"In the pail is what the future's made of" (267)—need not be devoid of hope as it first sounds, for, as he makes clear at another point, "it is also an illusion that what you throw (or push) into a river will be carried away, swallowed for ever, and never return. Because it will return" (127). Yet in order for Mary's dead child to "return," she would logically have to have another baby. The problem of Mary's infertility, represented by the old hen killed for no longer being able to lay eggs, is foreshadowed in Tom's dream, suggesting either that he has inherited Sarah Atkinson's prophetic power, or that his narration of this vision to his students is affected by current happenings. That is, similar to how his dream correlates the past and present in figurative terms that moderate the irreversible losses of his mother and his child, Tom's narrative unconsciously brings together Mary's youth and her adulthood, showing their hidden correspondences. Through its bypassing of the intervening time, this verbal "dialectical image" replaces the absence and death predominant in the two separate episodes with the symbolic promise of new life.

By recounting Mary's escapade with the stolen infant so that it is seen in conjunction with her past, Tom's tale reveals the redemptive undercurrent beneath the account of her ostensibly hopeless situation leading up to the theft. Mary revives from her long inertia following a discussion that she has with Tom concerning Price, who, she guesses, wishes to "save" (109) the world rather than just change it. This talk about a "homeless-looking" (109) boy with what Mary assumes are Messianic tendencies rekindles both her lost curiosity and her youthful interest in religion, abandoned after her emergence from self-imposed penance for the pregnancy. Mary the realist thus turns into a spiritualist, reading books with titles like "If Jesus Returned" (111), and withdrawing from her husband to pursue a "love-affair" (35) with God, from whom she seeks "New Life and Salvation" (111). Tom points out on several occasions that only God can perform "inexplicable wonders" (100) such as preserving Jack Parr from the trains when he lay drunk on the tracks (though He had some assistance from Mrs. Parr in that case), or giving a baby to an aging, infertile woman. Supplicating for God's intervention, Mary grows mysteriously younger, a development that Tom regards as a symptom of incipient mental illness; he thinks: "my wife is becoming a child again" (111).

Mary's rejuvenation does not only lead to madness, however; it also prepares the way for the "miracle" of the second baby. With this implausible reversal of time—"where history dissolves, where chronology goes backwards," Tom says (229)—Mary regresses psychologically to the lost period in her life when she was capable of bearing children. Like the Biblical Sarah whom God graces with a baby in old age, Mary becomes a "mother" by stealing the infant from the supermarket on God's instructions. (Swift's strategic juxtaposing of chapters puts the fruition of this "miraculous act" directly after Mary's fatalistic decision to terminate her earlier pregnancy: "'I know what I'm going to do'" [228].) Tom's description of the scene he discovers at home echoes the symbolism of his dream: he calls Mary a "Madonna" and the family grouping a "bizarre Nativity" (229), suggesting that Mary has, in some sense, become the "mother of god" as he imagined the day of the abortion. Clutching the baby to her breast, Mary metaphorically enacts the return to innocence and the forgiveness of evil implied by Henry's maxims about "mother's milk" and falling stars. As told by Tom, then, Mary's taking of the baby is not merely an act of desperation, a foolhardy attempt to reclaim what has been lost. Instead, it fulfills, in symbolic terms, the possibility of merciful rebirth latent in the narration of her youth, just as the story of her past reciprocally brings to light the concealed typological significance of her present pitiable state.

Yet the stolen baby must be taken away from Mary, suggesting that this provisional "resurrection" finally brings not salvation but only more doom. Tom must explain to Mary that miracles are extinct, that "God doesn't talk any more" (232), and he must force her to give up the baby she believes "will save us all" (284). While the removal of this would-be redeemer seems to annihilate hope, his brief presence as Mary's "child" establishes the figurative possibility of new life where only incontrovertible loss had existed before. We can therefore understand this incident as a failed "repetition" of the earlier sacrifice, a step in the regenerative sequence, leaving open the potential for future opportunities at which the past could be recovered.

Tom's narrative expands the prospects for such redemption by creating a further relationship between Mary's history and that of his brother Dick, the so-called "Saviour of the World." Like Mary, Dick tries unsuccessfully to use a baby that is not his as a means of reviving something that has been lost—in his case, his mother's love. On the other hand, Dick himself is supposed to be a "special" child, conceived by his parents in order to keep humanity from hastening its own extinction. While each of these efforts ends in failure, their conjunction in Tom's narrative—like that between Mary's past and present—produces a hopeful subtext that is not clearly discernible in either event individually, a subtext that intersects with Mary's story to form the novel's overall pattern of sacrifice and projected salvation.

With his simple-minded credulity, Dick cannot grasp the concept of loss; he genuinely thinks that whatever is missing will eventually be restored, if not intact, then in some analogous shape. He refuses to accept his mother's death as final, expecting her to materialize at any moment:

92         CHAPTER THREE: THE WHOLE STORY

But Dick won't believe she can have gone where she can't be retrieved. Perhaps she's hiding somewhere else. [...] And if she isn't in the chest (because she isn't) then perhaps she's inside those bottles [...] . Or perhaps what's inside those bottles will make her reappear.... (210–11)

Dick's formulation of how this conjuring trick will occur is based on unconscious association rather than on logic: he relates his mother's coffin to the chest that she left him, and guesses that one "box" may be able to undo the work of the other.[14] His dead mother gradually becomes inseparable in his thoughts from a series of interconnected symbols—the chest, the beer, and also the river, to which Henry began taking his sons every evening not long after Helen's "decampment" (211) to fish for eels. Dick intuits that this activity holds a clue to the riddle of his vanished mother, and could maybe even serve as a method of getting her back: "Perhaps the river can tell where Mother has gone and how she might return. [...] Perhaps one day when the traps are hauled in..." (211–12).

But while Helen is never among Henry's nightly catch, another "genie" (217) finally does show up in the form of Mary. When she appears at the "magic" spot and asks Dick for an eel, a "Gift" (216) that recalls his previous display of attraction (as well as phallic superiority) at the swimming contest, he transfers to her the symbolic significance which he has formed around his mother's memory. With this associative shift, like that from one "box" to another, Mary takes the place of the absent mother, and becomes the recipient (and, in Dick's mind, also the donor) of the same kind of "Lu-love" (222) that he shared with Helen. (Henry helps to validate Dick's transition between Helen and Mary by equating the "feeling" [222] between mother and child with love in general. This slip of the tongue also strays close to the subject of incest, which Henry has been at pains to conceal.) Despite the difficulties of "immaculate conception" (226) caused by his penile size, Dick confidently anticipates the baby which will be physical proof of his success in having replaced his mother's love. The "miracle" of Mary's pregnancy seems to confirm his belief in the inevitable, though transfigured, recuperation of that which has been lost.

---

[14]The association that Dick, in his child-like simplicity, makes between the two "boxes" recalls the parable that Benjamin uses in "The Image of Proust" to explain the opaque similarity of dream images. He writes that children intuitively recognize the relationship between a stocking's dual identities as "bag" and "present" (205)—between its emptiness and its fullness—without losing sight of the object's actual function. To Dick, the coffin and the chest are linked symbolically to his mother, and therefore should be able, as a "unit," to transfer her dead body and turn it back into a living one.

Dick, though, is forced to confront the fact that his triumph over loss is founded on a number of illusions, which come apart one by one. First, he must accept that neither Mary's baby nor her affections were his at all; even his use of the maternal talisman, the bottle of Coronation Ale, to kill the rival "father" Freddie Parr, does not regain his paternity. Second, he not only learns that Henry, his only remaining uncompromised familial tie, is not really his father, but also that his genetic background prevents him from ever having a child of his own who would fill the void opened by all of these disappointments. Like Mary (and Price, too), Dick too is cut off from the future, apparently beyond hope; but unlike Mary, he does not take refuge in delusions. Despite Tom's assessment that his brother has gone "barmy" (304), Dick's disillusionment leads not to insanity but to clear-sighted nihilism, culminating in suicide. The story of Dick's search for love seems to insist upon the harsh reality that the recovery of loss is impossible, even through figurative rather than literal replacements.

The account of Dick's origins also deals with an ostensibly misguided and disastrous attempt to bring about redemption. Ernest Atkinson arbitrarily assumes that he can change the movement of history by siring a "a very special sort of child" who will rescue the "dying" (196) world that he sees reflected in the atrocities of World War I.[15] Although Ernest's mission is to save humanity from its own wickedness, however, his method is itself somewhat retrogressive. The incestuous relationship that he has with his daughter as a means of conceiving this child involves (as does Mary's middle-aged "motherhood") a temporal irregularity, a generational displacement that skews the ordinary progression of things; Helen muses: "My life's stopped too. Because when fathers love daughters and daughters love fathers it's like tying up into a knot the thread that runs into the future, it's like a stream wanting to flow backwards" (197). While Mary's rupture of the temporal order results in her mental illness, Ernest and Helen's incest produces another kind of abnormality in the form of Dick's retardation, which makes him patently unfit for activities of Messianic consequence.

---

[15]Ernest's grimly accurate predictions about this conflict, whose coming to pass was experienced first-hand by Henry and his brother George, bring to the fore the way in which the World Wars—the First, the Second *and* the Third, as projected by Price and the Holocaust Club—repeat one another in the manner of the self-perpetuating cycle of revolutionary violence discussed by Tom in his class. Tom connects the French Revolution and the first two World Wars as consecutive "bloodbath[s]" (259) of escalating violence. While his narration does not envision a "successful" war that would "redeem" these "failures," it does suggest that Price and his fellows might come to see the future in a different light owing to their new understanding of the past.

His designation as "Saviour of the World," which is supposed to compensate for his solitariness, therefore appears to be, as Tom secretly thinks, a cruel joke, the idea of a "mad" (280) man. This outlandish legacy, which helps to precipitate Dick's suicide, seems to engender only pointless suffering and death rather than the salvation of which Ernest believes his son to be the "divine" instrument.

Regardless of its manifest failure, however, the tale of Ernest's procreational effort, when put together with the events from Dick's youth through the medium of Tom's narrative, sheds light on the potentially positive implications of Dick's sorry demise that would otherwise go unnoticed. Keeping in mind Ernest's unshakeable conviction that his offspring will save the world (he does, after all, seem to have inherited the Atkinson gift for prophecy), we should look closely at the circumstances of Dick's death for Messianic overtones. His fatal plunge into the water recalls his earlier dive in the contest for Mary's love, a dive of such duration that it gives signs of extending "into that wondrous and miraculous possibility For Ever" (164) before he finally surfaces. Indeed, Dick's prowess as a "fish of a man" (309)—an "amphibious" quality shared, in different forms, by Tom and Sarah Atkinson as well[16]—makes it conceivable that he has not drowned at all, but will simply reappear much later. Like the aborted fetus, Dick could eventually emerge from the river, a miraculous rebirth prefigured by the "seed" (165) that he ejaculates into the water during the swimming contest. (Dick's resurrection is further hinted at in the fact that his suicide takes place on Sunday.) If realized, this promise of new life, whose lastingness is represented by the motorcycle that lovingly awaits Dick's return, would mean that he had fulfilled his role as saviour through sacrifice, bringing about the absolution of humanity's sins and its rescue from eternal death. The revelation of Dick's origin suggests, then, that his hard lesson about the irreversibility of loss may be untrue, and that he may be the harbinger, if not the actual embodiment, of a universal redemption that would permit the kind of symbolic recovery that he tried to attain.

---

[16]As it is with Dick, the "amphibious" nature of both Sarah and Tom is related to an unusual ability to survive. One story that Tom reports as having circulated about his maternal ancestor is that she escaped from the asylum prior to her funeral, and "dived 'like a very mermaid' beneath the water never to surface again" (90); this legend becomes attached to those that would have her walking the earth long after her supposed death. Tom's "amphibious life" (179) has not to do with water but with books, to which he "escapes" from the trials of reality and in which he can "live" with equal facility.

When brought into dialectical relation with Mary's composite story, the combined account of Dick's life from conception to death adds to the sacrificial sequence while keeping open the possibility of further reclamations. Even though Dick himself may never return, becoming another failed "repetition" of the original lost child, his activities as "Saviour of the World"—however ineffectual—make him a forerunner of the *bona fide* redeemer who will make his appearance in the future, a necessary stage in the divine plan leading to ultimate salvation.

This open-ended pattern of regeneration is built up over the course of Tom's telling of these stories within the context of his own current, devastating circumstances: he faces the irretrievable losses of both his wife and of his job, which had served as a substitute family. Like those of Mary and Dick, Tom's predicament therefore is also seemingly beyond remedy, and his future without prospects; the oblique similarities between his bereft state and theirs in the past could account for the fact that these incidents "flash up" during his impromptu digressions from his history lesson. While the conjunction of others' experiences of loss within Tom's narration discloses their latent hopefulness, his act of narrating itself thus brings to light the positive potential concealed in his own case. Through his classroom (and extramural) yarn-spinning, Tom converts the "homeless-looking" Price into a believer in history and a personal supporter, almost a "son" (209). Tom may thus succeed in becoming a non-biological "parent" as both Mary and Henry (to Dick) try to do and fail, a "foster-father" as he says Napoleon Bonaparte was to the "orphaned" French (290). That is, Tom may redeem the death of his child, the loss that begins the entire sequence, through a figurative replacement along the lines of Dick's ill-fated bid to revive his dead mother through association. Ending with the anticipation of renewal prefigured by the "Easter" (287) deadline for his termination as a teacher, Tom's present situation therefore takes its place in the Messianic sequence of death and rebirth that emerges from his narration.

What begins as a conscientious attempt to present information about familial history to his students in a clearly logical way thus concludes as an unwitting endorsement of the mystical, the miraculous. After setting out to justify Mary's "crime," Tom realizes that there is something "inexplicable" at the heart of the matter that defies rational treatment, that "keeps him scurrying further and further into the past" (94) in the hope of happening upon some revelation. In the process of telling his tales, he illuminates not only Mary's recent loss (and his own) but also those from the past that he calls up in this supposedly random pursuit. For each of these past experiences, Tom's narration is, in

Benjaminian terms, the future "developer" that is "strong enough to bring forth the image in all its details" (qtd. in McCole 290); it remakes these moments, freeing them from the limitations of lived experience and exposing their hidden meanings, which depend upon their suddenly visible relation to other moments across time. While Tom's discourse appears as a series of extemporaneous anecdotes joined through spontaneous association, Swift's novel makes deliberate use of this structure to show how narrative can produce an effect similar to that which Benjamin ascribes to the chance occurrence of dialectical images throughout history.[17] *Waterland* demonstrates how narrative can act as a kind of "collective memory," holding open the possibility that lost events that would otherwise be forgotten can always be revived and seen anew. Further, *Waterland* suggests that narrative can record not only the "realistic" aspects of the past, but also its "inexplicable" nature as well—its "true" story, which only we, as readers, will recognize.

-iii-

In describing his eighteenth-century ancestor Jacob Crick, Tom details Jacob's movements at a specific point in time as if he had been there to see them:

> When the redcoats were storming Quebec, and the citizens of New England were rising up against their British masters [...] Jacob Crick was putting his cheek and ear to the air to feel the direction and force of the breezes. He was leaning and pushing against the tail-poles of his twin mills to set the sails in the right position. (12)[18]

Despite the liberties that it takes with the facts, though, Tom's description is not a deliberate attempt to deceive, to fill his address with falsified material that bears no relation to how things "actually" took place. The impetus behind

---

[17]In reaction to Proust's work, Benjamin rejects the novel as the ideal repository of involuntary recollection, arguing instead that the dialectical image had to occur—and be recognized—independently of its artistic immortalization (see McCole 264–65). While I do not intend to suggest that the sort of belated historical revelation theorized by Benjamin can *only* be captured in textual form, I am contending that Swift's novel presents a "product" that resembles that of the dialectical image, and that it openly thematizes the ability of all fictional narrative to do so.

[18]The "wind" felt by Jacob is, of course, also the *Zeitgeist* of his era, so Tom's description is perhaps less purely fanciful than it is figurative.

Tom's telling of his tales is, at basis, historical in nature: he sincerely wishes to communicate the past, both personal and ancestral, to his listeners. Tom's intention is to convey what Spence would call "historical truth," but his desire to hold his audience's attention constantly leads him to embellish and make things up. His message therefore becomes compromised by obvious inventions and conflicting representations, resulting in a depiction of events that seems to be, as Tom puts it, no more than "a lucky dip of meanings" (122).

The contradictory tendencies to truth-telling and fabrication at work in *Waterland* through Tom's narration correspond roughly to two interrelated sorts of memory, which Benjamin distinguishes as "remembering" and "forgetting" (7). While "remembering" is the conscious activity of trying to summon up a faithful image of an original occurrence, "forgetting" is an involuntary operation, associated with the nighttime domain of dreams, in which we "forget" our daily lives yet re-encounter aspects of them as "opaque similarities" that are unlike what we know when awake, yet hauntingly familiar. In his essay on Proust, Benjamin joins these two kinds of recollection through the metaphor of Penelope's weaving (from *The Odyssey*): each night, Penelope would undo that day's output at the loom. To Benjamin, however, it is our conscious efforts to recover the past that undermine the more productive handiwork of involuntary memory: "our purposive remembering each day unravels the web and ornaments of forgetting" (202). Still, the actions are interdependent, together creating the "woof" and the "warp" (202) of a complete "text" (from "*textum*," or web), whether in the form of an individual's total experience of remembrance, or of a written oeuvre in which such remembrance is recorded, as in Proust's case.

In *Fiction and Repetition*, J. Hillis Miller discusses Benjamin's trope of "Penelope work" in terms of its implications for how the fictional text "repeats" that which is outside itself in two complementary, though opposite, ways. Miller aligns "remembering" with the "presupposition" of literary realism that it creates a "mimetic copy" (6) of some version of the external world; and he compares "forgetting" with the "demystifying side" (15) of fiction, that shows up any claims to mimesis as "illusions" (16), since textualized phenomena appear as misleading "repetitions" that only seem to be grounded in the real but in fact have no solid origin there. This second kind of resemblance, he suggests, creates "a vast intricate network of lies, the memory of a world that never was" (7). Although each type of repetition "subverts" its counterpart, it cannot exist independently, "inevitably call[ing] up the other as its shadow companion" (16). Extrapolating from Miller's application of the Benjaminian concepts of "remembering" and "forgetting," we can clarify *Waterland*'s paradoxical urges to truth and falsity and what they say about its relationship to the representational modes from the literary past which it reproduces within its text, particularly those from the realist and modernist novel.

If, as Miller indicates, the belief that fiction can provide a "mimetic copy" of actuality coincides with the tenets of realism, then the view that the literary text cannot "repeat" except as a series of "'simulacra' or 'phantasms'" (6) without stable originals is closer to the modernist emphasis on competing interpretations of the same event. Through its overt references to Charles Dickens's *Great Expectations*, *Waterland* explicitly invokes the characteristics of the realist novel, especially those of the *bildungsroman*; Tom's story, like Pip's, has the apparently undeniable authority of a coherent, first-person narration delivered with the benefit of maturity and hindsight. This stability, however, is always at odds with Tom's lapses of memory and hedgings (note his frequent use of "perhaps" to qualify statements), as well as his suppositions in the place of actual data, as with his sketch of Jacob.

In this last habit, Tom resembles Mr. Compson in William Faulkner's *Absalom, Absalom!*, described by Brooks as a "rich scenarist" whose "imaging[s]" (295) of situations he never witnessed quickly take on the status of "fact" in the narrative, at least relative to the several other accounts in simultaneous play. While the assumption persists that there are "real" events behind the many fabrications and superimposed re-tellings in Faulkner's work, those events are permanently displaced by the very "repetitions" that are meant to represent them, but which finally open the way for endless additions and revisions to the "truth." Even though *Waterland* gestures toward recapturing the realist novel with its mimetic grounding and single-perspective narration, it also maintains the hermeneutic multiplicity of Faulknerian modernism, keeping the two reciprocally disruptive impulses of "remembering" and "forgetting" in constant tension.

Recalling the Benjaminian and Freudian models developed in the first two parts of this chapter, we can further evaluate *Waterland*'s internalization of these counteractive modes as the effect of two kinds of repetition. On the one hand, we can see *Waterland* as the "image" or "third thing" (Benjamin 205) created by the coming together of opaquely similar manifestations of the same object—that is, of the novel in both its realist and modernist modes. In this respect, Swift's text would be the product of the synchronous "flashing up" of two moments from the literary past within a distinctly new kind of novel that conjoins them, yet is more than their sum.

On the other hand, though, we can also detect in *Waterland* the workings of a more diachronic type of repetition, along the lines of Freud's theory that we compulsively repeat the past until it is mastered. For example, in *Dead Fathers: The Logic of Transference in Modern Narrative*, Nina Schwartz states that modernist fiction emulates "the parental pattern (or original)" of narratives from past literary periods (especially from the realist period, whose conventions, she argues, it repeats in the form of a repression or "negation"[19]) as part of an "oedipal dynamic" (2) in which the new texts seek to take over the authority of the old texts while rendering them obsolete. Adapting Schwartz's hypothesis to Swift's postmodern novel, we can say that *Waterland* replicates the "patterns" of its realist and modernist literary forebears, thereby enacting an Oedipal drama that has as its optimal outcome the passing down of authority from earlier "generations" to the present one. While Schwartz finds that modernism's attempt to overcome the past is a "doomed [...] rebellion," a situation mirrored in the texts' "impotent" characters who "struggle futilely" against "preexisting [...] forces" (2), we can speculate on the result of *Waterland*'s Oedipal passage by looking at how the novel represents the movement of authority between parents and children, particularly between fathers and sons. This intratextual figuration will suggest whether or not *Waterland* successfully comes to terms with its precursors through its internal reproduction of them.

As we saw in Part One, the central relationship of a child to parents in *Waterland*—that of Tom to his mother and father—is inextricably bound up with the process of narrative. Tom tries in vain to recover the meaningful storytelling that disappeared forever with his mother's death, the perfect *logos* admitting no breach between word and world. Although his father's tales— "Made-up stories, true stories" (1)—help Tom to deal with the loss, they themselves are insufficient to fill the absence. It is only when Tom acquires his own "knack," a facility demonstrated in his narration to his class, that he finds an appropriate substitute with which he can master the original trauma. Symbolically, this progression is made possible by his father's handing over of the right to speak at the scene of Dick's suicide. Brooks points out that, from the nineteenth-century onward, the novel as a genre "repeatedly concerns issues

---

[19]Schwartz's somewhat ingenious idea is that modernist fiction "repeats" realism's techniques and concerns (especially its cultural and political orientation) by effacing them, a tell-tale gesture that she views as a "reaction-formation [...] the *denial* of something that paradoxically speaks of its existence" (16).

of authority and transmission, and regularly plays them out in relations of fathers to sons" (292).[20] If we read this family triangle as reflective of the novel's own situation with regard to its literary antecedents, we can conclude that *Waterland* succeeds in subsuming the authorities of both realism (though with recognition that its supposedly direct representation of the "real" is no longer plausible) and modernism (but with renewed insistence that there is a "truth," however inaccessible, behind the myriad interpretations). Through its mastery of parental "patterns," Swift's postmodern novel, as does Tom, thus finds its own voice, which is at the same time imitative and original, formed by the examples of the past while conscious of their limitations and ultimate irreproducibility.

There is, however, a second transmission of narrative authority between a parent and a child that has implications for how *Waterland* intratextually constructs its relationship to historical reality. The "homeless-looking" Price is rehabilitated, we have seen, by Tom in the role of surrogate father,[21] who gives him what his actual parents cannot—that is, a sense of his own place in history. While Tom cannot eradicate the nuclear menace, he does enable Price to gain new perspective on his fears by putting them in the context of previous crises, and consequently to historicize his own situation.

Tom's re-integration of Price into the larger historical progression is reminiscent of Georg Lukács's notion about the compensatory effect that fiction can have on the human consciousness, which is inevitably beset, he says, by alienation and fragmentation. In *The Theory of the Novel*, Lukács contends that,

---

[20]It is significant that the two literary "ancestors" most clearly evoked by *Waterland*—*Great Expectations* and *Absalom, Absalom!*—also focus on the passing down of authority from fathers to sons, only in the virtual absence of mothers. As Brooks indicates, Pip's adventures are made up of unsuccessful attempts to recover the "authority" (115) taken from him with his parents' deaths; he discovers that his only option is the false "father," Magwitch, who is inadequate to replace the "missing patronymic" (140) and thus define Pip's identity. Faulkner's novel similarly deals with a failed transference of authority from a father to a son: Thomas Sutpen's refusal to recognize the legitimacy of his son, Charles Bon, leads to the murder of Bon's fiancée (his half-sister) by her own brother, an irreparable rupture in the family line symbolized by the fact that the paternal property, Sutpen's Hundred, does not descend as planned to the next generation. Quentin Compson, however, does succeed his father as the "authoritative" narrator, a textual dynamic suggesting that, despite its depiction of incomplete "transmissions," *Absalom, Absalom!* works out a new voice for the novel in a way that *Great Expectations* does not.

[21]The obvious parallel to Tom and Price's relationship is that of Bloom and Stephen in James Joyce's *Ulysses*, yet another indication that Swift's postmodern text picks up where the modernist novel leaves off and advances its preoccupations.

although the perfectly "self-sufficient" (112) interior life can never be fully recovered once it has come into contact with the destructive forces of time, the "transcendent homelessness of the idea" (121) can be mitigated by the novel's ordering of experience into temporally coherent configurations. The novel therefore provides readers with a new totality that replaces, but does not restore, the state of original bliss.

Similarly, although Price can never go "home" in the sense of achieving ideal security, he can take comfort in a story that makes it possible for him to see pattern and structure where before he saw only random annihilation, the "non-story" of the apocalypse. Although Tom's tales are self-admittedly partially fabulations, they give Price a means whereby he can reinsert himself provisionally in the historical process from which he had thought he had been completely cast out. This interaction between "father" and "son" is thus paradigmatic of *Waterland*'s self-referential concern with the role that postmodern narrative can play, notwithstanding its awareness of its own irreversible separation from the "real," in mediating our estrangement from history.

In *The Writing of History*, Michel de Certeau speaks of the novel as a "son" in exile from the property of its father—historical truth—whose murder is the "initial event that it silences in order to become a substitute in its place" (326). While the son can never return to the familial ground, "traveling farther and farther away from a ground of identity," it can also never escape its "debt" (319) to the murdered patriarch, to whom it is always bound by memory and name. With this double burden of "loss" and "obligation" (320), de Certeau says, comes fiction, unable to reproduce the history whose place it has taken, but unable to sever its ties with it, either. It is this set of opposite precepts—to remain loyal to history, and to recognize that such fidelity is impossible—that *Waterland* has inherited from the literary past, and that it dramatizes in Tom's narration in the form of both accurate historical documentation and exuberant yarn-spinning, of "remembering" and "forgetting." By keeping these impulses in play without attempting to resolve their contradiction, *Waterland* exemplifies the peculiar relation to history common to much contemporary British fiction. While relentlessly drawing attention to the unreliability of post-realist representation, *Waterland* nonetheless insists on the importance of telling stories about the past, stories that make us aware of that from which we are in exile, and help us to overcome and reclaim it.

These interpretations using the "systems" of Freudian psychoanalysis and Benjaminian historiography reveal that Swift's novel latently engages with the past, both social and literary, in ways that exceed its surface thematization of history's discursivity as identified by Hutcheon. In the next chapter, an extended consideration of the subtext of Vichian historiography in *Possession* illuminates a similar divergence between an apparently regretful acceptance of the alienating effects of postmodernity and the projection of revivifying historical contact made possible by that culture's extreme linguistic instability. Through the concept of the *ricorso*, Byatt suggests that self-conscious reading of the sort internally figured by her novel can reform contemporary society.

# Chapter Four
## *Corso, Ricorso:*
## Historical Repetition and Cultural Reflection
## in A.S. Byatt's *Possession: A Romance*

Giambattista Vico's *The New Science*, an eighteenth-century treatise on historical social theory,[1] makes an early appearance in *Possession* as the volume between the leaves of which Roland Michell, a young literary scholar, finds the first titillating letters from one Victorian poet, Randolph Henry Ash to another, Christabel Lamotte. The reasons for this initial mention seem plain enough: Vico was interested in the creative power of language not only to reflect reality, but also to shape it, an idea important to Roland's eventual discovery of his poetic vocation. Furthermore, *The New Science* proposes a repetitive model of history, with each generation mirroring those that have come before, much as the twentieth-century characters, Roland and his fellow academic Maud Bailey, openly resemble their nineteenth-century predecessors. The reference to Vico's work does more, however, than provide an element of thematic circularity and a basic pattern for the plot; it suggests a kind of

---

[1]Ivana Djordjević notes that early reviews of *Possession* made only passing references to Vico's role in the novel (44), a practice only somewhat improved on by later critics. Thelma J. Shinn devotes most of her argument to the cyclical nature of time in the narrative, yet does not mention Vico at all. Kathleen Coyne Kelly briefly suggests that Byatt uses Vico to invoke a model of history as repetitive without "an end point or denouement" (97), as demonstrated by the open-ended "Postscript"; she also senses a double allusion via Vico to James Joyce's *Finnegans Wake*. Bronfen sees the true significance of Vico's presence in the novel in the coalescence of passion, historical influence and creativity that occurs when Roland realizes that Ash's marginalia in *The New Science* was written as a direct result of his initial meeting of Lamotte. This recognition of Ash's romantic possession by Lamotte at the time he wrote *The Garden of Proserpina*, Bronfen argues, leads to a concomitant transformation in Roland, who "experiences a total loss of self" and receives Ash's message about "the poetic power and vitality of language" (128), a viewpoint with which I only partially agree. Djordjević's essay, which appeared during the writing of this article, promises a discussion of the concept of the *ricorso*, yet mostly catalogues correspondences of details among the various "generations" in the novel.

"master code" whereby we can better interpret the complex project underlying Byatt's apparently contradictory text. On the one hand, she vividly depicts Western postmodern society and adheres to some of its hallmark fictional techniques, and on the other she ostensibly favours an idealized conception of nineteenth-century England, and overlays her plot line with traditional literary conventions that ultimately seem to undermine the novel's contemporary form and content.

The protagonists, Roland and Maud, are exemplary postmodern citizens, discouraged by the inauthentic junk and venality of their times, and beset by anxieties about ideology, language, and sexuality unleashed by contemporary theory, which figures prominently in their professional lives. In their quest to discover the truth about the illicit relationship between Ash and Lamotte, Roland and Maud must confront the radical instability and historicity of all systems of signification, including their own identities, while being haunted by the desire for a coherent sense of themselves as individuals and as social beings. In the process of comparing themselves to their nineteenth-century counterparts, they confirm their impressions that their own culture, for all its advances, has actually regressed by creating an atmosphere of paralyzing skepticism with regard to intellectual curiosity, artistic endeavour, and interpersonal relations. Bereft of romance and convinced of their relative inferiority, Maud and Roland are seemingly unable to bridge the divide between the lost world of love, stable meaning, and communication they sense existed in the Victorian era, and the demoralizing condition of postmodernity.

In formal terms, the novel exemplifies several of the qualities often associated with postmodern fiction. *Possession* meets the criteria for "historiographic metafiction": it uses a high degree of literary self-consciousness to focus readers' attention on the inevitable processes of fabrication and interpretation involved in reconstructing historical events in narrative form. Not only does the novel self-reflexively center on literary writing and its commentary, those activities are also shown to be object lessons on the difficulties of representing the past. Ash, dubbed by his biographer "The Great Ventriloquist" (*P* 19), gives poetic voice to forgotten historical figures, in effect "resurrecting" them; yet he is keenly aware that, while each of his fictional renditions "lend[s] life to truth," as he says, it equally grants "verisimilitude to a colossal Lie" (185). The documents studied by Roland, Maud, and others in their efforts to understand the Victorians are prone to incompleteness, loss, suppression, and subjective misreading, and the narrative of the poets' interaction compiled from these documents is more an imaginative present-day construction than a faithful historical record. The proliferation of fragments—from poems, journals, letters—inserted into the narrative forms a "textual heterogeneity" (Holmes, "Historical" 321) that both creates the illusion of an extratextual reality and emphasizes the impossibility of gaining unmediated access to it. In addition to its thematization of historiographic issues, *Possession* openly parodies other literary forms, most notably detective and romance novels, throwing into ironic relief some of the accepted "master narratives" of Western culture; Jackie Buxton notes this deconstructive "generic pastiche" (200) as further proof of Byatt's postmodern style.

It is curious, then, that *Possession* also frustrates those same critics who applaud its postmodernism. For instance, Frederick Holmes discerns an abrupt reversion to "the discredited metaphysics of a Romantic idealism" ("Historical" 319) in Roland's sudden discovery, near the end of the novel, of his poetic ability, a discovery that brings with it a vivid sense of the power of words to describe and re-create the world. Holmes notes that

> It is important to acknowledge that the liberation provided by Roland's imagination from the [...] sterility of his intellectual sophistication is never satisfactorily accounted for in rational terms. It is not clear how he overcomes the post-structuralist positions on language, authorship, and identity. His claim that some signifiers are concretely attached to signifieds is simply asserted, not argued for [...] . It would seem, then, that Roland's dramatic alteration is validated by the very sort of emotional or existential experience that critical theory has conditioned him to dismiss as insubstantial. (330)

This "metamorphosis," which Holmes finally labels "problematic" ("Historical" 330) and "ambiguous" (*Postmodernism* 73), seems to mark a final capitulation to a nostalgic impulse in the novel that has been barely held in check to that point, the same impulse that paints the nineteenth century as vibrant in contrast to the desolate present. Buxton, too, is troubled by this aesthetic "epiphany," which she sees as "modernist-inflected" (215) since she believes that Roland must dissolve his personality *à la* T.S. Eliot before he can write. While Holmes views Roland's transformation as thematically and stylistically incompatible with the rest of the text, Buxton considers it ideologically suspect (to borrow one of the novel's own phrases). Roland's rejection of contemporary thought for an outmoded belief in "the creative poetic sensibility [and] the imagination," she argues, is only one symptom of *Possession*'s inherent conservatism, apparent also in the novel's embedded "heterosexual, humanist" ideology (215–16). As evidence, she cites Byatt's suppression of the lesbian Blanche Glover, "the one Victorian character whose story is *not* told" (216), and the clear gender bias of the ending, which has Roland evolving into an artist in his own right and becoming a successful academic, while Maud must be content with discovering her ancestral link to Lamotte and Ash and succumbing to Roland's sexual possession of her. Although Maud earlier had been Roland's superior academically and financially, she thus seemingly finishes up as the stock heroine of a romance, loved but outclassed by her man. Indeed, with its emulation of the nineteenth-century well-made plot and its irresistible movement towards tidy resolution and romantic closure, the novel's entire structure could be seen as indicative of a traditionalism in excess of any ironic coding on Byatt's part.

Must we, then, see *Possession* as a text ultimately at odds with its own postmodernism? Lured by the seductively readerly qualities of the Victorian novel, does Byatt finally lose the parodic distance implied with her reinscription of that narrative, capitulating to a genuinely traditional ending and thereby undermining the deconstructive effects of *Possession*'s historiographic self-consciousness? And is the representation of the twentieth century meant to be just a pale imitation, a debased repetition, of a glorious past for which the characters—and we as readers—must nostalgically yearn?

The problem with this interpretation is that it overlooks or misreads crucial aspects of the text. First, any argument that *Possession* consistently holds up the nineteenth century as superior to the twentieth disregards the fact that the Victorian characters ultimately fare badly in comparison with the modern ones. Glover, Lamotte's housemate and likely sexual partner, commits suicide in reaction to what she perceives as Lamotte's betrayal of their dream of the perfect female community, which would pursue artistic interests "without recourse to help from the outside world, or men" (*P* 333). Ash spends the latter part of his life cut off from Lamotte, deprived of his true love by a society that keeps him duty-bound to his wife Ellen, a repressive virgin who secretly reproaches him for his infidelity. The endings of the nineteenth-century plots are characterized by undelivered messages: Ash's last expression of affection to Lamotte is not communicated to her by their mutual child, whom Ash never openly recognizes; and Lamotte's final love letter to the dying Ash is confiscated by his wife. The suppression of this letter completes Lamotte's identification with her poetical creation based on Breton myths, the semi-monstrous Fairy Melusina, who, in various versions of the story, can bring salvation to men by visiting them on their deathbeds, or escape her own eternal damnation by marrying a mortal. Lamotte herself ends her days "in a Turret like an old Witch" (489), unmarried and prevented from acknowledging her relationship to her own child.

The twentieth-century characters, in contrast, all fail or triumph according to their merits, signalling a marked preference for the liberties of an ultimately more ethically-sound modern fictional world over the outmoded and inequitable restrictions of Victorianism. The unscrupulous critics, Mortimer Cropper and Fergus Wolff, are denied full participation in the final discovery of the poets' secrets, whereas Beatrice Nest, the dowdy editor of Ellen Ash's journal, who had felt estranged from her more progressive colleagues, regains the sense of community she enjoyed in her youth by gathering Maud, Roland, and others to protect Ash's grave from being desecrated by Cropper in his search for relics. In a conspicuous reversal of both Glover's and Lamotte's fates, she appears at the gravesite, flanked by her allies, "transfigured" "like some witch or prophetess" (539). Roland and Maud not only succeed in securing the last piece of their scholarly puzzle, Lamotte's missing letter to Ash, but also manage to foster their own love affair, with each partner respecting the other's ambitions. In true romance form, Roland's embittered ex-lover, Val, is magically granted exactly the happy ending that he had wished for her, that a "solicitor" (18) would sweep her off her feet.

The concept of romance, so crucial to the novel, raises a second objection to the reading of *Possession* as formally and ideologically reactionary. In the epigraph Byatt provides from *The House of the Seven Gables*, Hawthorne differentiates between the "Novel," by which he means the realist novel, which "is presumed to aim at a very minute fidelity, not merely to the possible, but to the probable and ordinary course of man's experience," and the "Romance," in which the author "claims a certain latitude [...] to present that truth [i.e. the truth of the human heart] under circumstances, to a great extent, of the writer's own choosing or creation" (n. pag.). By clearly modelling her text, with its central quest and fairy tale overtones, on the "Romance" and not the "Novel," Byatt claims that "latitude" for herself, opting for a symbolic rather than a mimetic mode of representation. To critique the romance ending for its seeming sexism makes the mistake of taking it literally as Byatt's preferred depiction of actual contemporary life, and misses the symbolic implications of the novel's conclusion.

Since Roland and Maud are established throughout as figures of contemporary culture, their final positions in the novel represent a fresh start imagined by Byatt for that culture and expressed in the fantasy terms of her text. With his discovery of his poetic ability, and especially the stubborn materiality of words,

Roland suggests the possibility of revived creativity and meaning in the slippery, contingent, Derridean landscape; this breakthrough comes in spite of, not
in place of, the principles of post-structuralist thought, which he acknowledges
yet feels ready to move beyond. The same spirit of compromise informs
Roland's final, practically utopian situation with Maud, which preserves their
need for solitude and individual accomplishment while readmitting sympathetic interaction to modern liaisons. As a couple, Roland and Maud finish the
novel as the "Adam and Eve" of a postmodern world on the verge of a cata-
clysmic new beginning and self-awareness; they awake post-coitus to a
"strange new smell [...] which bore some relation to the smell of bitten. It was
the smell of death and destruction and it smelled fresh and lively and hopeful"
(551).

This prospect of renewal with which Byatt concludes her text is entirely in
keeping, as Elisabeth Bronfen points out, with the traditional structure of
romance:

> Suffering leads to survival and regeneration, the fulfillment of wishes
> can create a complex yet harmonious world, in which nothing is ever
> lost which can't also be regained. The re-emergence of the hidden, the
> resurrection of the dead, to return once more to the theme of Byatt's
> novel, is always plausible and possible. (130)

Yet the "wishes" fulfilled by *Possession*'s ending—for imagination, selfhood,
love, and community—still seem anachronistic, or at least naive, in the postmodern context, with all its Lyotardian "incredulity" towards such master narratives. Rather than simply disregarding the longing for such things in the text
as hopelessly sentimental, we can view them instead in the way that Bronfen
proposes, in keeping with the novel's general thematization of matters psychoanalytic. She argues that these yearnings are "unconscious drives and desires
inherited from the past" (128), impulses that contemporary culture has
repressed in its enlightened deconstruction of meaning systems. These unconscious drives, which Byatt suggests continue to make themselves felt in the
present, motivate Maud and Roland in their actions as cultural representatives.
Their final attainment of these desires, in ways compatible with their status as
late twentieth-century people, marks the realization of Byatt's fantasized
redemption of postmodernity.

The transformation of this fictional world from arid skepticism to Edenic
possibility does not occur spontaneously, however. Rather, it is the consummation of an elaborate process of contact with those periods harboring the

traditions and desires that Roland and Maud, on behalf of their society, long to recover in some way. This work of creative retrospection resulting in cultural renewal closely resembles a concept developed by Vico in *The New Science*, the *ricorso*, which will help to illuminate *Possession* as an intensely contemporary text, despite its seeming backslidings. Before we can fully understand the *ricorso* and its applicability to Byatt's novel, though, we must first review the main principles of Vico's system.

-i-

Vico envisions history not just as recurrent or cyclical, but also as progressive, with the purpose behind each generational repetition being the ultimate preservation of humanity, albeit at the cost of near annihilation. Each generation or "time-form" occupies a space on an overall continuum, or "*corso*," which follows a trajectory over which a society develops from a primitive to a more advanced state. Paradoxically, the culture in question simultaneously deteriorates into ever greater social alienation and intellectual sterility, until, though seemingly more sophisticated than at its inception, it is on the verge of self-destruction.

According to Vico, this decline occurs parallel to shifts in how words are used to relate to the world. In language, Vico found the "master key" of his historiographic method, a "discovery [which] … cost [him] the persistent research of almost all [his] literary life" (*NS* 22). What Vico realized was that language was not just a practical medium of communication, but rather the formative element of a culture's basic concept of reality, its very consciousness.

In this sense, Vico contends, the documents of early civilizations, consistently phrased in mythic terms, were not literary contrivances distinct from people's actual manner of thinking, but rather, accurate expressions of the mindset of the age. In this primitive "logic," which Vico tells us is difficult for the modern mind to comprehend, all people "were poets who spoke in poetic characters" (21), "naming" and thereby "making" the world. This process entailed people's projecting their own anxieties and desires onto phenomena, and designating those phenomena with words that coincided with their emotions. For example, Vico hypothesizes that our early ancestors reacted fearfully to thunder, assuming that it must emanate from an angry deity, so thunder became endowed with divine power and named, or "remade," accordingly as Zeus or Jupiter. Vico associates this first time-form, the age of the gods, which is founded on a holistic interrelationship between language and reality, with the total identification characteristic of the linguistic trope of metaphor. Nonetheless, as Hayden White notes in *Tropics of Discourse*, Vico understood that this initial stage also contained within it the seeds of change, a "tension between things and the words used to characterize them" (206), which derived from "the sensed inadequacy of language to its object" (203); the word "thunder," for instance, while basically sufficient, would not adequately describe different types of anger. This nagging discrepancy soon necessitated revisions in the ways that people used language to relate to the world which, in turn, produced the new consciousness of the next generation.

Subsequent time-forms would then undergo societal changes that reflected the increasing strain in the correspondence between words and world, until both the culture and its language were at the breaking-point. Vico aligns these intermediate transitions with various tropes that typified the world view of the culture at each stage. In the first shift, from metaphor to metonymy, the superstitious consciousness that unified primitive humanity was replaced by a world view marked by division and class conflict, as dominant patriarchs gradually assumed the powers attributed to the gods, enslaving those weaker than themselves for their own gain. White specifies that "the act of ruling [was] taken for the agency of rule" (211) by both masters and slaves, so that the emerging aristocratic society was based on metonymic thinking. Over time, though, the lower classes came to recognize themselves as parts of humanity as a whole, using the logic of synecdoche to foment uprisings that would lead to the establishment of more democratically organized societies, with legal systems designed to promote equality. The explicit mediation between justice and injustice, however, exposed a widening gap between truth and falsehood, words and meanings, thereby causing another linguistic and social transition that would prompt the movement to the final stage in the cycle.

The increasingly divided relationship between language and the world that informs the consciousness of this last generation, the age of irony, is in direct contrast with the metaphorical unity of the first time-form, and produces the conditions for the culture's drastic decline. According to Vico, the earliest people "had the simplicity of children" and were "truthful by nature" (131), so were incapable of lying. With each passing time-form, though, as people became more and more aware of the symbolic nature of words, they started putting them to more sophisticated uses, including figurative ones. Whereas the primitives were poets by nature, artlessly creating metaphors in an effort to make sense of their world, the people of the last age understood that figurative language could be used deliberately for effect. This more self-conscious view of language, consistent with the trope of irony, had negative consequences for the culture. Since words no longer referred to phenomena in clear, uncomplicated ways, language lost forever its primitive power to correspond simply and directly with things in the world. The collapse of representationalism, Vico argues, led to rampant skepticism about formerly-held beliefs and the erosion of accepted values, such as justice, community responsibility, and honesty. Ironic speech also made possible deceit and hypocrisy, leading to a society whose thinking was predicated on manipulation, egotism, and cynicism. Vico calls this state of affairs "the barbarism of reflection," as opposed to "the barbarism of sense" characteristic of the first time-form:

> For such peoples, like so many beasts, have fallen into the custom of each man thinking only of his own private interests and have reached the extreme of delicacy, or better of pride, in which like wild animals they bristle and lash out at the slightest displeasure. [...] [T]hey live like wild beasts made more inhuman by the barbarism of reflection than the first men had been made by the barbarism of sense. For the latter displayed a generous savagery, against which one could defend oneself or take flight or be on one's guard; but the former, with a base savagery, under soft words and embraces, plots against the life and fortunes of friends and intimates. (423–24)

With its self-absorbed intellectualism, rhetorical excess, and social disaffection, the age of irony would rapidly descend into the chaos that signalled the approaching demise of that culture.

At this crucial point at the end of the *corso*, however, there would come a moment of retrospection, or *ricorso*, during which the society would save itself by repeating more primitive time-forms in their most valuable aspects. This act of repetition, immanent in the culture from its beginning, would not take place in any material sense, since it would be impossible for a people so advanced to return literally to the old ways. Rather, it would occur at an intellectual or spiritual level, as a function of the final age's heightened reflective powers. As A. Robert Caponigri explains, this act of cultural self-replication requires a specific kind of reading, in which historical documents are approached with a view to mentally recapturing the consciousness of earlier periods:

> [The ricorso] is the ideal repossession and assimilation by the human spirit of its past. [...] The spirit is confronted by the documents of that time-moment, but only in their immediacy, their 'certitude.' In order to

> penetrate them truly it must possess in idea the reality of that spontane-
> ity of which those documents are the expression and the historical sub-
> stance. (164–65)

Through this imaginative connection with the past, the culture would be able to regain stabilizing elements that previous time-forms had only experienced spontaneously, such as the possibility of forging an ethical community, the ability to interact in non-egocentric ways, and the belief in coherent systems of value and representation. With the application of these principles, although in a modified light, the society could redress its balance and begin afresh. A new cycle of decline and eventual recovery would then ensue.

It is just this kind of self-conscious cultural reflection that makes possible the salvation of postmodernity as depicted in *Possession*. The restorative link with the past is primarily achieved through the hermeneutic act of reading, which forms the central activity of the novel, as most of the characters study documents that provide access to previous modes of thinking. Not all kinds of reading are able to bring about the amelioration of the *ricorso*, however; as we shall see, the novel defines successful historical interaction as that which involves both a high degree of self-consciousness about the process of inquiry and a willingness to respect the past on its own terms.

-ii-

The community of twentieth-century scholars in *Possession* embodies the intellectual "barbarism" of Vico's last time-form, an era in which individuals are disassociated from each other, their immediate culture, and the world of the past. Both scholarship and sexuality become brutal struggles, with predatory types such as the aptly-named Wolff exploiting others for their own gain and pleasure. These characters flourish in the post-structuralist climate of destabilized language, for it allows them to manipulate people and ideas in selfish ways. This same climate, though, results in a situation in which other characters feel uncomfortable; Maud, for instance, ponders her existence as "a matrix for a susurration of texts and codes" (273) and longs, like Roland, for the sexual and personal autonomy symbolized by a "clean empty bed" (290). The uncertainty about identity reflects a general failure in this generation to think of things in terms of cohesive systems. After Val finds an unrelated collection of pornographic photographs and medical files in her employers' desks, she says to Roland, "None of them fit together, none of them makes any sense" (24). Cropper records in his biography how his father kept a private museum of artifacts, but "could never establish any guiding principle as to how they should be ordered" (112). Beatrice Nest's elaborate card index of Ellen Ash's journal degenerates from thoroughness to confusion, so that crucial details threaten to "slip" through her "web of categories" (132). This period's inability to form coherent sign-systems with which to make sense of the world, present and past, contributes to its social and spiritual decline, and in turn produces certain flawed approaches to the problem of historical inquiry.

Among the various kinds of "readers" created by this condition are those who still vainly hope that the past is both knowable and retrievable, and those who blithely embrace its essential inaccessibility, as posited by contemporary theory. James Blackadder, a holdover from the days of New Criticism, had been convinced as a young man that every one of Ash's myriad references could be deciphered, but he soon found that "the footnotes engulfed and swallowed the text" with "two [problems] to solve [springing up] in the place of one solved" (33). Through this endless forensic exercise, he discovers that Ash's words and thoughts have taken him over on an unconscious level, displacing his own tenuous modern selfhood, so that the past he had been confident of possessing ends up overpowering him instead. Cropper, on the other hand, voluntarily ignores his own identity and defines himself exclusively through the past, in the form of objects belonging to Ash, which he collects with fetishistic relish. Indeed, his outlook on the world around him and history is suffused with elements of sexual domination: voyeurism, pornography, and finally necrophilia. The American critic Leonora Stern, too, approaches the past in sexual terms, though not in Cropper's sense of physically possessing it, which she considers outdated. Instead, she analyzes Lamotte's poems with a view to finding in them certain symbols and motifs that conform to her preconceived feminist notions. After reading one of her essays, Roland complains that "Leonora Stern makes the whole earth read as the female body—and language—all language. And all vegetation in pubic hair" (276). This narcissistic habit of imposing her own critical views, regardless of their pertinence, is replicated in her personal relationships, as seen in her attempt to push an unwilling Maud into a love-making session. In all three cases, these critics are presented as faulty models of reading, unable to deal with the past or others without subjugating them to personal or contemporary priorities.

In contrast, Roland and Maud appear as figures who can succeed in their interpretive projects, creating the circumstances in which postmodernity can experience the benefits of the *ricorso* and reclaim the positive elements it needs in order to transform itself from a degraded copy of bygone times into an era of promise. To bring about this positive historical influence, they must learn to think of themselves and the past as participants in a dialogue or "conversation" (127), a word to which Byatt repeatedly draws our attention, always with associations of virtual equality and mutual respect between two parties. Clearly, Byatt means to point to the applicability of Mikhail Bakhtin's theory of dialogism to historical investigation, along the lines of Dominick LaCapra's Bakhtinian-inspired assertion that "the historian enters into a 'conversational' exchange with the past and with other inquirers seeking an understanding of it" (36).[2] Within this framework, the historian relinquishes monologic control over historical representation, and accepts that her or his own voice is in fact produced through the dialogue with the past, through the response to what is different from the self in its present context. This discovery generates both "self-critical reflection," as LaCapra points out (36), and awareness of the past's discrete and audible voice.

Hans-Georg Gadamer, in *Truth and Method*, similarly uses the analogy of a conversation to describe the encounter with history, and insists that the exchange should not be unbalanced in favour of the past as the privileged object of inquiry (303). Rather, the researcher is integrally important to the process, since his or her own situation influences what historical preconceptions and blindnesses—what Gadamer calls "prejudices" (269)—he or she brings to the dialogue. These prejudices are the basis of the historian's "horizon" in the present, "that beyond which it is impossible to see" (306), until he or she becomes aware of the past's "otherness," its unique horizon formed by its own set of prejudices. With this "historical consciousness," as opposed to "historical objectivism" with its empiricist assumptions, the historian develops new recognition both of the historical moment being studied and of the present, since his or her prejudices are challenged and adjusted as a result of contact with the past. Ultimately, the historian apprehends the connectedness of the past and the present, which "together constitute [...] one great horizon" (304), since "the horizon of the present cannot be formed without the past" (306). This "fusion" (306), however, does not neutralize the differences between the two points in time: "Every encounter with tradition that takes place in historical

---

[2] I am indebted to Holmes (*Postmodernism* 39) for this quotation, which he cites in the context of his discussion of the dialogic treatment of history in several British novels, *Possession* among them.

consciousness involves the experience of a tension between the text and the present. The hermeneutic task consists in not covering up this tension by attempting a naive assimilation of the two but in consciously bringing it out" (306). By accepting the past's separateness from themselves, Gadamer contends, historians enhance their historical understanding as well as their present circumstances through greater self-awareness.

Roland and Maud's ability to put into practice the sorts of ideal historical interaction theorized by Bakhtin and Gadamer comes with their realization that they must confront their own prejudices which have prevented them from seeing Lamotte and Ash except in terms consistent with postmodern epistemology. Once the twentieth-century characters have put aside their contemporary presumptions, they are able to enter into their predecessors' distinctly nineteenth-century "horizon," particularly their appreciation of the vibrancy of life in its immediate and historical aspects, and the power, albeit fading, of language to eliminate the imaginative distance between the present and earlier times. This respectful form of reading allows them not only to penetrate the secret of the poets' personal lives, but also eventually to develop a more "dialogic" relationship both with the past and with each other, as they become aware of the generational continuity and repetition that culminates in the *ricorso*.

-iii-

At first, Roland and Maud are at odds in their approaches to the past. As a scholar, Roland is out of step with his times, theoretically aware yet drawn to the connections between literature and reality, as suggested by his dissertation, *"History, Historians and Poetry? A Study of the Presentation of Historical 'Evidence' in the Poems of Randolph Henry Ash"* (13). When he smuggles Ash's letters out of the library, he is overcome by the sense that they are "alive" (56), part of a narrative that is still on-going and involves him in some vital way. Enigmatic and aloof, Maud immediately suspects him of having mercenary motives similar to her other colleagues', and is reluctant to embark on a collaboration that threatens to disrupt her established feminist notions regarding Lamotte and her work. When Roland first suggests that they read the correspondence between Ash and Lamotte as a dialogue, she refuses, arguing that they should each read their own poet's letters in isolation, since to do otherwise would be both "romantic" and a rejection of the "narrative uncertainty" that their period "value[s]" (144). Nonetheless, Maud is finally seduced into co-operation, attracted by the same redolent "life" that underlies their mutual fascination with the Victorians.

Maud and Roland initially want to believe that the nineteenth century enjoyed in unqualified terms everything that their own period has either lost completely or rendered hopelessly problematic. While people in the postmodern era are incapable of arranging things into coherent systems, their predecessors left behind monuments of order: libraries, museums, and exhaustive taxonomies and classifications, such as the "Key to All Mythologies" (35) compiled by Lamotte's father.[3] Ash stands as the exemplar of his time, his encyclopedic knowledge ranging over many fields, with a particular affinity to science, as realized in his narrative poem about Swammerdam, the inventor of the microscope. In science, Ash found one medium for expressing his conviction that "the universe [...] must be loved [...] for its universal life in every minute particular" (146). In typical Victorian fashion, his interest in natural phenomena was apparently fueled by purely objective inquisitiveness, unlike the narrower research of the twentieth-century characters, who bring to things the patterns they expect to find in them. The primary vehicle for his immense curiosity,

---

[3]The ironic reference here, of course, is to Mr. Causaubon's esoteric and ultimately useless "Key to All Mythologies" in George Eliot's *Middlemarch*, suggesting that even the apparently secure nineteenth-century systems in *Possession* are unstable at best. Ash seems to intuit the collapse of coherence in his own time in a letter to Lamotte: "I find it hard to shift without the Creator—the more we see and understand, the more amazement there is in this strangely interrelated *Heap* of things—which is yet not disordered" (180). Implicit behind Byatt's depictions of both Victorian order and postmodern chaos are modernist fictional representations of the intervening process of decline. Miss La Trobe's dismay in Virginia Woolf's *Between the Acts* over the modern world descending into "orts and fragments" is echoed in *Possession*'s description of Blackadder's fascination with a naturalist's efforts to reconstitute the digested contents of an owl's stomach. Woolf's Mr. Ramsey from *To the Lighthouse*, with his futile attempt to expand his range of understanding by imagining the ascending levels of human thought as an alphabet whose successive "letters" could be reached through mental exertion, is suggested by Byatt's emphasis early in the novel on the "felicitous alphabetical conjunctions" that Ash had encountered as a young poet in the London Library, where "Dancing," "Death," "Demonology" and "Dogs" (4) had been shelved in proximity. Those creative conjunctions from the past are replaced symbolically in the contemporary period by the second row of "ghost-desks" to which Roland is relegated in the British Museum, with their "stammering," out of sequence, double-letter designations, "DD GG OO" (31). Roland's disordered experience in the museum also invokes the absurd project of the Autodidact in Sartre's *Nausea*, who is reading his way through the library in alphabetical order, but without any sense of connection or context.

however, was his poetry itself, which, though composed of "merely words—
and the dead husks of other men's words" (174–75), was capable of "bringing
to life, *restoring* in some sense to vitality, the whole vanished men of other
times" (174). From Roland and Maud's perspective, there seems to have been
no serious disjunction in Ash's time between the power of the imagination to
resurrect the past and the ability of language to represent it. The nineteenth century, as envisioned by the twentieth-century protagonists, thus apparently precedes what Holmes calls the "schismatic fall into modernity" (*Postmodernism*
53), characterized by the severing of signifier from signified. Similarly, nineteenth-century feminism, in Maud's perception, had not yet fallen into the esoteric divisiveness of contemporary theory, but was still a burgeoning movement
deeply connected to women's lives, developing under the hands of pioneers
such as Priscilla Penn Cropper, the critic's great-grandmother. In Lamotte's
writing, Maud sees a proto-feminist reappropriating stories such as "The
Drowned City" and "The Fairy Melusina," which present women as evil and
monstrous, and revising them into narratives of empowerment. In personal
terms, the moderns believe that the Victorians were not only capable of romantic relations unhindered by the twentieth-century hyper-awareness of sexuality,
but were also endowed with a strong sense of identity; Maud says that "[t]hey
valued themselves" (277) in a way that members of her generation do not.

This vision of Victorianism, however, is partially a wishful one, for Ash
and Lamotte's own words reveal that their period was already undergoing some
of the changes that would lead to the modern state of malaise. Although the
nineteenth century might seem stable from a contemporary vantage point, Ash
and Lamotte were deeply aware that its fundamental values were collapsing
under the weight of growing skepticism, as witnessed by the poets' debate
about religion. Lamotte tries to defend Christianity from the implication in
Ash's poem *Ragnarök* that all tales of resurrection and the apocalypse are
equally fictional, simply accounts of what "Men […] Desire shall be or might
be, not what it is divinely, transcendently decreed Must Be and Is" (176). Ash's
response, though carefully devout, suggests that having absolute faith in mas-
ter-narratives like religion is becoming increasingly difficult in their age: "The
truth is […] that we live in an *old* world—a tired world—a world that has gone
on piling up speculation and observations until truths that might have been gras-
pable in the bright Dayspring of human morning […] are now obscured by
palimpsest on palimpsest" (181). He goes on to cite curiosity, the same quality
that the moderns think of as a sign of reassuring energy, as the driving force

behind this impetus to cultural change or "metamorphosis," which is not only both "good *and* evil" (181), but also inevitable. At the same time, Ash does not perceive in his own writing the unshakable representational certainty that Maud and Roland do, but instead sees his poetry as a form in transition, still imbued with Romantic imaginative potency, yet unable to convey the truth of the past without adulterating it with fiction. His poetic ventriloquism of historical figures is therefore both a revival and a distortion of their lives; as Blackadder realizes, Ash's versatile style conceals an "alienation from the voice of true feeling" (32), and his poems are precursors of postmodern simulacra. Ash's choice of subjects, "characters at or over the edge of madness, constructing systems of belief and survival from the fragments of experience available to them" (9), reveals what contemporary theorists such as Fredric Jameson would call the essential schizophrenia behind his ostensibly solid facade. Correspondingly, the incipient divisions in the women's movement are visible in Glover's self-centered, possessive treatment of Lamotte, who, for all her genius and progressive independence, is finally unable to detach herself from the "monstrosity" of sexual difference that stigmatizes her creations. Like their twentieth-century counterparts, the representative Victorian couple is therefore acutely aware of the unsettling shifts going on in their own era, and they look to the past in an effort to recoup what their culture has lost.

In their writing, Lamotte and Ash self-consciously evoke earlier times known to them through the study of historical documents, so that Maud and Roland are able to make contact with two generations at once when reading the nineteenth-century texts. These primitive periods are like Vico's first time-form: they comprise pre-reflective civilizations in which people conceptualize the world in terms of the projections of their own emotional states. The tales adapted by Lamotte depict women as embodiments of cultural fears, as in the spectral "whiteladies" (166) who harass travelers. In Lamotte's retelling of the stories, there is an emphasis on female power, but also on reconciliation and harmony between men and women, nature and humanity. Her poem "Psyche," about ants who help the mortal maiden to keep an assignation, begins: "In ancient Tales—the Creatures—helpful were / To taxed and fearful Humans in despair. / The World was One for those Men, which now is / A dissonant Congeries" (178). The theme of a world of unity, before the descent into difference and dissent, preoccupies Ash's poetry as well, only with a more linguistic orientation. In *The Garden of Proserpina*, he draws on his reading of Vico to lament the passing of a mythical time of completely meaningful signification, the same representational Eden that Roland looks for in Ash's own work:

> The first men named this place and named the world.
> They made the words for it: garden and tree
> Dragon or snake and woman, grass and gold
> And apples. They made names and poetry,
> The things *were* what they named and made them. (504)

Ash's longing to retrieve those traditions and elements of stability that his own era is rapidly losing also prompts his visit to Yorkshire, where he encounters the past in its most physical, and potentially salvational, form.

For Ash, Yorkshire is an opportunity to pursue an interest in origins that counterbalances his anxieties about his changing society. The "primaeval" (232) landscape he explores reverberates with early English culture, allowing him to feel part of an ongoing tradition with ancient roots. He writes to his wife about the Whitby legend of a giant, Wade, who was believed to have strewn the landscape with boulders during his fits of rage, and whose name, Ash surmises, is in fact an adaptation of the ancient Norse god Woden, among other things the god of battle. Ash concludes that the Anglo-Saxons combined their fear of military conquest with the existence of the local landmarks to create the legend; he suggests, "So the human imagination mixes and adapts to its current preoccupations many ingredients into new wholes—it is essentially poetic" (278). With his careful attention to the unique historical valence of language in Yorkshire, as in all his other researches, Ash gains imaginative access to the perspective of another time according to the Vichian model. One of Ash's modern-day defenders says of him, "He wanted to understand how individual people at any particular time saw the shape of their lives—from their beliefs to their pots and pans" (433) In resuscitating, through his poetry, the lives of "things long-dead but not vanished" (279), Ash brings his Victorian sensibility to bear on his subjects without losing sight of their essential strangeness, the divergence between their views of the world and his own. This willingness to see the past on its own terms, with his contemporary prejudices in abeyance, exemplifies a type of "reading" that gives him access to the disappearing foundations of his culture.

Ash is joined in this curious yet reverent attitude to the past by Lamotte, although her treatment of historical reanimation differs from his. While planning to write her epic, she says in a letter to him, "I would write, if I undertook it—a little from Melusina's—*own*—vision. Not, as you might, in the First

Person—as inhabiting her skin—but seeing her as an unfortunate Creature—of Power and Frailty" (192). The two poets therefore represent two contrasting approaches to the past: for Ash, the self imaginatively takes on the identity of the Other, as suggested by the novel's metaphors of ventriloquism and spiritual possession; for Lamotte, the self compassionately reaches out to the Other, acknowledging and caring for the Other's distress, as the Fairy Melusina does for the Knight Raimondin in her story.

In both cases, contact with the past is made with the assistance of what Lynne Pearce, in *Reading Dialogics*, calls "the Bakhtinian interlocutor [...] the 'listening other' whose presence is necessary for 'the word' to be spoken, for the past to be narrativized and hence *realized*" (187). That is, the historical characters and events about which Ash and Lamotte write would be lost to oblivion without the poets' attentive interest, their exemplary fulfillment of the role of recipient for messages sent long ago. To use Bakhtin's own term, there is a high degree of "addressivity" (95) in those historical moments; they are "directed" utterances, awaiting proper recognition in the future.

This same kind of addressivity is visible in the written correspondence between Lamotte and Ash at the onset of their affair, begun as a respectable way of getting to know one another, given Ash's marital status. When considering the correspondence, Roland thinks about how "true" letters are written "for *a* reader" (145) who will implicitly grasp the author's meaning and whose existence becomes a necessary precondition for writing. In Lamotte, a poet with similar thoughts on the creative act and its products, Ash discovers *his* reader, thereby achieving the shared understanding of language he idealizes in his poems on Ask and Embla, the Norse versions of Adam and Eve: "We two remake our world by naming it / Together, knowing what words mean for us" (127). Although both Lamotte and Ash had been active as creative writers before their initial encounter, they find in each other the perfect readers for their poetry and fiction as well as for their personal meditations. This compatibility is based partly on shared understanding; they both feel deeply about the "Life of Language" (189) and its power in the world. Nonetheless, the poets disagree about basic issues such as religious faith, as we have seen, and it is these disparities that inspire them in new directions. Ash tells Lamotte in a letter, "No other Poem of mine has ever in the slightest been written for a particular Reader—only for myself, or some half-conceived Alter Ego. Now, you are not that—it is your difference, your otherness to which I address myself—fascinated, intrigued" (206). As he does the past, Ash regards Lamotte the fellow author as both connected to him and completely distinct, knowable yet cryptic.

By responding to what is different in each other, the poets change the orientation not only of their writing, but of their personal relationship as well. Through this exchange, Ash breaks out of his solipsism and attempts to communicate with an "Other" in her own right; he calls himself "an author of Monologues—trying clumsily to construct a Dialogue" (195). With her extreme reticence and intricate mind, Lamotte exceeds Ash's ability to know her, to "become" her imaginatively as he does his resurrected historical figures, so that he discovers the limits of his own vision and becomes willing to complement it with that of another. He writes to her that she makes him feel "*unheimlich*, as the Germans have it, least of all *at home*, but always on edge, always apprehensive of failure" (146). For her part, Lamotte learns to move beyond her chosen characterization as a "self-satisfied Spider" (97) jealously guarding her privacy, to allow Ash to approach her with the same compassionate care that she brings to the story of Melusina.

The poets' relationship briefly survives its "papery" (209) inception, though it is already under siege from that which lies outside their insular paradise of the written word. Once the poets leave on their train trip together, Ash must relinquish his imaginings about Lamotte and deal with the reality of her paradoxical familiarity and foreignness. Byatt's model here is clearly *The French Lieutenant's Woman*, with Ash and Lamotte replaying the seduction between Charles and Sarah at Endicott's Hotel. Yet there are subtle variations between Byatt's rewrite and Fowles's original. In *Possession*, the "observer" (297) in the railway car is only hypothetical; there is no intrusive narrator insisting on a cameo, as in Fowles's famous passage. Rather, for the first time in the novel, Byatt abandons her contemporary vantage point, narrating the nineteenth-century events directly, without the intervening "filters" of found documents. Her narrator even assumes a Victorian mindset, commenting on the phrenological assets of Ash's head. Just as the shift in narration suggests the importance of viewing the past in its own context, so too does Lamotte provide a different kind of object for the reading process. Like Sarah, she is enigmatic; Ash regards her as a "text" to be interpreted: "He learned her. He studied the pale loops of hair on her temples" (301). Unlike Sarah, though, Lamotte is not secretly manipulating her lover to accomplish her own selfish purposes. Rather, Lamotte is honest and forthright, an equal partner in their planned intrigue.

In Yorkshire, temporarily freed from social obligations, they achieve parity intellectually, physically, and romantically. The inscrutable side of Lamotte's character is exposed in the lovemaking scene, in which she is described in mythological terms, as an enchanted "selkie" or seal-woman, and as "Proteus" (308), altering shape in Ash's arms. Nonetheless, he subdues the mystery, saying to her, "You see, I know you" (308), and she concedes that he does. The success of their relationship lies in the same kind of deference that Ash brings to his historical studies; though curious, he does not ask about her apparent sexual, likely lesbian, experience, but rather respects her privacy and separateness. Again, Ash's Ask and Embla provide the paradigm for their relationship: "Then he saw that she / Was like himself, yet other" (263). Despite the double-edgedness of their association, Ash and Lamotte find in one another the same sort of origin they seek in the past, both textually and physically; Lamotte judges Ash to be "the life of things" (310), and he calls her his "centre [...] where my desire has its end" (312). In Yorkshire, Ash and Lamotte therefore attain the same balance of self and Other that they bring to historical inquiry and creative endeavour.

As Pearce points out, though, the utopian model of dialogism, with its perfectly democratic interaction between the parties, is impossible to sustain in actual social relations, for "[i]t ignores the fact that in any exchange between two or more persons/discursive positions a power dynamic is inevitably involved" (12). In the case of Ash and Lamotte, this dynamic manifests itself primarily in terms of the patriarchal imbalance of Victorian society. Not only is Lamotte disadvantaged by her status as lover to a married man, but also her fragile autonomy as a female artist is threatened. Despite Ash's genuine regard for her privacy, she cannot long abide his intrusion into her creative work, however delicately handled, nor his overwhelming influence. Even before their tryst in Yorkshire, she regrets their meetings as an irreversible loss of "primaeval innocence" (215); after more intensive contact, she tells him, "I should fade and glimmer if long in your hot light" (310). The poets' inability to continue their affair beyond the glory days of Yorkshire signals a collapse of the ideal dialogic exchange when transferred to the Victorian social context with its differential power relations. Ash and Lamotte's final parting also marks their disconnection from the secure "origins," personal and cultural, they had so urgently sought.

It is striking, of course, that the poets' remarkable relationship does not give rise to any renewed sense of stability, but rather corresponds with a general descent into greater disarray, with all of the Victorian characters ending up dissatisfied and alone, as we have seen. In terms of the Vichian model that Byatt sets up, this failure is due to the period's placement in the cultural continuum:

the nineteenth century is not ready for the correction of the *ricorso*, just as it is not prepared to allow the relationship between Lamotte and Ash to continue. While the nineteenth-century characters cannot re-establish cultural equilibrium in their own time, though, the text does hold out the prospect of their future redemption. In the postscript, Ash meets his and Lamotte's daughter, representative of a coming generation of which the twentieth-century couple are symbolically and, in Maud's case, literally the descendants. The poets' failed historical union thus has its own addressivity, waiting like the concealed letters to be received by sympathetic readers in the future.

Through their critical fascination with Ash and Lamotte, Roland and Maud become the "listening others" who intercept and revive the poets' story in the twentieth century. While Lamotte and Ash gained a dialogical understanding of the past and each other in Yorkshire but could not sustain it, Roland and Maud learn from their predecessors, emulating their successes while arriving at the compromises they failed to reach. The modern characters are aided in this learning process by their era's extreme self-consciousness, an otherwise alienating quality that, in this case, makes them especially aware and critical of their own roles in the process of historical inquiry. During their parallel trip to Yorkshire, Maud and Roland extend their "reading" beyond the printed page, retracing the poets' movements with various texts as guides. The depiction of the physical environment as alive with significance literalizes the growing sense in *Possession* that the past *is* knowable, despite the problems of access and interpretation raised by recent historiographic theory and thematized by the novel itself. These issues, though never forgotten, are put aside temporarily as Roland and Maud act out the fantasy of recapturing particular historical moments.

They follow in the footsteps of Cropper, who made the same journey some years earlier. As Maud discerns from his account of the trip, Cropper came to the landscape with the intention of finding in it proof of his particular biographical slant. At first, Roland and Maud are in danger of duplicating Cropper's mistake; they allow their modern sense of "semiotics" (273) to colour their interpretations, seeing a sexual metaphor in everything, as Stern would. Then Roland rejects that kind of contemporary self-absorption, the arrogant imposition of one period's ideology on another; he says, "Everything relates to *us* and so we're imprisoned in ourselves—we can't see *things*. [...] It makes an interesting effort of imagination to think how they saw the world" (276). As the critics agree on this more responsive approach to the past, similar to that adopted by Ash and Lamotte, they also gain a more balanced understanding of one

another, a new reciprocity. Whereas Roland and Maud previously had reserva-
tions about each other's choice of literary study, they each spend time in
Yorkshire reading about the other's preferred writer, forming a common "language" in which they can communicate, similar to Ash and Lamotte's bond as
poets. They also begin to think of themselves as distinct from the Victorians
who have so dominated their lives. Maud notes that she and Roland can never
"see [desire] as [Lamotte and Ash] did" (290), leading to confessions of their
desire for freedom from the oppressive sexual demands of the contemporary
world.

Curiously, at this point when the twentieth-century couple decide to con-
centrate on their own relationship, to "get out of [the poets'] story" (291) for a
while, they unwittingly repeat the past. Both sets of characters are drawn to the
archaic Yorkshire language; we are told that Lamotte "had taken delight in the
uncompromising Northern words, which they had collected like stones, or
spiny sea-creatures" (311), and the critics later enthusiastically "comb[ed]"
(291) those words from the text of *Melusina*. Their mutual interest in accumu-
lating words as objects imbued with pastness differs, though, from the zeal that
Cropper brings to acquiring literary relics such as Ash's pocket watch, since
Cropper's collection is dedicated only to his own professional egotism, and not
to the appreciation of the life of the past which such objects can yield. When
the two couples decide one hundred years apart to go to Boggle Hole because
they like the word (291, 311) with its connotations of complexity and mystery,
their coincidental attraction opens up new understandings of Yorkshire history,
but also helps the moderns to identify imaginatively with their predecessors. As
a result of this connection, the contemporary characters can rediscover the vitality repressed by their overly-intellectualized world, symbolized by Maud's hair,
usually concealed because of professional taunts, but which is "glossy with
constricted life" (295) and which she and Roland agree to loosen and let free
before leaving Yorkshire. The dialogic relationship with the past and each other
achieved by Maud and Roland in Yorkshire therefore initiates the spontaneous,
revitalizing repetition of the *ricorso*, which has lasting positive effects for them
as representatives of their culture.

In the final portion of the novel, Roland finds himself steadily developing
a more clearly defined identity as a social being, an academic, and eventually
as a poet. No longer intellectually intimidated by Maud, who is gradually
becoming his lover, he joins her in their scholarly pursuit, the "Chase and Race"
(460) which monopolizes the rest of the plot, as an equal partner. At the same
time, he attains a new level of professional respect, with job offers that promise his release from the "Inferno" (31) where he serves as Blackadder's minion.

As he gains independence personally and professionally, Roland also acquires creative autonomy. Discouraged by professional rejection, Roland at first has little sense of self; he reluctantly accepts contemporary theories that human beings are all "made up of conflicting systems of beliefs, desires, languages and molecules" (513), and allows others to dominate him. This openness to outside influence is particularly acute in the case of Ash, whose voice "s[i]ng[s]" (99) in Roland's head to the point where he can no longer distinguish his own thinking from his literary idol's. Roland's susceptibility to "verbal ghosts" relates to his "word-obsessed mind" (161), which is always alert to the elaborate specificity and descriptive power of language. When Roland visits Lincolnshire, he is impressed by Tennyson's ability to capture the reality of the landscape perfectly in a poem: "[He] saw immediately that the word 'meet' was precise and surprising, not vague" (78). Gradually, though, Roland's linguistic fascination evolves, going beyond the lexical or even the aesthetic to a state in which language obtrudes on his consciousness (and subconscious, through dreams) in non-representational forms. In this condition, Roland perceives words like material objects, similar to Lamotte's collection of Yorkshire vocabulary, but without the historical resonance. Words spring unbidden into his mind, so many that he feels compelled to write them down as lists "that [resist] arrangement"; they compose a "primitive language" (467) whose meaning initially eludes him.

According to Julia Kristeva, this material aspect of language—its suddenly obtrusive, essentially alien, and unassimilable nature—discloses the workings of what she calls the semiotic order: the non-rational, disruptive force of desire normally repressed by dominant social discourses. As Brenda Ludeman points out in her essay "The Other of Language," the semiotic makes itself felt as "the presence of a palpable acuity, a bodily pulsion or rhythm," discernible in language as "aural and textual vicissitudes" inaccessible to the "historically privileged" "sense order" of the visual (27–28). When individuals intuit the existence of the semiotic through a sensory apprehension of words, they undergo both "pleasure and difficulty" (28) as they become aware of the previously unrealized limitations of their perception. In the process, they "acknowledg[e] [their] ability to access structures of meaning (rationality) while dissolving those structures in any given practice" (32). The self-conscious recognition of the materiality of language thus can have a "revolutionary" effect, prompting individuals to reclaim those desires deemed unacceptable by the dominant discourse, and to re-examine and modify the seemingly fixed identities assigned to them by the symbolic order with which the semiotic is in constant tension.

Roland's transformational encounter with the physicality of language, which begins with his list-making, crystallizes around his deeply affecting rereading, near the end of the novel, of *The Garden of Proserpina* while alone for the last time in his basement apartment. This experience does not, as Bronfen contends, "transform him into Ash, both encompassing him and being consumed by him" (128). Indeed, by the time Roland reads the poem, he has already begun the process of distancing himself from Ash's overpowering influence; he has looked at his cherished portraits of Ash and thought that there is now in them "not an angle, not a bone, not a white speck of illumination comprehensible by him or to do with him" (507). Nor is Roland's encounter with Ash's work a "modernist epiphany," as Buxton claims (215), sparked by an "impersonal reading" (*P* 512) of the kind recommended by the narrator as just one way of revisiting a familiar text, in which readers abandon themselves to the transcendent beauty of language. Rather, the narrator intrudes uncharacteristically at this point to define precisely the sort of unprecedented, materially-engaged reading required for Roland to find what he most needs, for himself and for his culture:

> Now and then there are readings that make the hairs on the neck, the non-existent pelt, stand on end and tremble, when every word burns and shines hard and clear and infinite and exact. [...] In these readings, a sense that the text has appeared to be wholly new, never before seen, is followed, almost immediately, by the sense that it was *always there*, that we the readers, knew it was always there, and have *always known* it was as it was, though we have now for the first time recognised, become fully cognisant of, our knowledge. (512)

This overt narratorial presence underscores the intense self-consciousness with which Roland approaches Ash's poem, an act of "reflective rereading" that Matei Calinescu would describe as the final stage of a "haunting" (*Rereading* xi-xiii) performed mutually by text and reader.

Although Roland knows the poem intimately, he genuinely appreciates its strangeness for the first time, in the way that the narrator describes. This visceral effect stems from his new sense of the words' radical otherness; he rereads them "as though [they] were living creatures or stones of fire" and is conscious of "the language moving around, weaving its own patterns, beyond the reach of any single human, writer or reader" (512). By seeing the text as separate both from himself and Ash, Roland gains a fresh understanding of the creative potency of language, especially in its earliest forms: "He heard Vico saying that the first men were poets and the first words were names that were also things" (512). With his unexpected insight into the primordial linguistic power behind the poem, Roland feels that he has received Ash's message for the future: "there was no privileged communication, though it was he who happened to be there, at that time, to understand it" (513). Simultaneously, though, he pulls himself away from Ash's domineering influence, finding his own personal and artistic voice, with the lists of words "arrang[ing] themselves into poems" (515) in his mind. His new-found aesthetic aspiration takes into account the representational crisis of his age, but is no longer constrained by it: "He had been taught that language was essentially inadequate, that it could never speak what was there, that it only spoke itself. [...] What had happened to him was that the ways in which it *could* be said had become more interesting than the idea that it could not" (513). At this moment, Roland becomes a poet both in the literal and Vichian senses; he imaginatively recaptures the linguistic sensibility of the first time-form and, with it, the representational stability that Ash himself had felt slipping away. He does so, however, in full awareness of his own period's apprehensions about the limitations of language, apprehensions that he acknowledges yet is ready to surpass.

By learning to look beyond the instability of meaning that debilitates his life and those of his contemporaries, Roland taps into his culture's lingering desire for a closer relationship between words and the world. As a result, he revises his own subjectivity and establishes himself as the "first man" of a new era in which language is recognized as a dynamic force in its own right that is also inextricably connected to human activity and perception, and is hence returned to contact, if only provisionally, with the reality it seeks to describe. Roland's symbolic re-entry into the previously forbidden garden above his apartment thus marks him as the "Adam" of his era, the first practitioner of a new kind of "naming" that promises to rejuvenate his skeptical, moribund world.

For her part, Maud also signifies a restabilized sense of personal and societal identity. In the end, she rejects the aggressive, self-serving feminism, based entirely on gender conflict, promoted by her colleagues, thereby exemplifying a more integrated model of self in relation to others that concedes sexual difference but allows for both desire and equitable treatment. This new sense of feminist self-definition is brought about by Maud's reading of Lamotte's work, in which she is finally able to recognize not only the individuality and power for women that Lamotte depicts in her mythically-based texts, but also the importance of avoiding self-righteous solipsism. Through these realizations, Maud suggests a different direction for women of her own time, as well as making up for Lamotte's foreshortened ability to benefit from the same insights in the past.

As the descendant of both Lamotte and Ash, Maud represents a chance for the failures of their entire generation to be redeemed, and her relationship with Roland after his poetic transformation symbolically unites past with present, restabilized language with more coherent personal and communal identity.

Maud and Roland develop a romantic bond similar to Lamotte and Ash's, based on the interplay of difference and similarity and on the primacy of mutual respect, but without the burdensome inequality that obstructed the Victorians as lovers. Rather, Roland and Maud take the best elements of that failed effort and combine them with a late twentieth-century awareness about power relations, arriving at "a modern way" (550) of managing their romance that accommodates individual career ambitions and the need for privacy. At an early stage in their liaison, Roland had indicated his willingness to be flexible regarding traditional gender roles, voluntarily taking the "inferior" bunk on their trip across the Channel to research Lamotte's past, claiming "I don't see that it matters, top or bottom" (361). Yet this liberal attitude seems to lapse in their later sexual encounter, where Byatt goes out of her way to insist on the ideological coding objected to by Buxton, having Roland gallantly offer to "take care" of the frightened Maud, and giving him the prerogative of taking "possession" (550) of her first. By staging the scene in this way, Byatt makes clear that the patriarchal dynamic that undermined the Victorians' relationship, however muted, unavoidably persists for the twentieth-century characters. Nonetheless, she self-consciously calls attention to the "outdated" (550) nature of that inequality, then accords to Maud the ultimate moment of the sexual conquest, "her clear voice crying out, uninhibited, unashamed, in pleasure and triumph" (551). With the final parallel to Adam and Eve as the lovers emerge into the garden, Byatt suggests that the twentieth-century couple's sexual union is both inextricably embedded in the patriarchal ethos of Western culture and as close to dialogic perfection as possible, owing to the characters' self-consciousness about their situation.

Their union epitomizes what Zygmunt Bauman, following Emmanuel Lévinas, calls the "ethics of caress" (92), the basis of a revivifying social order for the postmodern world. In Bauman's vision of contemporary ethics, a person is not motivated to moral action by self-interest, for example the avoidance of punishment; rather, she or he feels a primary obligation to the Other which, when reciprocated, meets the needs of the self as well. The model for this mutually satisfying relationship is the "caress," the figure of erotic love, a "hand" that "remains open, never tightening into a grip, never 'getting hold of'; it touches without pressing, it moves obeying the shape of the caressed body"

(92). In their sexual congress, Roland and Maud act out this moral stance; they achieve reciprocal fulfillment by taking "possession" of one another physically, expressing desire without denying or subjugating the other's selfhood. In so doing, they use the dialogic lessons they have learned from the past to lay the groundwork of a replacement social order.

In Bauman's erotic model of postmodern ethics, the future, like the loved one, is desirable by virtue of its "absolute otherness and perpetual elusiveness"; it is never completely knowable, but is "always a new birth, an absolute beginning" (93). Byatt completes her novel with symbols of a future about to unfold with unknown, but promising, potential for cultural rehabilitation. By positioning the story of Ash and Lamotte's child, with its undelivered message, at the very end after the contemporary characters' sexual consummation, Byatt opens up the possibility of yet another "generation" of progeny who could benefit from the self-conscious reflection on the documents of the past for which Vico's *ricorso* is the prototype. As readers of *Possession*, we fulfill the role of the text's projected addressee, and gain the opportunity to enter imaginatively into the consciousness of earlier times, and to make contact, at least in fantasy terms, with lost desires and traditions that could restore faltering aspects of our culture. In this way, *Possession* is, however paradoxically, a very postmodern novel indeed.

-iv-

In Lamotte's tale "The Threshold," a young knight sent on a quest to find a remedy for his father's illness encounters three ladies, the first two radiantly gold and silver, the third plain and dull in comparison. The Childe chooses the third lady with her casketful of soothing herb, Lamotte's narrator tells us, because his decision has been foreordained not only by fate and patriarchal decree, but also by earlier tales, known to the knight and the reader alike: "wisdom in all tales tells us this, and the last sister is always the true choice" (171). The knight's choice is therefore really not a choice at all, though the narrator hints that, in future, other endings may be offered:

> And one day we will write it otherwise, that he would not come, that he
> stayed, or chose the sparkling ones, or went out again onto the moors to
> live free of fate, if such can be. But you must know now, that it turned
> out as it must turn out, must you not? Such is the power of necessity in
> tales. (172)

Here, Byatt seems to be hearkening back to *The French Lieutenant's Woman,* with its three possible endings from which the reader is invited to choose. As we saw in Chapter One, however, the illusion of choice in that novel is in fact designed to make readers reflect on the latent desires that they bring to the text, desires that they have built up from their previous reading experiences and the expectations they have come to associate with various literary genres and periods. With this embedded tale and its intertextual evocations, Byatt calls attention to the "Necessity" propelling her own narrative, a drive towards a romance ending so powerful that even Roland (as a modern-day "Childe," descended from Robert Browning's original) is aware of it: "He was in a Romance, a vulgar and a high Romance simultaneously; a Romance was one of the systems that controlled him, as the expectations of Romance control almost everyone in the Western world, for better or for worse, at some point or another" (460). The question is thus not whether Roland's story will conclude conventionally, since it is clear virtually from the outset that it will, but rather what Byatt's deliberate use of tradition reveals about her vision of postmodernity.

In *Possession*, Byatt reproduces past literary forms, most notably from the realist and modernist periods, evoking the artificially-ordered world views of which those forms serve as reifications and thereby to realize in textual terms the postmodern desire for a provisional restoration of cultural coherence. At the same time, though, Byatt's evocation of those conventions, embedded as they are in various traditions of representationalism, could be seen as inimical to her project of fashioning a novelistic version of a postmodern world in which the collapse of linguistic stability is recognized and accepted, yet in which meaning and social structure can nonetheless be generated. It is important, therefore, to consider how Byatt's reinscription of realist and modernist forms is both internally figured and carried out in overtly self-conscious ways that allow her to recover from those traditions elements consistent with her work of cultural reformation.

For Maud, who stands at the end of the text as the embodiment of unconscious inheritance, the influence of the past is initially oppressive. Of her genealogical link to both Lamotte and Ash, she says, "There's something unnaturally *determined* about it all. Daemonic. I feel they have taken me over" (548). Maud's anxiety stems from the fact that she has discovered herself to be the product of biological programming, a replication of ancestors who have left their literal imprint on her features. In *The World, the Text and the Critic,* Edward Said, working out of Vico, describes this kind of involuntary generational repetition, guided by genetic memory, as "filiation" (114), and argues, using an analysis of Karl Marx's discussion of inherited language in *The Eighteenth Brumaire of Louis Bonaparte,* that the process of descent is usually a degenerative one:

> In language as in families, Marx implies, the past weighs heavily on the present, making demands more than providing help. The direct genealogical line is parenthood and filiation which, whether in language or in the family, will produce a disguised quasi-monstrous offspring, that is farce or debased languge [sic], rather than a handsome copy of the precursor or parent—unless the past is severely curtailed in its powers to dominate the present and the future. (123)

In order for a given "offspring" to ward off the past's retrograde pressure, Said asserts, it must intentionally struggle against its forebears, breaking free from its automatic heritage to forge a new identity. Said sees this process of repetition-with-variation as a key facet of Vico's system, as well as a prominent issue in eighteenth- and nineteenth-century European fiction, in which heroes such as Emma Bovary are portrayed in situations of rebellion against established orders, often represented as familial structures. The hero in turn acts as a symbol of the text itself in its relation to tradition: "To be novel is to be an original, that is, a figure not repeating what most men perforce repeat—the course of human life, father to son, generation after generation" (117). The defining features of the novel, Said contends, are its rejection of the kind of mechanical filiative repetition that Maud finds so troubling, its refusal to unthinkingly give rise to ersatz forms of historical literary patterns and its insistence on innovation at both the thematic and generic levels.

With its pronounced emulation of traditional literary models, *Possession* is in danger of sharing Maud's position of anxious descendant, and therefore of being not truly "novel" in Said's sense. In addition to the romance and detective genres, the text's evident antecedents include the modernist *künstlerroman,* whose plot line underlies Roland's development towards his poetic calling, though not as categorically as Buxton suggests. For just as Maud's recognition of her ancestry is a crucial stage in her growth into a new sort of late twentieth-century woman, so too is Roland's artistic insight a step, as we have seen, away from the influence of the Victorian past and towards his personal reconnection to the postmodern world in all its extra-textual materiality, in defiance of both the modernist aesthetic of authorial impersonality and the post-structuralist view of language. In the same way, *Possession* as a whole moves beyond the apparently compulsive reproduction of conventions to a more reflective consideration of how those traditions can help to work out in symbolic terms the failings of postmodernity and their possible solutions.

In this respect, Byatt's use of literary conventions more closely resembles the second, more self-consciously constructed form of repetition that Said identifies from his analysis of Vico's historiography, "affiliation" (118). While filiative procreation is the natural expression of biology, it does not entail any innate sense of obligation to perpetuate society; rather, Vico says, the instinctive response is to destroy, rather than to protect, the next generation: "Men mean to gratify their bestial lust and abandon their offspring" (*NS* 425). Contrary to this intention, though, people conjoin in the institutions of marriage and parenthood, acting out a preservative impulse that runs through the course of human history, as epitomized by the salvational effect of the *ricorso*. The affiliative bonds resulting from this involuntary urge to survive unite humanity in ways that are unregulated by mere genetics or temporal progression, and that are therefore stronger and more lasting. This kind of social cohesion, which is given greater force at the end of Byatt's novel than the menacing oppression of heredity, is typified by Roland and Maud's anticipated conjugal stability, and by the community of like-minded scholars working towards the common goal of saving Ash and Lamotte's secrets from commercial exploitation.

Said notes a similar valorization of affiliation over filiation in *The Eighteenth Brumaire*, in which Marx corrects Louis Bonaparte's putative claim to be the son, rather than the nephew, of the emperor Napoleon, thereby delegitimizing the descendant's right of succession. Rather, Said maintains, Louis's power of usurpation derives from a falsified rewriting of history, one which Marx's essay in turn repeats and further revises. Said concludes that

> Marx's is neither a natural feat nor a miraculous assertion: it is an affiliative repetition made possible by critical consciousness. It portends a methodological revolution whereby, as in the natural and human sciences, the facts of nature are dissolved and then reassembled polemically, as during the nineteenth century in the museum, the laboratory, the classroom, or the library facts are dissolved and then assembled into units of didactic sense, perhaps to illustrate human power more to transform nature than to confirm it. A parallel affiliative process takes place in philology, in fiction, in psychology, where repetition turns into an aspect of analytic structural technique. Probably repetition is bound to move from *immediate* regrouping of experience to a more and more *mediated* reshaping and redisposition of it, in which the disparity

between one version and its repetition increases, since repetition cannot long escape the ironies it bears within it. (124–25)

Affiliation, in Said's terms, can thus be a function of literary discourse, in which traditional forms are "dissolved" and "reassembled" as a collection of ironically-realized structures within the framework of a new text.

This kind of internalized reassemblage of past forms within literature can lead to a critical revaluation of tradition, an effect comparable to that of what Martin Heidegger calls, in a philosophical context, "destruction." In *Being and Time*, Heidegger proposes the dismantling of the Western philosophical canon, which he believes has become so culturally ingrained as to be passed on unquestioningly from generation to generation. One effect of this entrenchment is that the original motivation behind the development of various ideas and structures has become occluded: "When tradition thus becomes master, it does so in such a way that what it 'transmits' is made so inaccessible [...] that it rather becomes concealed. Tradition takes what has come down to us and delivers it over to self-evidence" (43). In order to expose what those "categories and concepts" (43) were designed to respond to and cover over—the dread induced by existence in its barest form—Heidegger undertakes an open critique of the origins of Western metaphysics. While this "destruction" may seem regressive, its purpose, Heidegger maintains, is ultimately constructive:

> If the question of Being is to have its own history made transparent, then this hardened tradition must be loosened up, and the concealments which it has brought about must be dissolved. [...] But this destruction is just as far from having the *negative* sense of shaking off the ontological tradition. We must, on the contrary, stake out the positive possibilities of that tradition. [...] On its negative side, this destruction does not relate itself towards the past; its criticism is aimed at 'today.' (44)

Heidegger's goal is not to discard the history of Western philosophy, but to create a new line of thought that retains the best aspects of that tradition while acknowledging the essential chaos underlying *Dasein*'s being-in-the-world. In this respect, Heidegger's project resembles the *ricorso*, with its discriminatory review of past time-forms for the sake of cultural reform.

In his application of the Heideggerian concept of destruction to postmodern literature, William Spanos, in *Repetitions*, recognizes that any writer working within the influence of Western culture is "inevitably the victim in some degree of the epistemological assumptions informing (concealed in) the language he inherits from the past" (55). For contemporary authors, Spanos argues, the assumptions that assert themselves most insidiously and persistently are those from the realist and modernist traditions, both of which he regards as exemplars of the West's logocentrism, its attempt through language in its various manifestations to "domesticate—to at-home—the threatening realm of Nothingness" (17).

The realist tradition, Spanos contends, presents life as a well-made plot, a seamless sequence of events in which the law of cause-and-effect infallibly operates. All unexplainable, contingent, or absurd occurrences are stripped away, leaving a perfectly ordered, linear narrative removed from the messiness of temporal existence. Within this positivistic view of the world, the detective reigns, implicitly or explicitly, as the "Transcendental Signified" (47), the agent of logical discovery who brings about reassuring closure. In the modernist tradition, on the other hand, the ethos of the "biologist" (33) dominates. Just as a phylogeneticist makes connections among species and generations across vast periods of time, the modernist writer, Spanos suggests, creates a spatialized text in which events take place and characters interact in a state of mythic or artistic transcendence, abstracted from ordinary time.[4] While literary modernism began largely as a reaction against teleological rationalism, the influence of its symbolist precursors led to its evolution of a new form which, while not linear in the same sense as realist texts, still shapes existence into an aesthetic whole, an object meant to replace and deny the discomfort of being-in-the-world.

Spanos advocates that contemporary authors should recognize and ultimately reject the influence of both these traditions, and instead follow the precedents set by writers who have eschewed "*art*-ificialized nature in behalf of the recovery of its primordial terrors" (48). These writers—who range from Cervantes and Shakespeare through the absurdists to late modernists and postmodernists such as Samuel Beckett, Charles Olsen, and Thomas Pynchon—all deliberately disrupt and reconfigure conventional notions of literary structure, both the teleological narrative associated with realism and the "re-centered 'anti-Aristotelian' line" (49) of modernist spatialization. Instead, these authors have experimented with "dis-closive or de-structive (open) forms to 'world' the text, to retrieve a radically temporal perceptual stance, *i.e.* to *defer* presence"

---

[4]This conception of modernist textuality was first critically described by Joseph Frank in his "Spatial Form in Modern Literature," *Sewanee Review* 53 (Spring, Summer, Autumn 1945): 221–40, 433–45, 643–65.

(58). Spanos identifies Jean-Paul Sartre's late modernist novel *Nausea* as an exemplary model of how postmodern fiction can break with tradition and uncover the terrifying contingency of temporal experience; it also, as we shall see, helps to illuminate *Possession*'s paradoxical reversion to literary conventions from the past.

While *Nausea* has been described by critics as a novel about an existential crisis that is finally resolved in aesthetic terms, Spanos argues that the text's seeming capitulation to modernist form at the end is in fact misleading, and that Sartre's design, intentional or otherwise, is to "destroy" that tradition as well as the realist one through what Said would call an "affiliative" representation of both. The main character, Antoine Roquentin, attempts to write the biography of a certain marquis from the period of the French Revolution, to arrange the disparate and fragmentary facts concerning that historical personage's life into a seamless, coherent narrative that would emulate the conventions of the realist novel, epitomized by the copy of Honoré de Balzac's *Eugénie Grandet* that Roquentin tries unsuccessfully to read. At the same time, though, Roquentin begins to have unsettling glimpses into the fluid, alien nature of the reality around him, which eventually leads him to abandon his writing project and to disdain the bourgeois façade of the city in which he lives. Roquentin's sense of disorientation or "nausea" culminates in an experience in a public park where he suddenly perceives the existence of a tree so powerfully that he feels overwhelmed, deprived of the ability to use language to describe and order the external world. Spanos cites this scene as a reversal of the Biblical story of the Garden of Eden, in which God gives Adam the power by God to name the beasts and thereby to safely place them, and the rest of earthly reality, into a totalizing, objective system of signification. Roquentin, in contrast, is characterized, Spanos explains, as an "anti-Adam" (65) who "un-names" the world and consequently negates the comfortable but illusory orderliness of Western logocentric thought.

Despite his undeniable discovery of the formlessness of existence, Roquentin still yearns for something to lift him out of his dread, to make sense of the world and his place in it. Initially, he gets relief from his alienation in an American jazz tune, which he hears repeatedly at a café. In the song's "geometric" (Spanos 82) form, Roquentin believes he has found an image of timeless perfection, unaffected by life's vicissitudes. This song provides the inspiration for the novel that Roquentin decides, at the end of *Nausea*, to write as a more durable form of escape from his existential turmoil. As Spanos elaborates, Roquentin necessarily rejects the realist mode for his project, since it is too closely aligned with the false bourgeois order that his disturbing visions have shattered. Rather, he aspires to write a book as transcendent as the jazz tune; in his journal, which comprises the text of *Nausea*, he describes it as "another type of book. I don't know which kind—but you would have to guess, behind the printed words, behind the pages, something which didn't exist, which was above existence" (252). Clearly, Roquentin's intention is to emulate the spatialized integrity of the modernist novel, and his epiphany puts him in company, as Spanos points out, with other *künstlerroman* heroes of that period, such as Stephen Dedalus in Joyce's *A Portrait of the Artist as Young Man*.

Spanos begins his analysis by citing critics, including Iris Murdoch, who equate Roquentin with Sartre, and the modernist novel projected in the journal entry with *Nausea* itself. In this formulation, which presumes a circularity in the novel's structure similar to that ascribed to the jazz song, Sartre's text seems to obliterate the vivid effect of Roquentin's insights into existence, suggesting an aesthetic reordering of the contingent world that would quell both the character's and the reader's experience of uneasiness. Spanos, on other hand, views these equations as contradictory of both the message and form of Sartre's work. Instead, he calls attention to the fictional "Editors' Note" prefacing the novel, which claims that Roquentin's journal had been found among his papers, left behind following his disappearance from Bouville. Rather than providing circular completion, then, the ending of the text opens onto fragmentation and absence, indicative of a form which, Spanos suggests, is the "fictional counterpart" (101) of the existential revelations in the novel's main narrative. Unlike the conventionalized modernist *künstlerroman* imagined by Roquentin, Sartre's text fulfills Spanos's call for a new kind of fiction, an "antinovel" that discloses the ideological reifications of both the realist and modernist traditions while "demystifying the reader's logocentric expectations of formal unity" (100).

*Possession*, on the other hand, would seem to defy Spanos's admonition by restoring unified forms that conceal temporality and direct readerly desire in conventionally familiar ways. Roland and Maud, with their gradual revelation and piecing-together of the mysteries of Ash and Lamotte, accomplish the biographical ordering that Roquentin fails to achieve with the Marquis; the poets' histories, embedded within the teleological unfolding of Roland and Maud's own romantic plot line, exemplify what Barthes calls the "preterite mode" (qtd. in Spanos 75), which "transform[s] life into adventure, the superfluous into a logocentric, a predictable and thus reassuring well-made world, in which all the pieces are integral and rigorously justified" (Spanos 75). The contemporary chaos briefly visible in Val's unexplainable photographs recedes behind the linearity of the text's realist structure. Similarly, the intergenerational repetitions and resemblances in the novel create a mythic resonance that allows the reader to see the characters and actions *"all at once"* (Spanos 37) in the transcendent manner associated with the modernist aesthetic. As a *künstlerroman* hero, Roland, with his epiphanic experience in the garden, seems to undo the process of "un-naming" undergone by Roquentin in the park, to reassert the Adamic power of language to order the world, just as *Possession* itself reinstates literary conventions.

As we saw earlier, however, Roland's "re-naming" of the universe is carried out in full consciousness of language's attenuated relationship with the world it seeks to represent, and only after his recursive contact with the past has made him aware of the desireability of recapturing elements of earlier periods, regardless of their inevitable provisionality in the contemporary context. Byatt's use of realist and modernist forms in *Possession* can be seen as analogously self-conscious and therefore "destructive" in Heideggerian terms: by ironically re-presenting those traditions within the discursive field of her text, she exposes the sedimented epistemological stances underlying their aesthetic structures while "stak[ing] out the[ir] positive possibilities." Among the beneficial elements revealed by this process of affiliative reproduction is the potency of readerly desire, as evidenced by *Possession*'s enormous marketplace popularity, for stories that suggest the potential for a renewed sense of order in postmodernity, one that draws on tradition while not concealing its ideological frameworks. Through her re-writing of Sartre's pivotal garden scene, Byatt goes beyond Spanos's call for "open form" to propose a new direction for contemporary fiction, in which the reclamation of convention is a metonym for cultural restabilization.[5]

While Byatt's text shows postmodernity and its connection to the past, both on the cultural and aesthetic levels, in a redemptive light, Rushdie's *The Satanic Verses* and *Midnight's Children* seem to exemplify contemporary cultural practices that threaten to dilute historical understanding, if not render it completely obsolete. In response to the arguments of prominent theorists such as Jameson, however, Chapter Five will demonstrate that Rushdie's historiographic novels do not foreground their intertextual composition or mix fictional with actual

---

[5]In her essay on her novel *Still Life*, Byatt acknowledges the park scene from *Nausea* as "[o]ne of the powerful forces behind [her] interest in naming and describing" (*Passions* 12).

events for the purpose of contributing to postmodern culture's increasingly dehistoricized, image-ridden relation to reality. Rather, in these texts, Rushdie embeds spatial images that allegorize the representational issues that he confronts as a British author of contemporary fiction working within a postcolonial worldview.

# Chapter Five
## Unfinished Business: Intertextuality and Historiography in Salman Rushdie's *The Satanic Verses* and *Midnight's Children*

In *Postmodernism, or, The Cultural Logic of Late Capitalism*, Fredric Jameson tells a fairy tale about the process leading up to what he perceives as the postmodern era's generalized estrangement from historical reality. The process began, he claims, "Once upon a time," with the sign, which emerged with the birth of capitalism, and which initially enjoyed "unproblematic relations with its referent" (95). This harmony was quickly disrupted by another capitalist by-product, reification, which severed the referent from the sign, placing the world and representations of it at an unbridgeable distance. With this second stage, the realist period gave way to the modernist, marked by the "semiautonomy of language" (96).[1] Yet the force of reification persisted, driving a wedge between the component parts of the sign itself, consigning the referent and its attendant reality to oblivion, and leaving the signified in a position of radical instability. The result of this third stage is postmodernism:

> We are left with that pure and random play of signifiers that we call post-modernism, which no longer produces monumental works of the modernist type but ceaselessly reshuffles the fragments of preexistent texts, the building blocks of older cultural and social production, in some new and heightened bricolage: metabooks which cannibalize other books, metatexts which collate bits of other texts [...] . (96)

The target of Jameson's critique here is intertextuality, especially as it appears

---

[1]Jameson's misgivings about modernism and its rejection of the world here seem to be at odds with his earlier, more subtle defence of it in *The Political Unconscious*: "[I]t is evidently wrong to imagine, as Lukács sometimes seems to do, that modernism is some mere ideological distraction, a way of systematically displacing the reader's attention from history and society to pure form, metaphysics, and experiences of the individual monad; it is all those things, but they are not so easy to achieve as one might think" (266). His simplified explanation in *Postmodernism* seems to be necessary to the "logic" of his "fairy tale," which has modernism as the point at which things began to go seriously wrong in terms of the sign.

in postmodern fiction. In his earlier essay "Postmodernism and Consumer Society," he describes contemporary artistic intertextual practices as taking the form of "pastiche" or "blank parody," in which the styles of previous generations are aimlessly copied owing to the current exhaustion of "stylistic innovation" (114–15). This state of affairs, he says, "means that one of [postmodern art's] essential messages will involve the necessary failure of art and the aesthetic, the failure of the new, the imprisonment in the past" (115–16). He is not suggesting, though, that contemporary art is enriched by direct contact with an actual tradition, but rather that it can only reproduce simulacra of the artistic past, which take the place of the referent lost with the double shift from realism through modernism to postmodernism: "[W]e are now, in other words, in 'intertextuality' […] as the operator of a new connotation of 'pastness' and pseudo-historical depth, in which the history of aesthetic styles displaces 'real' history" (*Postmodernism* 20). Intertextuality, then, is seen by Jameson to be symptomatic of postmodern culture's inability to represent the "real" except as images emptied of historical significance.

This uniform "depthlessness" (*Postmodernism* 6), Jameson argues, extends even to cultural productions that promote themselves as overtly engaged with the past, including novels of "postmodern fantastic historiography" (*Postmodernism* 367) such as those written by E.L. Doctorow, to cite his example, or Salman Rushdie. In these novels, Jameson insists, "the making up of unreal history is a substitute for the making of the real kind," and they are "allergic to the priorities and commitments, let alone the responsibilities, of the various tediously committed kinds of partisan history" (369). Because he refuses to differentiate how intertextuality and historical representation are manifested in contemporary fiction from how they are treated in less self-conscious postmodern cultural artifacts, however, he fails to take into account the potential for texts like Rushdie's to bring about the "critical distance" (*Postmodernism* 48) that he believes is so desperately needed as a corrective to the obliteration of history.

Even though Rushdie, in his writing, produces the very effects that Jameson believes contribute to historical amnesia—parodic imitations of older works, recastings of actual events in fictional terms—he does so in such a way that they make visible what would otherwise be implicit or transparent: the continuity between the contemporary text and its literary antecedents, and the ramifications of that relationship for the complexities of historical referentiality in the aftermath of realism and modernism. In *The Satanic Verses* and *Midnight's Children* respectively, Rushdie addresses these points in allegorical passages that fit into his overall thematization of how the novel needs to be made "new" to accommodate the ineluctable problems of postmodern representation while still reflecting in a meaningful way on extratextual reality. Both of these passages rely on spatial metaphors to demonstrate how the postmodern text can act as a "laboratory" in which the parameters of the new novel are worked out in relation to unresolved issues from the past, literary and historical.

Jameson recognizes space as the contemporary cultural dominant that has come to replace the modernist obsession with time, a change he associates with the postmodern lapse in historicity.[2] Rushdie, on the other hand, employs space self-consciously as a means of artificially bringing elements from different times and places into simultaneous interaction, and thereby subordinates it to his historical purposes. In the "Rosa Diamond" episode of *The Satanic Verses*, he uses a haunted house to symbolize how the intertextual presences of realism and modernism still make themselves felt in the postmodern context, particularly through their representational legacies. With the "Conference" in *Midnight's Children*, a gathering of characters within Saleem Sinai's mind, Rushdie deals with representation through another spatial image; this meeting space, which I compare to the computer-generated worlds of virtual reality technology, serves as a figure of how the versatility of the postmodern historiographic text makes it possible to mix phenomena from different ontological backgrounds in order to formulate alternative versions of actual occurrences. By presenting these concerns in conspicuously allegorical forms within self-reflexive fictions, Rushdie creates what Linda Hutcheon calls the "irony that

---

[2]Jameson contrasts the postmodern tendency to use space as a superficial replacement for historical depth with the politically-oriented theories propounded by Henri Lefebvre in *The Production of Space*, which responds to Michel Foucault's injunction that "[a] whole history remains to be written of *spaces*—which would be at the same time a history of *powers*" (*Power* 149). Lefebvre suggests that new understanding can be gained through attention to the social spaces, such as cities and houses, in which history actually takes place: "Vis-à-vis lived experience, space is neither a mere 'frame', after the fashion of the frame of a painting, nor a form or container of a virtually neutral kind [...] . Space is social morphology: it is to lived experience what form itself is to the living organism" (93–94). More recently, Edward Soja in *Postmodern Geographies: the Reassertion of Space in Critical Social Theory* (London: Verso, 1989) has extended Foucault and Lefebvre's ideas to contemporary society, stressing the need to recover the geopolitical and cultural realities suppressed by traditional historicism. Jameson himself urges greater individual consciousness of the globalized spaces of postmodern culture through a vague system called "*cognitive mapping*" (*Postmodernism* 51ff.) to which art potentially could contribute, but he finds contemporary historiographic fiction inadequate to the task.

allows critical distancing" (*Poetics* 89), engendering a renewed awareness of the history behind the texts that in turn counteracts the forgetfulness induced by the surrounding culture.

-i-

As Jameson remarks, postmodern historiographic fiction often takes the form of a "genealogical" (*Postmodernism* 368) chronicle, which has as its trope for historical progression the descent of a series of characters over several generations. His observation is confirmed by the appearance of extensive "family trees" in the opening pages of novels such as Gabriel García Márquez's *One Hundred Years of Solitude* and Rushdie's later work, *The Moor's Last Sigh*. This fascination with genealogy also manifests itself in critical attempts to theorize the relationship between contemporary fiction and its literary precursors. Hutcheon describes postmodern fiction as parodically "*us[ing]*" and "*abus[ing]*" (*Poetics* 130) a canon to which it is necessarily posterior; she thereby positions it as the impertinent offspring of a lineage or tradition in the modernist conception.[3] While Hutcheon has the fiction standing at the end of a line of tradition over which it casts its ironic glance backward, the model of intertextual praxis proposed here shifts the emphasis away from the strictly temporal to the "genealogical" in the more spatially-oriented sense defined by Michel Foucault.

Foucault regards genealogy not as a tracing back through time to a "secret" origin (a pursuit, he says, which inevitably produces disillusionment), but rather as a perspective that discourse is always "fabricated in a piecemeal fashion from alien forms" ("Nietzsche" 78). This view of each discursive unit as a collection of disparate parts relates to the Foucauldian notion of a "heterotopia," as elaborated for the literary context by Brian McHale: a "space where fragments of a number of possible orders have been gathered together" (18). With

---

[3]The standard modernist lineal paradigm is, of course, from T.S. Eliot's "Tradition and the Individual Talent," in which he theorizes: "The existing monuments form an ideal order among themselves, which is modified by the introduction of the new (really new) work of art among them" (38). As does Eliot's model, Harold Bloom's Oedipally-based system in *The Anxiety of Influence: A Theory of Poetry* (New York: Oxford UP, 1973) focuses on the relationships among authors rather than texts. Without doing away entirely with the idea of authorial agency—it is, after all, Rushdie who chooses to imitate other writers—my model is more textually-centered, with the various stylistic and allusive references in the contemporary text representing works exemplary of certain periods in literary history.

this revised genealogical definition in mind, it is possible to leave off thinking of postmodern intertextuality as primarily retrospection and instead imagine it as a cumulative activity, with the contemporary text acting as a present site of discursive assemblage.

Within the heterotopic fictional space of a postmodern novel, intertexts representing many periods and cultures can co-exist synchronously. When these intertexts are literary in nature, they reveal themselves as "ghostly" presences, flickering through the very fabric of the contemporary text. This "haunting" of the postmodern "house" suggests an intertextual relationship that is not exclusively parodic in Hutcheon's sense of a "stylistic confrontation" (*Theory* 8). For instance, when James Joyce's *Ulysses* appears in "spectral" form in *The Satanic Verses*, it does so as a revered ancestor whose influence perceptibly lingers in the present, much like the brilliant but mad patriarch in *One Hundred Years of Solitude* with whom conversations continue to be held long after his death. If, as Nina Schwartz argues following Paul de Man, modernism assumed a "parricidal" (5) attitude,[4] seeking to secure its own originality through the overthrow of the literary "parents" to which it was unavoidably linked, postmodernism on the other hand recognizes its continuity with the past, shaping the terms of its own textuality through internalized dialogues with the ancestral "spirits" of earlier works, movements, and genres. In this way, postmodern fiction is paradoxically, as Hutcheon makes clear, at the same time "oedipally oppositional and filially faithful" (*Poetics* 88) to the phantom progenitors that inhabit its texts, and whose authority, as we saw in Chapter Three, it attempts to inherit and make its own. In Rushdie's fiction, as in *Waterland* and *Possession*, these intertextual apparitions frequently signify both realism and modernism as persistent forces whose aesthetic implications are still in the process of being understood. As Rosa Diamond puts it, "What's a ghost? Unfinished business, is what" (129). The sequence in Chapter Three of *The Satanic Verses* that deals with this elderly Englishwoman's conjurings of her past into present-day England provides an allegory of how the postmodern novel summons other texts into its uniformly contemporary fictional space, thereby making possible interdiscursive relations on the genealogical terms indicated by Foucault's definition.

---

[4]Schwartz predicates her discussion on de Man's observation in "Literary History and Literary Modernity" that "[m]odernity exists in the form of a desire to wipe out whatever came earlier, in the hope of reaching at last a point that could be called a true present, a point of origin that marks a new departure" (148). Like de Man, Schwartz asserts that this desire for absolute originality is compromised from the outset, since it must define itself against the past and thus acknowledge its own fundamental "derivativeness" (5).

On one level, *The Satanic Verses* acts as a forum where multiple, and usually incommensurable, cultural intertexts are brought into contact.[5] The novel
brings together discursive fragments from East and West, from history, literature, and myth, religion and secularism, high culture and pop culture, in the
eclectic manner favoured by one of its characters, the art critic Zeenat Vakil:
"[W]as not the entire national culture based on the principle of borrowing whatever clothes seemed to fit, Aryan, Mughal, British, take-the-best-and-leave-the-
rest?" (52). Philip Engblom describes Rushdie's writing as a "carnivalized
space" in which "a multitude of voices" expressing "innumerable, irreducible
claims, visions, and ideologies" (295) compete and conflict with one another.
The text's central questions—"How does newness come into the world? How
is it born? Of what fusions, translations, conjoinings is it made?" (8)—point to
its interest in the depiction of contemporary heterogeneity and change, particularly in light of the interpenetration and migration between English and former-
ly-colonized cultures after the demise of imperialism. The main characters,
Gibreel and his counterpart/nemesis Chamcha, both of whom are in flux
between the old and new "worlds," serve as figures of the postcolonial subject
in transition. In his essay "In Good Faith," Rushdie defends the novel's plural-
istic content:

> *The Satanic Verses* celebrates hybridity, impurity, intermingling, the
> transformation that comes of new and unexpected combinations of
> human beings, cultures, ideas, politics, movies, songs. It rejoices in
> mongrelization and fears the absolutism of the Pure. *Mélange*, hotch-
> potch, a bit of this and a bit of that is *how newness enters the world.*
> (*Imaginary* 394)

---

[5]In *Salman Rushdie and The Third World: Myths of the Nation*, Timothy Brennan criticizes
Rushdie's mixing of intertexts as a pernicious "flattening of influences" (52) that degrades all of the
cultures involved, but particularly those from the Third World, whose national identities are leached
in the process. Brennan treats Rushdie not as an individual artist per se but rather as the representative *par excellence* of a group of international writers whom he dubs the "cosmopolitans."
Working out of Edward Said, Antonio Gramsci, and Jameson, Brennan lambastes the cosmopolitans (among whom number García Márquez, Carlos Fuentes, and Bharati Mukherjee) for their col-
lusive role as Third World authors who, as intellectual elitists, serve up palatable "pop" images of
their nations, usually written in English, for the First World to consume. My major disagreement
with Brennan's argument, beyond its rather patronizing tone, has to do with its logical extension,
which would seem to imply that "Third World" authors should be ghettoized in their own cultures,
writing exclusively for native audiences and fastidiously blocking out all foreign influences.

This cultural interplay realizes in fictional form what Calinescu calls "the vast dialogue" ("Ways" 169) characteristic of postmodern reality.

*The Satanic Verses* is dialogic, however, on the specifically literary level as well as on the cultural. The text's ability to be about several things at once is captured in the image of the "lenticular badge," worn by an anonymous character, "the sort that changed its message as you moved" (413). Rushdie's questions about "newness" are equally about the current state of the novel: how can the novel renew itself in the postmodern era? of what "fusions" and "conjoinings" of styles and representational modes will it be made up? By stressing hybridization in the context of renewal, Rushdie states tacitly the postmodern recognition that the new is necessarily composed of the old. The intrinsicality of the past to any innovation is thematized in the novel's insistent concerns with matters of evolution and reincarnation: "To be born again," sings Gibreel Farishta at the novel's beginning, "first you have to die" (3). He and Chamcha are likewise figurations of the text's reflection on its own development, and the novel's in general, as a literary form.

Most significantly, though, *The Satanic Verses* foregrounds its ongoing dialogue with literary history through constant intertextual evocations. Using stylistic echoes and allusions, Rushdie changes "voices" as deftly as do Chamcha and his colleague Mimi for the voice-over business. These "voices" from other literary works can be heard fleetingly beneath Rushdie's own prose, ephemeral but audible. For instance, in one paragraph describing Chamcha as a young adolescent playing on the rocks at Scandal Point (37–38), there are intimations of a number of exemplary modernist texts, including Virginia Woolf's *Mrs. Dalloway* and *Jacob's Room*, as well as Joyce's story "Counterparts" and the "Nausicaa" episode of *Ulysses*. Despite their temporally anterior derivations, these ghostly intertexts exist simultaneously with the present text, appearing in the heterotopic space of Rushdie's novel as representatives not only of the individual works to which they refer, but also of the periods in which they were written; as John Frow suggests, "reference to a text implicitly evokes reference to the full set of potential meanings stored in the codes of a genre" (157). This intertextual exchange between the contemporary novel and various unresolved aspects of the literary past is one of the subtexts of the Rosa Diamond episode.

When Gibreel and Chamcha show up on the English shoreline following their miraculous descent from an exploded aircraft, they immediately encounter the eighty-eight year-old Rosa, on whose property they have happened to land, and who initially mistakes Gibreel for the "incarnation of her soul's most

deeply buried desire" (133–34), her long-lost paramour Martín de la Cruz. After
Chamcha has been taken away by the immigration police, she therefore invites
Gibreel to stay with her and participate in her reminiscences. Rosa has the rare
ability of being able to see the past as if it is still occurring in the present; for
instance, she habitually watches the arrival of William the Conqueror on her
beach, where he originally invaded nine hundred years earlier:

> When the full moon sets, the dark before the dawn, that's their moment.
> Billow of sail, flash of oars, and the Conqueror himself at the flagship's
> prow, sailing up the beach between the barnacled wooden breakwaters
> and a few inverted sculls. — O, I've seen things in my time, always had
> the gift, the phantom-sight. — The Conqueror in his pointy metal-nosed
> hat, passing through her front door, gliding betwixt the cakestands and
> the antimacassared sofas, like an echo resounding faintly through that
> house of remembrances and yearnings […] . (130)

With the entrance of Gibreel, however, Rosa turns her attention away from
Norman ghosts to more personal history.

At the spinsterish age of forty, she had married an Englishman named
Henry Diamond, who "knew much about birds and little about women" (143)
and who owned a large estate in Argentina. Once in Buenos Aires, Rosa became
attracted to Martín, one of Henry's gauchos, and may—or may not—have had
an affair with him. Up to the point at which Gibreel arrives, she has not been
able to settle in her mind which version of events she wishes to preserve as
"really" having happened: did she willingly make passionate love to Martín on
the day of their picnic lunch together, or did he force himself on her? were they
interrupted *in flagrante delicto* by Aurora del Sol, a rival for Martín's affections? or did her husband arrive in time to slay her would-be lover? All of these
possibilities are played out over and over, as Gibreel, who is possessed of some
extraordinary visionary powers of his own, becomes the passive medium for
Rosa's relivings of her youth. Like Rosa, Gibreel becomes aware of the presence of figures from the past: he is alarmed to come upon "an archaic pony-
trap" (149) and Argentinians in old-fashioned dress in the local village, especially when he realizes that no one else can see them. Only as Rosa nears death
can Gibreel free himself from her phantom history, but not before, playing
Martín to her rejuvenated ghost, he has taken part in her final re-enactment of
the day of the picnic, whose outcome we are never told, though it is hinted that
the seduction is mutual and successful.

In *The Location of Culture*, Homi Bhabha reads this passage as a demonstration of how other cultures can subtly infiltrate and undermine the solidity of national self-identity. Bhabha sees Rosa as the figure of "the atavistic national past" of "the English *Heim* or homeland," and Gibreel, sporting Henry's smoking jacket, as an impersonator who "mimics the collaborative colonial ideologies of patriotism and patriarchy, depriving those narratives of their imperial authority" (167–68). As the Indian postcolonial subject in disguise, Bhabha argues, Gibreel disrupts Rosa's solipsistic myth-making, forcing it into new directions; his intrusion into her English enclave "articulates the narrative of cultural difference which can never let the national history look at itself narcissistically in the eye" (168). Bhabha's interpretation thus confines itself to the episode's significance in revealing the subversive potential of the postcolonial citizen's presence in the colonizing culture.

While Bhabha's exegesis identifies a political allegory behind Rosa's experiences with Gibreel, it leaves out in the process certain aspects that do not neatly support his reading. Gibreel's other crucial role as the surrogate for Martín, who is colonized rather than colonizer, is not mentioned; similarly, Bhabha's monolithic characterization of Rosa as English nationalism overlooks her triple marginalization as a woman who is old and who was temporarily exiled in another country. Beyond these omissions, however, Bhabha completely ignores the passage's overt intertextuality, especially as it relates to the allegorical importance of Rosa's numerous retellings of her story.

This episode also functions as a general reflection on the role of literary intertexts in the contemporary novel. Rosa's late twentieth-century house, busy with all sorts of poltergeists, parallels the "haunted" textuality of postmodern fiction, in which the "ghosts" of many earlier texts make intermittent appearances. However, the intertextual "conjuring" here is also quite precise: like Rosa with her love triangle, Rushdie's novel has some "unfinished business" with which it wants to deal.

Without limiting the text to a set of prescriptive "matrices" in the mode of Michael Riffaterre's theories,[6] I would like to posit that this episode intertextually evokes certain works of fiction which, in turn, signify the aesthetic practices of the periods in which they were written. While the South American setting and fantastic occurrences indicate Rushdie's usual fascination with magic realism, the intertexts specific to this episode derive from English literary

---

[6]See, for example, Riffaterre's *Text Production*, Trans. Terese Lyons (New York: Columbia UP, 1983).

realism and modernism, those two periods with whose representational implications the British postmodern novel particularly attempts to come to terms. These intertexts center on Rosa, who, as a composite of female characters from canonical realist and modernist fiction, represents Rushdie's negotiation with literary history.

On the one hand, she recalls Charles Dickens' Miss Havisham from *Great Expectations*: disappointed in love, estranged from her family, she spends her old age alone in a house stopped in time. On the other hand, she brings to mind Joyce's Eveline from his story of the same name in *Dubliners*, and William Faulkner's Rosa Coldfield from *Absalom, Absalom!*. Both of these characters are associated with modernist uncertainty: Eveline is "paralyzed" over whether or not to run off with her lover from dreary Ireland to exotic Buenos Aires (a dilemma given a different twist in Rushdie's rewriting), while Miss Rosa's narration is archetypal of the epistemological difficulties central to modernist storytelling. By having one character summon all of these intertexts, Rushdie simultaneously introduces into the contemporary field of his own text the related problematics of representation left over from both realism and modernism: can the "real" truly be represented by fiction, or is it always subject to multiple perceptions, interpretations and tellings? In other words, can the novel recover some of the supposed referential confidence of realism, or is it to be forever and increasingly beset by the modernist consciousness of epistemological instability and textual relativism?

These issues are openly thematized in this episode as Rosa, with Gibreel's assistance, tries to determine the final version of her own story. Before Gibreel's arrival, Rosa was trapped in her own history, unable to move forward, a plight emphasized by her continual repetition of "well-worn phrases" (130) and by her belief that "in an ancient land like England there was no room for new stories" (144). While Rosa symbolizes the past as permanent and unalterable, Gibreel on the contrary represents change; he lands on the beach like a latter-day William the Conqueror: "Turning his back on the sea, blotting out the bad memory in order to make room for the next things, passionate as always for newness" (131). Gibreel enables Rosa finally to break out of her repetitions and tell her old story afresh; with his visionary co-operation, she can literally re-create the events however she chooses, decide which account is "true." Whether or not Rosa's ultimate version corresponds with what "really" occurred, she goes beyond her previous hesitation to recount her history in a new way that sets her free from the past.

The issues raised in the "Rosa Diamond" episode, both thematically and intertextually, permeate *The Satanic Verses*. Indeed, the novel's claim to fame (if not infamy) is its scrutiny of the discursive processes that produce and shape truth. Just as the specific realist and modernist intertexts present in this passage, when recognized by the reader, provide an added awareness of the problems attendant upon restricting history to one particular version, so too do self-conscious gestures throughout the text highlight contemporary fiction's ongoing efforts to come to terms with post-realist representation.

For example, the final confrontation between Gibreel and Chamcha, those transitional figures between the old and the new, begins in the reconstructed "Dickensian London" (421) of a movie set, recalling how Fowles uses the framework of a nineteenth-century realist text in *The French Lieutenant's Woman* to reinvent the parameters of the British novel. In a more direct intertextual evocation of this postmodern forerunner, Rushdie has his devilish narrator echo Fowles's narrator's pretense of non-interference in the characters' activities, as well as his disclaimer about "fight-fixing." Commenting on Gibreel's confusion at "moving through several stories at once"—his concurrent visions from different levels of "reality"—and at having to determine the best course of action, the narrator says: "I'm giving him no instructions. I, too, am interested in his choices—in the result of his wrestling match" (457). As we saw in Chapter One, the narrator's feigned neutrality in *The French Lieutenant's Woman* actually conceals a deliberate agenda involving the novel's ending; Rushdie's doubly ironic imitation should thus draw the reader's attention to the outcome of *The Satanic Verses*.

In this case, it is the triumph of one adversary over the other that has implications for the state of the novel as a form. As actors, both Gibreel and Chamcha are skilled at assuming various roles and at exploiting the money-making enterprises associated with their talents—popular film, television, advertising, publicity, theater—that dominate the life of the city. As a result of Gibreel's tendency to serve as the projection of others' desires, particularly those of the capitalist system that has given him his fame, he literally falls victim to the role of archangel that he played in Bombay-made "theological" movies. Consequently, he finds himself overwhelmed in the form of retributive ghosts and divine visions by the personal history and religious heritage from which he thought to have neatly severed himself. Gibreel's unstable sense of self and infiltration by the past leave him shattered, mentally precarious to the point of suicide. Chamcha, on the other hand, chooses his own role as "goodandproper Englishman" (43), rejecting his Indian background in favour of an idealized notion of British superiority. This cultural deference, however, leaves him vulnerable to being reconstructed by English racism, "the power of description" (168) that turns him into a devilish goat-man; the London underworld of night-time police raids and immigrant hide-outs provides the forum for his humiliation and eventual recovery. While Gibreel's perceptions of London grow manifold and increasingly phantasmagoric, Chamcha's experiences follow the opposite trajectory, with the city changing from nightmarish to more manageable as he regains control over his splintered identity. Chamcha survives by learning to embrace the ruthless tactics of self-preservation and promotion of Thatcher's Britain, and to manipulate for his own benefit the fluid self-image that had been taken over by cultural and market-driven forces. Whereas Gibreel never manages to master or enjoy his visions, a failure that ultimately proves fatal to him, Chamcha gradually takes control of his fantastic metamorphoses, reclaiming his identity from others and uniting his current English life with his Indian heritage. Like Rushdie's novel, Chamcha is "a creature of *selected* discontinuities, a *willing* reinvention" (427) that takes from the past that which allows it to adapt itself to the present. Through self-conscious evocations of *The French Lieutenant's Woman*, Rushdie emphasizes the symbolic importance of Chamcha's survival, which concludes the novel's self-referential working-out of the terms of a new kind of postmodern textuality—one that acknowledges the legacy of literary history while trying to move beyond representational anxiety.

*The Satanic Verses* insists on the inextricable and evolving relationship between contemporary fiction and its literary ancestors, a relationship that is figured most suggestively in the Rosa Diamond sequence. By having intertextual visitants carry on animated exchanges within the space of his novel, Rushdie re-examines the loss of referential certainty, and attempts to reconcile the lessons of modernism about textual autonomy with the need to tell stories about the past in ways that have lasting significance. It is this compromise between history and fiction, between actuality and how it is told and remembered, that is allegorized in *Midnight's Children*.

-ii-

The second type of postmodern historiographic fiction discussed by Jameson encompasses novels about "imaginary people and events among whom from time to time real-life ones unexpectedly appear and disappear" (*Postmodernism* 369). *Midnight's Children*, with its insertion of political figures such as Indira Gandhi into a fictional reworking of modern Indian history, obviously falls into this category, as does Jameson's example, Doctorow's *Ragtime*, in which "real-life" characters are mingled with those drawn from intertextual sources and those who are purely imaginary. Jameson feels that such fictional syntheses are signs of a retrograde, depoliticizing tendency in contemporary writing that debases the referent and "derealize[s]" (370) the historical record into a series of equally superficial fabrications. Despite its overt political content, he argues, *Ragtime* undermines its own validity as a representation of history by conjoining characters that, he says, "are incommensurable and, as it were, of incomparable substances, like oil and water" (*Postmodernism* 22). This textual fusion essentially decontextualizes and spatializes the past, since actualities are combined on one plane without regard for their original "historical or existential" (*Postmodernism* 373) distance from the other phenomena replicated in the same fictional dimension. Doctorow's novel, though "seemingly realistic," is, in Jameson's view, therefore "a nonrepresentational work that combines fantasy signifiers from a variety of ideologemes in a kind of hologram" (*Postmodernism* 23). Jameson asserts that *Ragtime*—and other similar postmodern texts, by extension—convey only "pop history" (*Postmodernism* 25) that distorts the underlying "real" history that is their ostensible subject matter, and consequently occludes that history from their readers' sight. Instead, readers are mesmerized by "the simultaneous preservation of just such incompatibles, a kind of incommensurability-vision that does not pull the eyes back into focus" but rather melds disparate objects into a continuous blur in much the same way that "switching channels on a cable television set" (*Postmodernism* 372–73) does.

As is evident from his cable television analogy, Jameson considers this sort of historiographic fiction to have effects comparable to those of late twentieth-century cultural products that inundate consumers with images without drawing attention to the uniform artificiality of those images in contrast to the varying "realities" they reproduce. To clarify the distinction between the fiction and other cultural manifestations of the "mixing" Jameson finds so disturbing, I shall compare postmodern textuality with the recent technology commonly known as "virtual reality" or "cyberspace."[7] This technology has made possible a new kind of free-standing ontological sphere that stands in paradoxical relation to exterior reality, much as do the concretized "worlds," or heterocosms, of contemporary novels that integrate the realist urge to reflect actual happenings

---

[7]For an introduction to virtual reality technology, see: Michael Benedikt, Ed., *Cyberspace: The First Steps* (Cambridge, Mass.: MIT, 1991); Michael Heim, *The Metaphysics of Virtual Reality* (New York: Oxford UP, 1991); Sandra K. Helsel and Judith Paris Roth, Eds., *Virtual Reality: Theory, Practice and Promise* (Westport: Meckler, 1991); and Ken Pimentel and Kevin Teixeira, *Virtual Reality: Through the New Looking Glass* (New York: Windcrest, 1993).

and the modernist appreciation of self-referentiality. As we shall see, the overtly textual "virtual meeting space" of *Midnight's Children*, of which the Conference acts as a *mise en abyme*, facilitates a revision of events that alerts readers to look beyond the official account to the underlying history. It is thus on the level of subject recognition that Jameson's second type of historiographic writing differs from apparently similar, but less self-conscious, dehistoricizing aspects of postmodern culture, such as virtual reality.

-iii-

The process of creating a virtual reality program, referred to by its practitioners as "world-making," entails the designer's having to make a series of decisions: what sort of milieu should the user discover? what capabilities and restrictions should delimit the user's movements? what forms of objects should be present? The determining factor in these decisions is not the need to achieve "realism" in the sense of producing a convincing facsimile of an hypostasized external world; instead, the impetus is to create a program that the user will apprehend as intrinsically "real." The technology accomplishes this illusion by giving shape to a new kind of materiality, composed entirely of computer-generated images. Since all objects in a virtual world are made up of one essential "substance," images simulating unrealistic or "abstract" phenomena are equally as "real" as those recognizable from the outside world. In fact, realistic phenomena are often distinguishable from "abstract" only by virtue of their enhanced texturing. Users can project images of themselves that are substitute identities, images that they can alter from one appearance in that program to the next. As well, users can interact in seemingly close proximity with users from remote places, and encounter simulations representing diverse phenomena from many periods of time. So long as a program's images are persuasive to its users, they are perceived as "real" and therefore *are* real in the context of the experience.

Because the technology can grant unilateral and independent "reality" to things of widely varying degrees of verisimilitude, it has made "virtuality"— previously only a theoretical ideal—realizable in practical terms. "Virtuality" in this case does not indicate an existence completely removed from that of the external world, but rather the formation of an adjunct and self-contained "reality" in which actual phenomena are reconstituted as simulations and combined with other simulated phenomena. This concept of an independent sphere with its own ontological parameters provides a foundation for discussing the nature of postmodern textual representation.

Although postmodern fiction recognizes the schism between text and world made evident by modernism, it nevertheless assumes a complex relation with regard to the outside world: it neither pretends to be a faithful transcription of some pre-existent reality, nor does it entirely negate that reality from its textual worlds. That is, while postmodern texts depict the "real," they do not do so in the straightforward manner which Jameson suggests fiction was once capable of doing and should now aspire to recover. Like technological virtual worlds, the heterocosms of postmodern fictional texts are precisely conceived constructions with their own criteria for what is "real," a representational mode that can also be described as a type of "virtuality." As with the technology, "virtuality" here signifies a supplementary ontological level on which actual figures and objects, converted into textual "matter," can mix with various other, similarly converted entities in undifferentiated ways.

As in technological virtual worlds, the phenomena in these textual worlds behave as fluid presences or projections instead of as stable, realistic entities. When actual historical figures participate in postmodern heterocosms, they do so not as realistic characters *per se* but rather as images adapted for the constructed worlds of the texts. Actual events are also modified so that they take on "virtual identities" in the texts, and these events can occur simultaneously with events projected from other times and other realities, including fictive ones.

The heterocosms of many postmodern texts are therefore constructed such that combinations of phenomena that could not occur in either conventional historical fiction or fantastic fiction proper can take place. While Napoleon can appear as a character in an historical novel, for instance, a creature from outer space would seem out of place; similarly, the space creature would be at home in a science fiction story, but Napoleon would likely seem anomalous there, unless he had been dislocated from his original historical setting by some plausible scientific wizardry. In each case, there are certain kinds of characters and actions that are "indigenous" to that textual world; any departure from those classifications would fundamentally shift the text's compositional basis. (If, for example, the "Megalosaurus" mentioned in the first paragraph of Dickens' *Bleak House* were to escape from the simile that confines it, the text would be curiously changed.) Because postmodern historiographic fiction does away with the stipulation that only particular phenomena can be endemic to a specific heterocosm, what it makes imaginable is that Napoleon and the space creature can not only co-exist in one world, but also interact uninhibitedly because there are no physical or logical barriers to limit them. This unrestricted bringing together of different sorts of textual components can happen in postmodern fiction owing to the fact that, as in cyberspace, everything possesses the same essential "reality."

Unlike its parallel occurrence in virtual reality, though, the convergence of different kinds of phenomena in postmodern texts can lead to renewed consciousness of the "real." Virtual technology attempts to seduce users into believing in the inherent "reality" of its programs, a "reality" whose authenticity is inseparable from each user's experience and does not correspond to any empirical standard. Cyberspace therefore temporarily diverts users away from the external world by immersing them in a self-enclosed medium removed from social and political concerns. Postmodern novels such as *Ragtime* and *Midnight's Children*, on the other hand, draw attention to external reality by emphasizing the artificial nature of everything represented in their textual worlds. By forcing together "incommensurable substances," these texts make clear that the signifiers used to represent actual people and things can inconspicuously occupy the same semantic field as those used to represent phenomena not derived from empirical reality, and are thus equally "fictional." This apparent attenuation of historical actualities does not result in the glossiness of Jameson's "pop history," but rather in the sudden visibility of signification: the texts reveal historical signifiers *qua* signifiers, illuminating in the process "the particular nature of the historical referent" (Hutcheon, *Poetics* 89) that always exceeds containment in any one discursive form, even in those forms that seemingly represent the past in a direct and total way, such as conventional historical accounts. Instead of devitalizing the referent or distancing readers from it, then, this kind of postmodern fiction insists on the discursivity of all historical representations in order to show how those accounts that lay claim to objectivity and universal validity are in fact subjective constructions that can never fully embody the reality of the events they represent, and that inevitably reshape those events into culturally selective and biased narratives in the course of recording them. As a result, readers become newly aware of the reality concealed or suppressed by the apparent neutrality of traditional historical writings.

As a means of demonstrating how historical reality can be obfuscated by official accounts whose seeming "naturalness" dulls our perception of them, these texts let readers look at the same events recast in new forms. Novels such as *Midnight's Children* reconstruct history by acting as "virtual meeting spaces": discrete artificial environments whose representational plasticity makes it feasible for historical actualities to be brought into improbable conjunctions with phenomena from several ontological origins. These "virtual meetings" enact what Hans Kellner calls "historical dialogues," "imaginary encounter[s]" (45, 43) that could never take place in other circumstances. They can be thought of in terms of historiographic premises known as "counterfactual statements," which are formulated as "if … then," with the understanding that the first term is logically untrue (Kellner 47–48). For instance, in *The Infernal Desire Machines of Doctor Hoffman*, Desiderio contemplates paintings in which "Van Gogh was shown writing 'Wuthering Heights' in the parlour of Haworth Parsonage" and Milton is depicted "blindly executing divine frescos upon the walls of the Sistine Chapel" (198). Sensing his bewilderment, Albertina explains: "When my father rewrites the history books, these are some of the things that everyone will suddenly perceive to have always been true" (198). What these paintings make it possible to visualize, therefore, are not simply strange coincidences, but "truths" about the artists and their art that would not be discovered if they had not been brought together in this fashion.

Similarly, postmodern fiction allows readers to witness meetings between disparate figures from history and elsewhere, and to imagine the revelations about the past that these meetings could uncover. While such fanciful conjunctions would normally be discounted by historians—Jameson repudiates them as "comic book juxtaposition[s]" (*Postmodernism* 370)—Kellner assigns them to a legitimate category of historical information, "information *nonexistent in time and space*" (43), and he defends their significance in this way: "they are authentic creations of one type of historical imagination; to exclude them from any consideration as products of valid historical thought is to limit and perhaps to desiccate future thought about the past" (43). In other words, these imaginative renditions of actual occurrences do more than merely aestheticize historical representation or disclose the fragile distinction between history and fiction: they suggest dissident accounts of history that could never otherwise be produced and that disrupt complacent acceptance of the official record by making available multiple versions of events that invite speculation about the ideological bases of the single versions hitherto held to be incontestably true. We can now examine how the "Conference" in *Midnight's Children* can be seen as a paradigm both for postmodern fictional "meeting spaces" and for the relation between textual "virtuality" and the external world.

The "Midnight Children's Conference" held in the mind of Saleem Sinai, the central character and narrator, operates very much as a virtual world does: it serves as a space in which images can interact unhindered by obstacles such as distance. The Conference participants, the other 580 surviving children born all over India during the first hour of the nation's independence, assemble in this mental space whenever Saleem makes it available. As convenor of the Conference, Saleem maintains ultimate authority over the space, but not over the participants, who can enter and exit at will, or choose not to join a particular session. Although the "Midnight Children" remain physically in their locations around the country, the Conference allows them to converse as if they are all in the same physical vicinity by bringing together their projected presences. Much like visually-oriented cyberspace "aliases," the images of the Children within the Conference space tend to change or conceal their identities rather than reveal them. For example, Saleem realizes from the others' reactions that the original image of himself that he projected into the Conference "was heavily distorted by [his] own self-consciousness about [his] appearance," since it was "grinning like a Cheshire cat" (262) and his facial features were exaggerated. Like Saleem, each of the participants, though endowed with miraculous powers, has an actual, or at least an implied, "real" identity outside of the confines of the Conference, in the "real" world that is the heterocosm of the novel proper. The Conference therefore neither negates nor displaces the "reality" of the textual world, but rather provides a forum in which the "real" can be temporarily modified and combined in unusual ways. In this respect, the Conference bears a similar relationship to the rest of the textual world of *Midnight's Children* as does a technological virtual world to the real world in which it exists.

Taking the analogy one step further, we can say that the novel *Midnight's Children* likewise acts as a "virtual meeting space" in relation to historical reality. Just as the Conference in Saleem's mind brings together images in seemingly inconceivable ways, so too does the text itself. Some of the projected presences that the novel assembles within its textual space are actual historical events, such as the creation of the state of Pakistan, and personages, such as Indira Gandhi. Despite the corresponding names, however, the "Indira Gandhi" in Rushdie's novel, also known as the "Widow," is not identical with the historical figure. The character has instead what Umberto Eco calls a "transworld identity" (230), which McHale defines as a "fictional projection[s]" (17) whose differences from the original figure are foregrounded rather than concealed. Like Saleem's self-image within the Conference, Gandhi's virtual identity within Rushdie's text is exaggerated. She is described as having "had white hair on one side and black on the other" (501), as did the historical Indira Gandhi; but in Saleem's perception, the Widow's sharply divided hair not only symbolizes, but may also be responsible for, the disparity between the "white part—public, visible, documented" (501) of her activities as Prime Minister and her "secret" political ruthlessness. The Widow, as well as the other actualities modified for their appearances in the textual world, interact with characters and fictional occurrences that are without historical precedents, and in many cases are completely unrealistic.

The resulting configuration of events is implausible, fantastic: it rejects collective action and causality as the bases of historical understanding in favour of the personal, the idiosyncratic, and the arbitrary. As chronicler, Saleem reorganizes the major events of modern India so that they are either directly caused by him (such as the language riots precipitated by his bicycle crash) and/or reflected in some material way on his body (such as the cracks that symbolize the nation's gradual disintegration).[8] Admitting that he has incorrectly recorded the date of Mahatma Gandhi's assassination to suit his narrative purposes, Saleem wonders: "Does one error invalidate the entire fabric? Am I so far gone, in my desperate need for meaning, that I'm prepared to distort everything—to re-write the whole history of my times purely in order to place myself in a central role?" (198). By having his narrator concoct such a wildly self-centered tale, though, Rushdie is advocating neither that this specific version replace the accepted one, nor that history should be dispersed into numberless subjective perspectives. Rather, he uses this extreme as a method of debunking the pretext of objectivity that surrounds conventional historiography.

In "Nietzsche, Genealogy, History," Foucault contrasts traditional historians with the "new historians" or "genealogists." The former "take unusual pains to erase the elements in their work which reveal their grounding in a particular time and place" (90) in order to bolster the illusion that the past as recorded is unitary, unchanging, and "true," when in fact it is subject to the forces of power in play at the time. The latter, conversely, "refuse[s] the certainty of absolutes" and acknowledges that history is actually comprised not of "profound intentions and immutable necessities" but of "haphazard conflicts" and "countless lost events" (87–89).

As Hutcheon notes (*Poetics* 162–64), Foucault's ideas are apposite to *Midnight's Children* in several respects, but especially because they help to underscore how the text works to keep modern Indian history from being

---

[8]For a thorough exploration of the role of the body, both personal and politic, see Jean M. Kane, "The Migrant Intellectual and the Body of History: Salman Rushdie's *Midnight's Children*," *Contemporary Literature* 37.1 (Spring 1996): 94–118.

reduced to one unchallenged account. Unlike the traditional historian, who concentrates on the distant past in order to devise retrospectively coherent and universalized narratives, the genealogist "studies what is closest, but in abrupt dispossession, so as to seize it at a distance" (Foucault, "Nietzsche" 89); that is, the new historian refrains from making far-reaching patterns for the sake of "diagnosing" the particular influences that formed a given moment in the recent past. The unique hermeneutical difficulties posed by contemporary history that Foucault identifies are echoed by Saleem:

> Reality is a question of perspective; the further you get from the past, the
> more concrete and plausible it seems—but as you approach the present,
> it inevitably seems more and more incredible. Suppose yourself in a
> large cinema, sitting at first in the back row, and gradually moving up,
> row by row, until your nose is almost pressed against the screen.
> Gradually the stars' faces dissolve into dancing grain; tiny details
> assume grotesque proportions; the illusion dissolves—or rather, it
> becomes clear that the illusion itself is reality [...] . (197)

Through its emphasis on the subjective and the random, Rushdie's novel magnifies events in the manner indicated by Saleem's movie screen analogy, focusing on the inconsistencies and localized abuses of power that threaten to disappear into the larger historical picture. *Midnight's Children* therefore functions like Foucault's genealogist, counteracting the traditionalist impulse by showing that other versions of real events are possible, and that those versions, even if they are the products of "imaginary encounters" or "virtual meetings," can disclose truths that would otherwise never be known.

The tension between single and multiple historical perspectives is thematized in different ways throughout the novel. Saleem frequently differentiates the "real" from the "true," noting on one occasion that they "'aren't necessarily the same.' *True*, for me, was from my earliest days something hidden inside the stories Mary Pereira told me" (90). The implication here is that the truth can be reproduced in a number of fictional forms without suffering loss of validity. As Hutcheon argues, Saleem himself is guilty of trying to restrict the past to one story, "to reduce history to autobiography, to reduce India to his own consciousness" (*Poetics* 162); his failure "to make the multiple single" (Hutcheon, *Poetics* 164) is figured in his unsuccessful attempt to unify the disparate Midnight's Children, who cannot agree on a guiding political philosophy for their group. The Conference, of course, is also a metaphor for India itself, with its numerous factions, classes, religious divisions, and so on; as Saleem says,

"Midnight's children can be made to represent many things, according to your point of view" (240). Similarly, Saleem's lineage mirrors the evolution of his nation post-Independence, particularly with its joint Indian/British heritage as symbolized by Vanita and William Methwold. This same lineage, though, additionally signifies how seemingly indisputable truths can conceal repressed information. Saleem's inadvertent discovery of his real parentage after years of being deceived suggests how Foucault's genealogical analysis reveals the "accidents, the minute deviations [...] the errors, the false appraisals and the faulty calculations" (81) hidden behind the uniformity of the historical record: "The search for descent is not the erecting of foundations: on the contrary, it disturbs what was previously considered immobile; it fragments what was thought unified; it shows the heterogeneity of what was imagined consistent with itself" (82). Through Saleem's descriptions of the Conference, his family background, and so on, Rushdie's novel thus not only provides an alternative account of actual events, but also reflects figuratively on the impossibility of limiting historical reality to one representation.

While *Midnight's Children* advocates the need for multiple stories about the past, however, it does not do so in the irresponsible manner attributed by Jameson to postmodern historiographic fiction, in which the official version is displaced by interchangeable fantasies having no obligation to the facts.[9] As Gasiorek makes clear, the real events of modern Indian history are the "scaffolding" (167) against which Rushdie's narrative is consistently constructed; and while Saleem intermittently makes mistakes and omits certain details, his forgetfulness is a matter of great concern to him, and he frequently upbraids himself for his inaccuracies. Although Saleem from time to time becomes enthralled with his storytelling abilities, he always eventually recalls that the past he is recounting is not pure fabulation, just as, with "hindsight," he perceives his misconception about the early days of his telepathic adventures:

---

[9] In his essay "Fictions of History," Bernard Bergonzi suggests that recent British novels are more factually responsible than their American counterparts, which treat history, he claims, as if it is "infinitely malleable" (15). His reasoning for why this discrepancy exists is that Americans "have less history" (45) than Europeans, who therefore tend to be more respectful of the past. Whether there is any validity to Bergonzi's distinction is questionable; certainly, Jameson would view any fictional tampering with historical facts, regardless of degree, as equally reprehensible.

> [T]he feeling had come upon me that I was somehow creating a world;
> that the thoughts I had jumped inside were mine, that the bodies I occu-
> pied acted at my command [...] that [...] I was somehow making them
> happen ... which is to say, I had entered into the illusion of the artist [...]
> . (207)

Saleem's realization that fidelity to external realities must underlie his creative
endeavours is intensified by his political experiences, as he becomes aware of
the general amnesia being fostered by the reporting of those with power:

> Divorce between news and reality: newspapers quoted foreign econo-
> mists—PAKISTAN A MODEL FOR EMERGING NATIONS—while peasants
> (unreported) cursed the so-called "green revolution", claiming that most
> of the newly-drilled water-wells had been useless, poisoned, and in the
> wrong places anyway [...] . (399)

By writing his manuscript, then, Saleem does not actively set out to mislead any
more than Tom Crick does, but rather to call attention to others' misrepresenta-
tions of the facts that would otherwise be accorded instant credibility. This
agenda extends outward to the novel as a whole. In "'Errata': or, Unreliable
Narration in *Midnight's Children*," Rushdie explains that he intentionally left in
errors, favouring the "remembered" over the "literal" truth (*Imaginary* 24), as
a means of highlighting the fallibility of memory, whether personal or cultural.
The novelist's role, as he articulates it in the essay "Imaginary Homelands," is
to record history, not realistically, but in such a way that the deliberate false-
hoods of the accepted accounts are exposed:

> [R]edescribing a world is the necessary first step towards changing it.
> And particularly at times when the State takes reality into its own hands,
> and sets about distorting it, altering the past to fit its present needs, then
> the making of the alternative realities of art, including the novel of mem-
> ory, becomes politicized [...] . [T]he novel is one way of denying the
> official, politicians' version of truth. (*Imaginary* 14)

Despite its blatant fabrications, the novel's aim, according to Rushdie, is to
redirect attention to the real historical events obscured behind standardized representations.

In *Midnight's Children*, this recognition is aided by ironic distancing that
the text establishes in several respects. In addition to casting new light on the
historiographer's craft through Saleem's subjectivity and unreliability, Rushdie
clarifies the reader's role through the use of an intratextual "foil," Padma, who
is the immediate recipient of Saleem's creative endeavours. Although Padma,

with her uneducated tastes and demands for straightforwardness may be an adequate (if occasionally dissatisfied) audience for Saleem's tale, she is not the sort
of reader that the novel implicitly theorizes for itself, just as in *The French
Lieutenant's Woman* and *The Infernal Desire Machines of Doctor Hoffman* the
characterized readers are distinct from the implied readers. Rather, as was the
case in those texts, the implied readers which *Midnight's Children* projects for
itself are able to look beyond the deficiencies of the characterized position to
deduce how they, in contrast, must react to the narrative they are reading with
a combination of interpretive and intertextual awareness, as Keith Wilson
points out: "Rushdie's ideal reader is deemed to have a facility at intertextual
cross referencing of kinds that most contemporary self-conscious readers
might, in one form or another, be assumed to have" (65). Rushdie's key intertexts here, reviewed at length by other critics,[10] include Laurence Sterne's
*Tristram Shandy*, Günter Grass's *The Tin Drum* and García Márquez's *One
Hundred Years of Solitude*, all of which are non-realist "ancestors" of postmodern historiographic fiction, refigured in this case with the same double ironic
remove seen earlier with *The French Lieutenant's Woman* and *The Satanic
Verses*. By activating these intertextual references, readers are reminded of the
novel's history as a form that openly confronts the problematics of depicting
historical reality in a medium that acknowledges its own artificiality.

In Jameson's terms, these ironic textual elements in *Midnight's Children*
combine to "pull the eyes back into focus," precluding the dazzled distraction
he fears will result from the reading of postmodern historiographic fiction in
which characters and events taken from actuality appear in tandem with those
either derived from other sources or completely made up. As Kellner's ideas
suggest, the kind of "virtual mixing" epitomized by the Conference and elaborated by the novel as a whole provide alternative visions of the past which,
though only notional, can inspire genuine reassessments. Instead of vanquish-
ing the "real" for the sake of "pop images" (Jameson, *Postmodernism* 25)
drained of any historical significance, *Midnight's Children* insists on its

---

[10]On Sterne, for example, see Clement Hawes, "Leading History by the Nose: The Turn to the
Eighteenth Century in *Midnight's Children*," *Modern Fiction Studies* 39.1 (Spring 1993): 146–68.
On Grass, see Patricia Merivale, "Saleem Fathered by Oskar: Intertextual Strategies in *Midnight's
Children* and *The Tin Drum*," *Ariel* 21.3 (July 1990): 5–21. For a discussion of magic realism in
*Midnight's Children*, see James Harrison, *Salman Rushdie*, Twayne's English Authors Series 488,
New York: Twayne, 1992, 55–60.

primacy, showing how it can be obfuscated by instruments of power that masquerade as objective truth.

-iv-

What Jameson's "fairy tale" about postmodernism makes evident is the need for a revived awareness about the "real" in an image-based culture where it is being progressively neglected and adulterated. The challenge facing Rushdie, as well as other postmodern authors, is to find a way of incorporating historical reality into their writing while taking into account the knowledge about the nature of textuality gained since the Victorian period. According to David J. Herman's gloss on Hutcheon's theories, this approach should involve a reshaping, but not an alienation, of the referent: "[P]ostmodernism, through self-consciousness about representation, contests and defers the given in order to remodel it, not to abandon it in favour of some modernist abyss of auto-referentiality" (171). This necessary reconciliation between realism's groundedness and modernism's inwardness is what Rushdie attempts to work out, both intertextually and historiographically, in the textual worlds of *The Satanic Verses* and *Midnight's Children*. The embedded spatial metaphors of Rosa Diamond's house and the Conference illuminate how Rushdie overtly attempts to resist the forces of dehistoricization within a literary context.

# Conclusion

As we saw in Chapter One, *The French Lieutenant's Woman* contains within its narrative structure a reaction to the critical perception that the British novel could not sustain itself as a respectable literary form in an era dominated by metafiction, experimentalism, and anti-realist sentiment. Since the appearance of Fowles's ground-breaking work, authors such as Carter, Swift, Byatt, and Rushdie have consistently attempted to define the parameters of a new textuality that would make it possible for them to maintain the British inclinations towards readability, tradition, and history at the same time that they incorporate the contemporary trends towards self-consciousness in interpretation, intertextual reference, and representation. In the novels studied here, these efforts to mediate between the ways of the past and the present have taken the form of self-referential theorizing that works against surface content, which often gives the impression that the texts have deliberately and unanxiously removed themselves from extratextual realities. Through such "allegories of telling," these writers suggest some of the means by which the British novel has tried to adapt itself to the challenges raised by its post-war critics while remaining true to its domestic conventions and audience expectations.

Although the terms of the debate have changed somewhat in the intervening years, the subject of the British novel's vitality is still under vigorous discussion.[1] In a recent essay, Rushdie takes issue with a speech given by George Steiner at a conference of the British Publishers' Association, in which Steiner proclaimed that the European novel, and presumably the British variety especially, is once again in mortal danger. This time, however, the threat apparently does not emanate from within, as it did during the period of realist backsliding, but from without—from authors writing in non-European countries, as well as from film and other electronic media.

---

[1]A conference held on "The Novel in Britain, 1950-2000" at the Huntington Library in Pasadena, California on April 27–29, 2000 attests to the current interest in the fate of the British novel. The conference, organized by Zachary Leader, brought together such luminaries as Rushdie, Martin Amis, Ian McEwan and Hilary Mantel, to discuss the evolution of British fiction since the 1950s. Proceedings are expected to be published by Oxford UP in 2002.

The first "peril" Rushdie dismisses as a typically "Eurocentric lament" that overlooks the growth of "a postcolonial [...] decentered, transnational, interlingual, cross-cultural novel" ("Defense" 49–50), the positive effects of which have already made themselves felt in England through the works of authors such as Kazuo Ishiguro, Hanif Kureishi, Timothy Mo, Zadie Smith, and Rushdie himself. These novelists have injected a new set of perspectives on the importance of tradition which holds such perennial interest for contemporary British writing; and, like the feminist fiction of Carter, Jeanette Winterson, and others, their texts provide an increasing number of alternatives to the kinds of singularly hegemonic representations of history debunked by *Midnight's Children*, as the analysis in Chapter Five shows. Whether based in England or appreciated from abroad, Rushdie stresses, the international influences decried by Steiner have in fact rejuvenated the British novel rather than crowded it out of existence.

Rushdie's responses to Steiner's second charge echo some of the shared concerns of contemporary British writing that have emerged throughout this study. To the warning that traditional readers of fiction are being enticed away by technology, for instance, Rushdie replies that "literature—good literature—has always been a minority interest [...] . And this minority—the minority that is prepared to read and buy good books—has in truth never been larger than it is now. The problem is to interest it" (54). The latter difficulty arises, he claims, because "good" fiction must compete in a late-capitalist marketplace where thousands of new books of widely divergent quality are promoted for profit each year. As a result of this over-proliferation, the reader is not so much "dead" as "bewildered" (54), often unable or unwilling to sort through the choices available. In effect, Rushdie is saying that the British literary novel, which turned to the arts of "writerliness" with *The French Lieutenant's Woman* to endure as a viable commodity in the market of its day, must now learn to practise different kinds of seduction in order to survive.

Among those alternatives with which the novel must increasingly contend are what Steiner designates "hybrid forms, what we will call rather crassly fact/fiction [...] . What novel can today quite compete with the best of reportage, with the very best of immediate narrative?" (qtd. in Rushdie, "Defense" 48). Rushdie assumes that Steiner's classification includes generic crossovers such as American New Journalism, travel writing, and various types of literary non-fiction, and submits that "[t]he novel can welcome these developments without feeling threatened. There's room for all of us in here" (50). Nonetheless, the question of "hybrid forms," of "fact/fiction," raises anew the

issue of reconciling world and text, reality and artifice, which figured
nently in the preceding considerations of intertextuality and historiography, and
which continues to intrigue novelists currently writing in England. In conclusion, I would like to look briefly at the recent texts of one such writer—Pat
Barker—as a means of demonstrating how this representational problem is still
being worked out in contemporary British fiction.

-i-

In Barker's trilogy—*Regeneration*, *The Eye in the Door* and *The Ghost
Road*—we find an example of what is seemingly a straightforward realist narrative, reminiscent of the post-war revival of the 1950s and 1960s. The trilogy
focuses on the experiences of a few young men during the First World War,
with the action taking place primarily in Great Britain, where they are treated
by a prominent psychiatrist, Dr. William Rivers, for various neurasthenic disor-
ders. The historical subject matter is infused with a conspicuous class-con-
sciousness, covering a range of characters from the *literati* to poor women
working in munitions factories. As in many nineteenth-century novels, the narration is delivered from an apparently objective, third-person point of view,
without diegetic interruptions of any kind. The most strikingly "realist" feature
of these books, though, are the "Author's Notes" concluding each volume, in
which Barker clarifies the authenticity of certain characters and incidents, and
lists materials on which she has drawn for her research and which the reader is
invited to consult for further information. The effect of these authorial additions
is to create an aura of verisimilitude and fidelity to the "facts" that works
against the kind of historiographic liberty popularized by *Midnight's Children*
and other works of contemporary British metafiction.

Regardless of these traits, however, the trilogy subtly undercuts its own
mimetic pretences, suggesting how the oppositional impulses signified by realism and modernism are both in play even in novels that appear to have aligned
themselves clearly with one pole or the other. What those verisimilar listings
reveal is that the majority of the main characters are based on actual literary figures of some reknown (such as Siegfried Sassoon and Wilfred Owen), and that
they and the other characters derived from real people (like Dr. Rivers) have
been constructed on the basis of texts written by and about them. This blurring
of historical and literary sources, along with the mixing of "real" and "fictional" characters within the stories themselves, produces a tacit intertextual and
ontological confusion not unlike that which Jameson disparages in *Ragtime*. In

*The Eye in the Door*, for example, Robert Ross is correctly identified as "Oscar Wilde's devoted friend and literary executor," known at the time as 'the leader of all the sodomites in London'" (279–80); but the "Note" fails to point out Ross's second incarnation as the lead character in Timothy Findley's World War I novel, *The Wars*. By presenting the stories of homosexuals as well as those of pacifists who were persecuted for their opposition to the war, the trilogy also retrieves some of the history suppressed, as Benjamin would say, by the ruling classes, and makes available alternative versions of events that would otherwise never be imagined. The realist surface of these novels thus conceals a form of textuality that, while not overtly self-conscious, has internalized the lessons learned since modernism concerning the value of representing the past even in the absence of genuine mimesis.

Modernism's latent but influential presence in this contemporary trilogy is evident in the ways in which the novels draw on their early twentieth-century setting for more than war-related material. The spotlighting of Sassoon and Owen, whose work was defined and, in Owen's case, cut short by the conflict, provokes comparison with the high modernist poets who superseded them. This contrast is brought to the fore by a passage in *Regeneration* modelled on the final lines of "A Game of Chess" in Eliot's *The Waste Land*: a group of women sitting in a bar discuss the "demobbing" of one of their husbands; the wife in question, Lizzie, is unhappy with the husband's constant sexual attentions, and is more interested in getting herself a set of false teeth so that she can have "a bloody good time" (110); the bar's manager calls "Time, ladies" (111). With this single and obvious parody in an otherwise fairly unallusive set of texts, Barker hints at how her novels "repeat" and try to "master" modernism in psychoanalytic terms appropriate both to that period and the trilogy's content.

Psychoanalysis forms the core of the texts' plots, with Rivers listening to and interpreting the stories told by the various men as they attempt to overcome the repressed traumas that have resulted in symptoms of hysteria and, in one case, split personality (Robert Louis Stevenson's *The Strange Case of Dr. Jekyll and Mr. Hyde* is another key modernist subtext). In an interview with Stephen Smith of *The Globe and Mail*, Barker points out how this particular analyst/analysand relationship approximates that between readers and the subject matter of her novels: "Rivers, of course, has never been in a trench, and neither have we. His standpoint is ours: he's hearing about it" (C8). As Chapter Three demonstrated, the embedding of the reader/text interaction as a kind of psychoanalytic encounter can indicate a self-referential thematization of fiction's reconstructive power over historical reality.

An incident spanning the second and third volumes will illustrate how the trilogy uses psychoanalytic narrative as the major motif for its own, ambiguously referential storytelling. In *The Eye in the Door*, we discover that Dr. Rivers too suffers from an hysterical disorder, brought on not by the war but by an event in his childhood, the recollection of which he has repressed: he has lost his power of visual memory, and in particular is unable to remember the interior of any building he has ever been in, with the exception of one childhood home, the downstairs of which he can recall, but not the upstairs. When Billy Prior, a patient with whom Rivers develops a close professional acquaintanceship, hears about this problem, he invites the doctor to switch "chairs," and plays analyst to Rivers' analysand, creating a new readers' position in the process. Prior's guess is that Rivers was raped or beaten in the house's upper story, and that the trauma caused him to "put [his] mind's eye *out*" (139). Rivers resists this interpretation, however, distrusting the Freudian tendency to project "monsters" (139) onto every blank space in the memory. In *The Ghost Road*, we find that Rivers' suspicion may be correct, and that the traumatic occurrence may be somewhat less sensational than those suggested by Prior. The doctor's sister reminds him of a portrait of an ancestor, also named William Rivers, whose leg is being cut off because of a battle wound, and cauterized with hot tar. This portrait, which hung in the stairwell of the childhood home, is used by his father as a way of reprimanding him for crying at the barber's: "'*He* didn't cry,' his father had said, holding him up. '*He didn't make a sound*'" (95). Unsure as to whether this incident, with its overtones of paternally-imposed symbolic castration, is the cause of both his stuttering and his loss of visual memory, Rivers is nevertheless capable, from that point on, of recalling in vivid detail his experiences as a young researcher in the South Pacific.

These recollections, which form a counterpoint in *The Ghost Road* to Prior's present-day reportage of life at the front, involve a number of occasions on which Rivers witnesses horrifying sights that took place in narrowly confined interiors. The body of a local chief is left to decompose in a ritualistic stone enclosure; the chief's widow submits to a mourning custom in which she sits for many days in a separate enclosure in the same position as her dead husband; and, in a scene redolent of E.M. Forster's *A Passage to India*, Rivers is swarmed by bats in a small cave. These events, all of which happened years after the reprimand with the portrait, take on the power of "screen memories," such as those in the Wolf Man case study: they are either repetitions of the original trauma, subsequent "causes" of the same effect, which need to be traced backward in order to effect a proper cure; or they are isolated occurrences that are retroactively endowed with traumatic significance by being successively linked. In either case, the reader as "analyst" becomes engaged in the act of reconstituting Rivers' life, making connections among these childhood and adult incidents not on the basis of their empirical reality, but according to their ability to fit together into a coherent and meaningful story, to convey "narrative truth" in the same way that Tom Crick's narration to his class does.

Even though Barker uses psychoanalysis as a vehicle for presenting essentially realistic content about the war and other experiences, it also provides a counterbalance to the trilogy's seemingly untroubled referentiality, introducing a subtextual commentary on fiction's inescapable effect of reshaping the past as it retells it. Although Barker's trilogy is not as clearly "allegorical" as the fiction of Swift or Rushdie, it thus implicitly confronts the questions concerning contemporary literary narrative's status as a "hybrid" representational form—paradoxically both "fact" and "fiction" at the same time—that arose from the analyses of their works. Further, Barker carries on the thematization of hermeneutic self-awareness by providing identifiable positions within her texts that prompt readers to reflect on their role in the fictional reconstruction of the past.

These related concerns remain central as the British novel continues to evolve, in defiance of the ever-changing pronouncements of its obsolescence. By theorizing, in and through the act of storytelling, the ability of contemporary narrative to transcend metafictional self-absorption, the texts of Fowles, Carter, Swift, Byatt and Rushdie have called attention to some of the pressing issues facing the next generation of writers working in England.

# Bibliography

Bakhtin, Mikhail. "The Problem of Speech Genres." *Speech Genres and Other Late Essays*. Trans. Vern W. McGee. Ed. Caryl Emerson and Michael Holquist. Austin: U of Texas P, 1986. 60–102.

Barker, Pat. *The Eye in the Door*. New York: Plume, 1993.

——. *The Ghost Road*. London: Viking, 1995.

——. *Regeneration*. New York: Plume, 1991.

Barthes, Roland. *The Pleasure of the Text*. 1973. Trans. Richard Miller. New York: Hill and Wang, 1975.

——. *S/Z*. 1970. Trans. Richard Miller. New York: Hill and Wang, 1974.

Bauman, Zygmunt. *Postmodern Ethics*. Oxford UK and Cambridge USA: Blackwell, 1993

Benjamin, Walter. *Illuminations*. Trans. Harry Zohn. Ed. Hannah Arendt. New York: Schocken, 1968.

Bergonzi, Bernard. "Fictions of History." *The Contemporary English Novel*. Malcolm Bradbury and David Palmer, Eds. Stratford-upon-Avon Studies 18. London: Edward Arnold, 1979. 43–65.

——. *The Situation of the Novel*. London: Macmillan, 1970.

Bhabha, Homi. *The Location of Culture*. London and New York: Routledge, 1994.

Binns, Ronald. "John Fowles: Radical Romancer." *Critical Quarterly* 15 (Winter 1973): 317–34. Rpt. in *Critical Essays on John Fowles*. Ed. Ellen Pifer. Boston: G.K. Hall, 1986. 19–37.

Bradbury, Malcolm. *The Modern British Novel*. London: Secker and Warbury, 1993.

—— and David Palmer, Eds. *The Contemporary English Novel*. Stratford-upon-Avon Studies 18. London: Edward Arnold, 1979.

Brée, Germaine. *Marcel Proust and Deliverance from Time*. 1950. Trans. C.J. Richards and A.D. Traitt. New Brunswick, N.J.: Rutgers UP, 1955.

Brennan, Timothy. *Salman Rushdie and The Third World: Myths of the Nation*. London: Macmillan, 1989.

Bronfen, Elisabeth. "Romancing Difference, Courting Coherence: A.S. Byatt's *Possession* as Postmodern Moral Fiction." *Why Literature Matters: Theories and Functions of Literature.* Eds. Rüdiger Ahrens and Laurenz Volkmann. Heidelberg: Universitätsverlag C. Winter, 1996. 1774–34.

Brooks, Peter. *Reading for the Plot: Design and Intention in Narrative.* Cambridge: Harvard UP, 1992.

Buxton, Jackie. "'What's Love Got to Do With It?': Postmodernism and *Possession*." *English Studies in Canada* 22.2 (June 1996): 199–219.

Byatt, A.S. *Passions of the Mind: Selected Writings.* New York: Turtle Bay, 1992.

——. *Possession: A Romance.* New York: Random House, 1990.

Calinescu, Matei. *Rereading.* New Haven and London: Yale UP, 1993.

——. "Ways of Looking at Fiction." *Romanticism, Modernism, Postmodernism.* Ed. Harry R. Garvin. Lewisburg: Bucknell UP, 1980. 155–70.

Caponigri, A. Robert. *Time and Idea: The Theory of History in Giambattista Vico.* Notre Dame and London: U of Notre Dame P, 1953.

Carter, Angela. *The Infernal Desire Machines of Doctor Hoffman.* London: Penguin, 1972.

Chambers, Ross. *Story and Situation: Narrative Seduction and the Power of Fiction.* Minneapolis: U of Minnesota P, 1984.

Clayton, Jay and Eric Rothstein. *Influence and Intertextuality in Literary History.* Wisconsin: U of Wisconsin P, 1991.

Dällenbach, Lucien. *The Mirror in the Text.* 1977. Trans. Jeremy Whiteley and Emma Hughes. Cambridge: Polity P, 1989.

de Certeau, Michel. *The Writing of History.* Trans. Tom Conley. New York: Columbia UP, 1988.

de Lauretis, Teresa. *Alice Doesn't: Feminism, Semiotics, Cinema.* Bloomington: Indiana UP, 1984.

Deleuze, Gilles. *Proust and Signs.* Trans. Richard Howard. New York: George Braziller, 1972.

de Man, Paul. *Allegories of Reading: Figural Language in Rousseau, Nietzsche, Rilke, and Proust.* New Haven and London: Yale UP, 1979.

——. "Literary History and Literary Modernity." *Blindness and Insight: Essays in the Rhetoric of Contemporary Criticism.* Second Edition. Minneapolis: U of Minnesota P, 1983. 142–65.

Djordjević Ivana. "In the Footsteps of Giambattista Vico: Patterns of Signification in A.S. Byatt's *Possession.*" *Anglia* 115.1 (1997): 44–83.

Eco, Umberto. *The Role of the Reader: Explorations in the Semiotics of Texts.* Bloomington and London: Indiana UP, 1979.

Elias, Amy J. "Meta-*mimesis*? The Problem of British Postmodern Realism." *British Postmodern Fiction.* Eds. Theo D'Haen and Hans Bertens. Postmodern Studies 7. Amsterdam and Atlanta: Rodopi, 1993. 9–31.

Eliot, T.S. "Tradition and the Individual Talent." 1919. *Selected Prose of T.S. Eliot.* London: Faber, 1975. 37–44.

Engblom, Philip. "A Multitude of Voices: Carnivalization and Dialogicality in the Novels of Salman Rushdie." *Reading Rushdie: Perspectives on the Fiction of Salman Rushdie.* Ed. M.D. Fletcher. Cross/Cultures: Readings in the Post/Colonial Literatures in English 16. Amsterdam and Atlanta: Rodopi, 1994. 293–304.

Foucault, Michel. *The Archaeology of Knowledge and The Discourse on Language.* 1969 and 1971. Trans. A.M. Sheridan Smith. New York: Pantheon, 1972.

——. "Nietzsche, Genealogy, History." 1971. Trans. Donald F. Bouchard and Sherry Simon. *The Foucault Reader.* Ed. Paul Rabinow. New York: Pantheon, 1984. 76–100.

——. *Power/Knowledge: Selected Interviews and Other Writings 1972–1977.* New York: Pantheon, 1980.

Fowles, John. *The French Lieutenant's Woman.* New York: Signet, 1969.

Freud, Sigmund. *Beyond the Pleasure Principle.* 1920. Trans. James Strachey. New York: Liveright, 1950.

——. *From the History of an Infantile Neurosis* (the "Wolfman" case study). 1918. Vol. 17. *The Standard Edition of the Complete Psychological Works.* Trans. and Ed. James Strachey. London: Hogarth, 1953-74. 7–122.

——. *The Interpretation of Dreams.* 1900. Vols. 4 and 5. *The Standard Edition of the Complete Psychological Works.* Trans. and Ed. James Strachey. London: Hogarth, 1953–1974. 1–627.

——. "Remembering, Repeating, Working Through." 1914. Vol. 12. *The Standard Edition of the Complete Psychological Works.* Trans. and Ed. James Strachey. London: Hogarth, 1953–1974. 147–156.

Frow, John. *Marxism and Literary History.* Cambridge: Harvard UP, 1986.

Gadamer, Hans-Georg. *Truth and Method.* Second Revised Edition. Trans. Joel Weinsheimer and Donald G. Marshall. New York: Crossroad, 1991.

Gasiorek, Andrzej. *Post-War British Fiction: Realism and After*. London: Edward Arnold, 1995.

Gindin, James. *Postwar British Fiction: New Accents and Attitudes*. Berkeley: U of California P, 1962.

Grass, Günter. *The Tin Drum*. 1959. Trans. Ralph Manheim. Harmondsworth: Penguin, 1965.

Harding, D.W. "Psychological Processes in the Reading of Fiction." *British Journal of Aesthetics* 2 (April 1962): 133–47.

Heath, Stephen. "Realism, modernism, and 'language-consciousness.'" *Realism in European Literature: Essays in Honour of J.P. Stern*. Eds. Nicholas Boyle and Martin Swales. Cambridge: Cambridge UP, 1986. 103–22.

Heidegger, Martin. *Being and Time*. Trans. John Macquarrie and Edward Robinson. New York: Harper and Row, 1962.

Herman, David J. "Modernism versus Postmodernism: Towards an Analytic Distinction." *Poetics Today* 12.1 (1991): 55–86. Rpt. in *A Postmodern Reader*. Eds. Joseph Natoli and Linda Hutcheon. Albany: State U of New York P, 1993. 157–92.

Higdon, David Leon. *Shadows of the Past in Contemporary British Fiction*. London: Macmillan, 1984.

Holmes, Frederick. "The Historical Imagination and the Victorian Past: A.S. Byatt's *Possession*." *English Studies in Canada* 20.3 (Sept. 1994): 319–34.

——. *The Historical Imagination: Postmodernism and the Treatment of the Past in Contemporary British Fiction*. ELS Monograph Series 73. U of Victoria: English Literary Studies, 1997.

Hutcheon, Linda. *Narcissistic Narrative: The Metafictional Paradox*. New York and London: Methuen, 1980.

——. *A Poetics of Postmodernism: History, Theory, Fiction*. New York and London: Routledge, 1988.

——. "The 'Real World(s)' of Fiction: *The French Lieutenant's Woman*." *English Studies in Canada* 4.1 (Spring 1978): 81–94. Rpt. in *Critical Essays on John Fowles*. Ed. Ellen Pifer. Boston: G.K. Hall, 1986. 118–32.

——. *A Theory of Parody: The Teachings of Twentieth-Century Art Forms*. New York and London: Methuen, 1985.

Huyssen, Andreas. "The Search for Tradition: Avant-Garde and Postmodernism in the 1970s." *New German Critique* 22 (Winter 1981): 23–40.

Jameson, Fredric. "The Ideology of the Text." *Salmagundi* 31–32 (Fall 1975/Winter 1976): 204–46.

——. "Metacommentary." *PMLA* 86.1 (January 1971): 9–18.

——. *The Political Unconscious: Narrative as a Socially Symbolic Act.* Ithaca: Cornell UP, 1981.

——. "Postmodernism and Consumer Society." *The Anti-Aesthetic: Essays on Postmodern Culture.* Ed. Hal Foster. Seattle: Bay, 1983. 111–25.

——. *Postmodernism, or, The Cultural Logic of Late Capitalism.* Durham: Duke UP, 1991.

Johnson, B.S. *Aren't You Rather Young to be Writing Your Memoirs?* London: Hutchison, 1973.

Kellner, Hans. *Language and Historical Representation: Getting the Story Crooked.* Madison: U of Wisconsin P, 1989.

Kelly, Kathleen Coyne. *A.S. Byatt.* New York: Twayne, 1996.

Kostis, Nicholas. "Albertine: Characterization through Image and Symbol." *Critical Essays on Marcel Proust.* Ed. Barbara J. Bucknall. Boston: G.K. Hall, 1987. 70–92.

Kristeva, Julia. *Revolution in Poetic Language.* 1974. Trans. Margaret Waller. New York: Columbia UP, 1984.

——. *Sêmêiôtikê: Recherches pour une sémanalyse.* Paris: Seuil, 1969.

Lacan, Jacques. *Ecrits: A Selection.* Trans. Alan Sheridan. New York: Norton, 1977.

——. *The Language of Self. The Function of Language in Psychoanalysis.* Trans. Anthony Wilden. Baltimore: Johns Hopkins UP, 1968.

——. "Du sujet supposé savoir, de la dyade première, et du bien." 1964. *Le Séminaire— Livre XI: Les Quatres concepts fondamentaux de la psychanalyse.* Ed. Jacques-Alain Miller. Paris: Seuil, 1973. 209–20.

LaCapra, Dominick. *History and Criticism.* Ithaca: Cornell UP, 1985.

Lee, Alison. *Realism and Power: Postmodern British Fiction.* London: Routledge, 1990.

Lefebvre, Henri. *The Production of Space.* 1974. Trans. Donald Nicholson-Smith. Oxford: Blackwell, 1991.

Lessing, Doris. "The Small Personal Voice." 1957. *Declaration.* Ed. Tom Maschler. London: MacGibbon and Kee, 1959. 13–27.

Lodge, David. *"The Novelist at the Crossroads" and Other Essays on Fiction and Criticism.* London: Routledge and Kegan Paul, 1971.

——. "The Novelist Today: Still at the Crossroads?" *New Writing*. Eds. Malcolm Bradbury and Judy Cooke. London: Minerva, 1992. 203–15.

Loveday, Simon. *The Romances of John Fowles*. London: Macmillan, 1985.

Ludeman, Brenda. "Julia Kristeva: The Other of Language." *The Judgment of Paris: Recent French Theory in a Local Context*. Ed. Kevin D.S. Murray. North Sydney: Allen & Unwin, 1992. 23–37.

Maltby, Paul. "Excerpts from Dissident Postmodernists." *A Postmodern Reader*. Eds. Joseph Natoli and Linda Hutcheon. Albany: State U of New York P, 1993. 519–37.

McCole, John. *Walter Benjamin and the Antinomies of Tradition*. Ithaca: Cornell UP, 1993.

McEwan, Neil. *The Survival of the Novel: British Fiction in the Later Twentieth Century*. London: Macmillan, 1981.

McHale, Brian. *Postmodernist Fiction*. New York and London: Methuen, 1987.

Miller, J. Hillis. *Fiction and Repetition: Seven English Novels*. Cambridge: Harvard UP, 1982.

Mitchell, Juliet. *Psychoanalysis and Feminism: Freud, Reich, Laing and Women*. New York: Vintage, 1974.

Murdoch, Iris. "Against Dryness." 1961. *The Novel Today: Contemporary Writers on Modern Fiction*. Ed. Malcolm Bradbury. London: Fontana, 1990 (1977). 15–24.

Nash, Cristopher. *World-Games: The Tradition of Anti-Realist Revolt*. London and New York: Methuen, 1987.

Pearce, Lynne. *Reading Dialogics*. London: Edward Arnold, 1994.

Polkinghorne, Donald E. *Narrative Knowing and the Human Sciences*. Albany: State U of New York P, 1988.

Proust, Marcel. *Remembrance of Things Past*. Trans.C.K. Scott Moncrieff and Terence Kilmartin. 3 vols. Harmondsworth: Penguin, 1983.

Rabinovitz, Rubin. *The Reaction Against Experiment in the English Novel, 1950-1960*. New York and London: Columbia UP, 1967.

Rankin, Elizabeth. "Cryptic Coloration in *The French Lieutenant's Woman*." *Journal of Narrative Technique* 3 (Sept. 1973): 193–207.

Rushdie, Salman. *Imaginary Homelands: Essays and Criticism 1981-1991*. London: Granta, 1991.

——. "In Defense of the Novel, Yet Again." *The New Yorker* 24 June and 1 July 1996: 48–55.

——. *Midnight's Children*. New York: Penguin, 1980.

——. *The Satanic Verses*. New York: Viking, 1989.

Said, Edward. *The World, the Text and the Critic*. Cambridge: Harvard UP, 1983.

Sartre, Jean-Paul. *Nausea*. Trans. Robert Baldick. Harmondsworth: Penguin, 1965.

Scholes, Robert. *The Fabulators*. London and New York: Oxford UP, 1967.

Schwartz, Nina. *Dead Fathers: The Logic of Transference in Modern Narrative*. Ann Arbor: U of Michigan P, 1994.

Shinn, Thelma J. "'What's in a Word?': Possessing A.S. Byatt's Meronymic Novel." *Papers on Language and Literature* 31.2 (Spring 1995): 164–83.

Smith, Stephen. "*The Ghost Road* aims a spotlight at English writer." *The Globe and Mail* 16 December 1995: C8.

Soja, Edward. "History: geography: modernity." *The Cultural Studies Reader*. Ed. Simon During. London and New York: Routledge, 1993. 135–150.

Spanos, William. *Repetitions: The Postmodern Occasion in Literature and Culture*. Baton Rouge and London: Louisiana State UP, 1987.

Spence, Donald. *Narrative Truth and Historical Truth: Meaning and Interpretation in Psychoanalysis*. New York: Norton, 1982.

Stevenson, Randall. "Postmodernism and Contemporary Fiction in Britain." *Postmodernism and Contemporary Fiction*. Ed. Edmund J. Smyth. London: B.T. Batsford, 1991. 19–35.

Suleiman, Susan and Inge Crosman, Eds. *The Reader in the Text: Essays on Audience and Interpretation*. Princeton: Princeton UP, 1980. 3–45.

Swift, Graham. *Waterland*. London: Picador, 1983.

Tarbox, Katherine. *The Art of John Fowles*. Athens and London: U of Georgia P, 1988.

Todd, Richard. "The Presence of Postmodernism in British Fiction: Aspects of Style and Selfhood." *Approaching Postmodernism*. Eds. Douwe Fokkema and Hans Bertens. Amsterdam and Philadelphia: John Benjamins, 1986. 99–117.

Vico, Giambattista. *The New Science of Giambattista Vico*. Unabridged Translation of the Third Edition (1744). Trans Thomas Goddard Bergin and Max Harold Fisch. Ithaca and London: Cornell UP, 1984.

Wallerstein, Robert S. Foreword. *Narrative Truth and Historical Truth: Meaning and Interpretation in Psychoanalysis*. By Donald Spence. New York: Norton, 1982. 9–14.

Waugh, Patricia. *Metafiction: The Theory and Practice of Self-Conscious Fiction*. London and New York: Methuen, 1984.

White, Hayden. "Historical Text as Literary Artifact." *The Writing of History: Literary Form and Historical Understanding*. Eds. Robert H. Canary and Henry Kozicki. Madison: U of Wisconsin P, 1978. 41–62.

——. *Tropics of Discourse: Essays in Cultural Criticism*. Baltimore and London: Johns Hopkins UP, 1978.

Wilde, Alan. *Horizons of Assent: Modernism, Postmodernism, and the Ironic Imagination*. Baltimore and London: Johns Hopkins UP, 1981.

Wilson, Keith. "*Midnight's Children* and Reader Responsibility." *Critical Quarterly* 26.3 (1984): 25–33. Rpt. in *Reading Rushdie: Perspectives on the Fiction of Salman Rushdie*. Ed. M.D. Fletcher. Cross/Cultures: Readings in the Post/Colonial Literatures in English 16. Amsterdam and Atlanta: Rodopi, 1994. 55–68.

Wilson, W. Daniel. "Readers in Texts." *PMLA* 96.5 (Oct. 1981): 848–63.

Žižek, Slavoj. *The Sublime Object of Ideology*. London and New York: Verso, 1989.

# Index

This index includes most personal names (with the exception of the names of fictional characters) and publications referred to in this book. In the case of multiple authors or editors the book or article in question is listed under the name of the first author or editor; frequently titles are shortened.